The BEASTIE BOYS *Companion*

The
BEASTIE BOYS
Companion

Edited by

J O H N   R O C C O

Assistant Editor

B R I A N   R O C C O

Schirmer Books
New York

Schirmer Books
An imprint of The Gale Group
1633 Broadway
New York, New York 10019

Library of Congress Catalog Number: 98-42818
Printed in the United States of America

Printing number
1   2   3   4   5   6   7   8   9   10

Library of Congress Cataloging-in-Publication Data

The Beastie Boys companion / edited by John Rocco : assistant editor
  Brian Rocco
      p.   cm.
  Includes bibliographical references and index.
  Discography: p.
  ISBN 0-02-865334-3
  1. Beastie Boys.   I. Rocco, John (John M.)   II. Rocco, Brian.
ML421.B39B43 2000
782.42164'092'2—dc21
[B]   99-42818
                                                                   CIP

This paper meets the requirements of ANSI/NISO Z39.48-1992 (Permanence of Paper).

Again,
For Mary Clancy

Beastie Boys and Public Enemy, '87; Front row: DJ Hurricane, MCA, Chuck D; Back row: Adrock, Mike D, Flavor Flav, and Terminator X.

Contents

PART THREE   Smarter Than Spock

Acknowledgments

MUCH DEBT, MANY PROPS: Thanks to Richard Carlin for letting me do this and Richard Kassel and everybody else at Schirmer who supported and helped. Thanks to Mark Gallagher for all the help.

Thanks to Tim Ross for the great *Tuba Frenzy* piece and Adam Heimlich for all his writing and help. Dave Marsh helped me get in touch with my *Creem* contributors, and Bill Holdship was kind enough to write a preface to his review, and he also hooked me up with his great *Revolution* interview. John Kordosh got back to me and let me reprint his e-mail looking back at his twelve-year-old Beastie show.

Thanks to Chuck Eddy, Ann Powers, Frank Owen, and Adam Beyda for their words. Blair Jackson was an invaluable help over at *Mix*. *Tikkun* made it easy—it's never easy!—to reprint Akiba Lerner and Mark LeVine's great interview with Adam Yauch. The *New York Times* helped and Eric Miller was my man over at *Magnet*. And Rob Weiner provided invaluable library stuff.

Thanks to James and everybody at POPsmear.

I owe a great debt to Robert Christgau for letting me reprint his words and, more important, for the blazing trail of music writing he has ignited for all of us.

Everett True lent his fascinating critical gaze, his humor, and his e-mail to this book; I owe him thanks *again*.

Thanks to Glen E. Friedman for the amazing photos.

George Kaplan provided mad Zubov and reminds me to thank our Queens crew—Tommy Dracula, Vinny Knickerbockers, Tommy Z, Biff Don't-Be-Stupid, Mark Daily Paging, and Steve Rangers—for all the inspiration.

This book was Brian Rocco's idea.

Thanks, Dana, for everything and it wouldn't have happened without you.

Thanks, Beastie Boys, for the sounds.

Introduction

Mirror, Mirror: Beastie Boys Go AWOL in America

IT NEVER MEANT JUVENILE DELINQUENTS; IT MEANT CHARACTERS OF A SPE-CIAL SPIRITUALITY WHO DIDN'T GANG UP BUT WERE SOLITARY BARTLEBIES STARING OUT THE DEAD WALL WINDOW OF OUR CIVILIZATION.

— Jack Kerouac, *"Aftermath: The Philosophy of the Beat Generation"*

"I . . . AM A FOOL. MY TRICORDER IS CAPABLE OF RECORDING EVEN AT THIS SPEED. I'VE MISSED TAPING CENTURIES OF LIVING HISTORY NO MAN BEFORE HAS EVER—"

— Mr. Spock in *"The City on the Edge of Forever,"* directly preceding Dr. McCoy's leap into the Guardian of Forever

Mirror 1: hip(hardcore)hop

That's Mix Master Mike on a raft, his turntables piled up and swaying as his hands move over vinyl: In fades Geddy Lee, then Neil Peart's intricate drum cage, then Tom Sawyer and Huck along for the ride. And Jim. The lights are blinding and they emerge from a mid-'80s Rush show complete with rolling pot smoke. Smoke on the water and the restless Mississippi. Mark One. Mark Twain. Mark Three. Mix Master Mike moves a digit and all is gone, all the river gone as the Beastie Boys[1] take the stage gripping mics.

---

[1] A note on the name: This book is about a band called "Beastie Boys" without the "The." Just as we wouldn't call Led Zeppelin "The Led Zeppelin" or Bad Brains "The Bad Brains," Beastie Boys should be written without the article. And yet it's difficult not to use the "the": From the beginning, the "the" has been attached to the band by the press and

This is what happens before a performance by the Beastie Boys, at least a current performance. The DJ breaks apart Rush's "Tom Sawyer," a song from a 1981 album called *Moving Pictures*. (As the story goes, the Beastie Boys formed in 1981 at a birthday party for Adam Yauch.) It's a reference, a sample, half joke, half nostalgia ride, half serious. The combination of 80s rock and Mark Twain is there and not there. Meaningful and meaningless. There and gone. America in the early '80s (Rush is from Canada) and America in the late '90s (the Beastie Boys are from New York City). America in the nineteenth century and the adventures of Tom Sawyer and his buddy Huck. And Jim. Sound has a history.

This book is a history of the Beastie Boys. This is a history compiled from different voices at different times, a chronicle beginning with the blastoff of the first Beastie space cake, Carvel's Cookie Puss, to the Boys going Intergalactic themselves at the close of the millennium ("In the next millennium, I'll still be old school"). As one of the most influential musical forces in American pop, the Beastie Boys have always commanded attention; they first caused a stir when listeners to their first hip hop recordings found out that they were white (this was before "Fight for Your Right [to Party]" put their faces everywhere). Then came the gargantuan success of their first album, and the music industry's growing recognition of the huge crossover potential of rap music. These are just two of the important "shocks" the Beastie Boys gave the system of modern pop music: They broke the color line and the money line. In the Age of Reagan this was a considerable cultural achievement, and the Beasties represented new possibilities for mainstream American music. But for many, the Beastie "shock" was puzzling or frightening. Even listeners who understood that the Beastie Boys were hip hop innovators were often prone to discomfort at their attack upon the propriety of rock/hip hop/pop convention ("I'm selling sex rhymes by the pound"). In the beginning, music critics were for the most part amused and often interested in the experiment; some were intensely appalled. (John Kordosh in *Creem* from 1987: "I think the critics who have embraced the Beastie Boys have actually lost their minds." See his 1999 e-mail to me on page 64.) The Beastie Boys were shocking and their music was shocking. The Beasties tapped into a

---

during the course of chiseling out English, one is almost compelled to use it. So know that it's wrong, but it can't be helped, and remember what Michael Diamond once told us about the meaning of the band's name: "For the record, Beastie Boys stands for: Boys Entering Anarchistic States Towards Internal Excellence."

For those without a scorecard: Michael Diamond = Mike D; Adam Horovitz = King Ad-Rock or Adrock; Adam Yauch = MCA.

resource lurking at the center of pop/youth culture and everybody (Madonna, every British tabloid, Run-D.M.C.) had to listen, at least for a little while. It was a wild mix of rap and hardcore and the music had a presence in skating culture as well as on *Soul Train*. Then they evolved and turned more shocking through musical experimentation. Then they demonstrated that William Blake's proverb really works: The Road of Excess Leads to the Palace of Wisdom. Or at least from White Castle to the Nile. A history of shocks is what follows.

In a certain respect, most modern popular music is shocking. Beginning with Elvis's hips on TV or Jerry Lee Lewis screaming about great balls of fire, rock and roll began as a blatant gesture against post-war American culture. But rock didn't begin with Elvis shaking his pelvis or Jerry Lee hitting the keys with his feet. Rock emerged out of the protean music of African Americans. Without black folk music, spirituals, and the blues, there is no rock 'n' roll. ("I know this music comes down from African descent.") When Elvis walked into Sun Studio that day in 1953 to record a song for his mother, Sam Philips knew he had the white voice that would give the music of Howlin' Wolf to the world. For Philips, the music of Howlin' Wolf and other black bluesmen was a magical force in which "the soul of man never dies." And Elvis became a vehicle for the transmission of this music. This is not to say that Elvis walked into Sun that day without any idea of the music he would soon give to the rest of the world. Elvis knew his roots: The recordings of bluesmen such as Arthur "Big Boy" Crudup and the great Roy Brown were early and lasting influences. Brown had this to say about Elvis: "[W]hen I first saw him on 'The Ed Sullivan Show,' all that wiggling and stuff, man, the blacks had been doing that for years. But there was something about Elvis that was different from the Fabians and them other guys. Elvis could *sing*. And he had a heart."[2] But everyone didn't admire the heart of the new popular music.

Some called the music of Elvis "voodoo" and, in a famous enunciation of racist reaction, the Citizen's Council of Greater New Orleans issued a warning: "DON'T BUY NEGRO RECORDS." "Negro records" were all rock and roll records, regardless of the musicians who produced the music. And the reason for this boycott: "The screaming, idiotic words, and savage music of these records are undermining the morals of our white youth in America." Now consider this from the British tabloid *The Daily Star* thirty

---

[2] Quoted in Robert Palmer, *Rock & Roll: An Unruly History*. New York: Harmony Books, 1995.

years down the line: "Their kind of trash is obviously very dangerous . . . our children will be corrupted by this sort of thing." The "trash" here is the music of the Beastie Boys and the speaker is a member of Parliament; the event he is reacting to is the arrival of the *Licensed to Ill* tour in 1987.[3] But we don't have to go twelve years in the past to see this kind of reaction to the Beasties. An editorial in the 1999 April/May issue of *Magnet* blasted Rage Against the Machine and the Beastie Boys for the Mumia Abu-Jamal Benefit held at the Continental Airlines Arena in January of 1999. The writer's reactionary stance toward the case—he seems to have gotten his "facts" about Abu-Jamal's trial and what many believe was a brutal mis- carriage of justice entirely from the *New York Post*—is mirrored in his sec- ondary attack upon the *music* of the Beastie Boys: "And then there are the Beastie Boys, who made their careers by pretending they were black, by co- opting black music and slang, processing it then selling it back to teenagers."[4] Now this is not the dumbest thing ever said about the Beastie Boys; it just seems like it is because it appears in a *rock and roll* magazine. (And a pretty dope rock mag at that: See the interview Larry Kay did with the Beasties from *Magnet* on page 000.) But this "commentary" is indica- tive of the kind of criticism the Beastie Experiment has triggered since the beginning. (There is even some "negative" Beastie writing in this book; for a *very* bad review of an early Beastie performance, see Bill Holdship and John Kordosh's "High School Equivalency Test," and for a recent critique of Beastie politics see Adam Heimlich's "Sensitive B-Boys.") And the reac- tion to the Beastie Experiment begins with the reaction to hip hop.

As with many of the truly revolutionary art forms, hip hop began at a party.

There is something about the human search for *transgressive* fun (Rabelais's carnivals, Robert Johnson's wandering songs, John Waters's Baltimore) that breeds politically charged and challenging art ("gravy to potatoes, Luke to Darth Vaders"). Exploding out of African-American music and culture, hip hop was born in the post–civil rights era and in many ways it embodied a new form of social protest. As Tricia Rose describes it, the new genre was postgenre and "postindustrial": "Hip Hop is an Afro-diasporic cultural form which attempts to negotiate the experi- ences of marginalization, brutally truncated opportunity and oppression within the cultural imperatives of African-American and Caribbean his- tory, identity and community."[5] Or, to put it another way: Hip hop began

[3] Quoted in Liz Philips, "This Trash Will Harm Our Youth," *The Daily Star,* April 15, 1987.

[4] Phil Sheridan, "Check Your Head," *Magnet,* April/May 1999.

with people breaking up records to dance, people dancing by breaking up moves, and people bustin' rhymes to represent frustration, passion, anger, love, style, and communal pride. Or again, to quote Chuck D, "Hip-Hop is a subculture of Black culture. It's another form of Black creativity."[6] From block parties in the Bronx in the early eighties to Public Enemy's 1988 *It Takes a Nation of Millions to Hold Us Back,* hip hop moved from fun and musical experimentation to the *politics* of fun and musical experimentation. (And P. E. laid down the line by responding to the Beasties with "Party for Your Right to Fight.") When N.W.A. began their reaction to the "marginalization" of their own communities on the West Coast, a new and aggressive form of rap took the attention of the mainstream and amplified popular reaction in sales and criticism. But hip hop was always political and always controversial—one origin of the form still bangs this history out for us. The Last Poets began at a birthday party for Malcom X and the power in their work is a resilient echo; Amiri Baraka: "The Last Poets are in the tradition of Revolutionary Art for Cultural Revolution. The razor."[7] This was the razor the Beastie Boys picked up.

The booklet inside the *Some Old Bullshit* CD includes an early fan letter to the original hardcore band called Beastie Boys. (The early tune "Beastie Boys" is a *hardcore* song.) The letter writer goes right to the point: "This pathetic, feeble imitation of Minor Threat and the Necro's should not be permitted." By bringing up these two hardcore bands, the letter writer placed the Beastie Boys in a tradition: Minor Threat formed in 1980 and their intense dedication to the hardcore aesthetic produced several influential recordings and popularized the "Straight Edge" philosophy of abstaining from drugs, booze, and tobacco. The Beasties have never been accused of being Straight Edge ("I'm so high, they call me your Highness"), but the letter is indicative of early reactions to the Beasties as a hardcore act who were "co-opting" an existing sound and style. This would become a mantra for those who later couldn't grasp or accept the Beastie move into hip hop; but it is significant that they were never criticized for embracing rap by members of the hip hop community. (Chuck D went as far in the reverse as to call them the white Jackie Robinsons of

[5] Tricia Rose, "A Style Nobody Can Deal With: Politics, Style and the Postindustrial City in Hip Hop" in *Microphone Fiends: Youth Music and Youth Culture.* Andrew Ross and Tricia Rose, eds. New York and London: Routledge, 1994.

[6] Chuck D with Yusuf Jah, *Fight the Power: Rap, Race, and Reality.* New York: Delta, 1997.

[7] Amiri Baraka's foreword to Abiodun Oyewole and Umar Bin Hassan with Kim Green, *On a Mission: Selected Poems and a History of the Last Poets.* New York: Henry Holt, 1996.

The Razor: Milford Graves and Amiri Baraka in '99. Photo by Brian Rocco.

rap.) It is the legacy of hardcore and the fecund music scene in NYC in the late '70s and early '80s that is vital for understanding the Beastie Evolution/Revolution/Constitution. We begin with a guy in the Kitchen.

His name is Rhys Chatham and he was the music director of the Kitchen, a space where NYC's experimental music lived in the early 80s. Chatham played in several "groups" that combined rock with conceptual and pop art. As director of sounds from the Kitchen—and Sheena reports in the first article in this book that the Beasties first met a bubble-machine-wielding Rick Rubin at the Kitchen—Chatham was centered in a place where the music of NYC was experimenting with itself. It was a movement into something new after NY punk left CBGBs, and after pop art became what Andy Warhol referred to as a man's first name. This experimental music became known as No Wave.

No Wave had two branches: the art/SoHo No Wave of Glenn Branca and bands such as Theoretical Girls and the harder, East Village stuff from Lydia Lunch (who christened herself after William S. Burroughs's masterpiece of dark addiction) and her important No Wave band Teenage Jesus and the Jerks (who embodied "violent expression and reaction against the stagnancy of music and culture").[8] The music of these bands and others such as DNA, Mars, Red Transistor, and the Contortions was explicit in its stance toward commercial music and the movement from punk to New Wave. Chatham was also explicit in the direction of the Kitchen's music: "Cage taught us that we can do anything we want. So the question becomes, What do we want?"[9] The Cage here is John Cage (1912–1992), the avant-garde composer who opened up an entire cosmos of "found" sounds (Cage's $4'33"$ is a composition for piano entirely made up of sounds coming from everywhere in the concert hall—and the street outside it—*except* the untouched piano) and musical experiments.[10] The fact that Chatham brings up Cage as artistic motivator/metaphor is indicative of the

---

[8] This is how Lester Bangs described the 1980 *Teenage Jesus and the Jerks* EP:

> Guys in my sixth-grade neighborhood used to entertain themselves by tying the head of a cat to one hot-rod fender and its tail to another and driving the cars apart slowly, which sounded a lot like part of this. Unless it's for Catholic-school beatings by nuns, nostalgia doesn't account for Lydia's passionate "Baby Doll" wailing. If you only want to try one, make it this—nothing more deathly shrill has ever been recorded.

For Bangs's look at what he calls "horrible noise," see "A Reasonable Guide to Horrible Noise" in *Psychotic Reactions and Carburetor Dung* (Greil Marcus, ed. New York: Vintage, 1987). Every time I accidentally watch MTV I think of Bangs and how much we *need* him today. Remember, Bangs *invented* punk by writing about it.

[9] Quoted in Alec Foege, *Confusion Is Next: The Sonic Youth Story*. New York: St. Martin's Press, 1994.

[10] Cage provided a stunning example of what can be done with music, or what music can do to us. A major aspect of his attack upon musical convention was a concern with the tools of music—his "prepared piano" turned the instrument into a different tool. He also anticipated later experiments of "sampled" music and sound. Here's a description of a Cage piece by Richard Kostelanetz from *John Cage (ex)plain(ed)* (New York: Schirmer Books, 1996):

> Rozart Mix (1965), originally composed for the Rose Art Museum at Brandeis University, employs six live performers, thirteen tape machines, and a pile of at least eighty-eight tape loops (where the two ends of a piece of recording tape are glued together) of varying lengths. Cage specified the unusually large number, he explained, "to make sure that the performers wouldn't select tapes only of their favorite pieces."

Bad Brains backstage at CBGBs, 1981. Photo © Glen E. Friedman.

kind of experimentation that was occurring in NYC during this period. And, as Kostelanetz describes it, Cage's work goes beyond mere shock and the crunching of crumbs in public: "His principle theme, applicable to all arts, was the denial of false authority by expanding the range of acceptable and thus employable materials, beginning with non-pitched 'noises,' which he thought should be heard as music 'whether we're in or out of the concert hall.'"[11] In the late '70s and early '80s, No Wave bridged the gap

---

> At the beginning of Rozart Mix, *each of the performers picks a tape from the pile of loops and places it on the machine; when a tape breaks or gets tangled, she or he replaces it with another tape chosen from the pile: "What you want, you see, is to get a physically confused situation." Although the machines are tuned to various amplitudes, the piece itself is a paralyzingly loud chaos of sounds. As frequently happens at Cage's concerts, unenlightened spectators trickle out after every cacophonous climax. At the premiere performance, refreshments were served when the audience dwindled to twelve; and the piece terminated, by prearrangement, when the last spectator left the Rose Art Museum, approximately two hours after* Rozart Mix *began. (The hors d'oeuvre to this main course consisted of Cage's munching a sandwich whose sound was picked up by contact microphones strategically distributed around his face, so that excruciatingly loud crunching noises penetrated every nook in the hall.)*

Compare Cage's sandwich with the Beasties hitting the bong or playing ping pong on *Paul's Boutique*.

[11] Richard Kostelanetz, "CAGE, John (1912–1992)" in *Dictionary of the Avant-Gardes* (New York: a cappella books, 1993).

between punk and the art gallery to resist the "false authority" of commercial music and commercial culture. Then there was hardcore.

Glenn Branca came to NYC to listen to punk, but CBGB's was empty of the bands he was looking for. So he made his own music. He formed Theoretical Girls and other bands that took a punk ethos and combined it with experimental compositions. Branca later turned to the guitar—the classic instrument of rock—and formed a series of "guitar armies" that pushed the instrument to its limits. In 1981—the same year the Beasties formed—Branca released *The Ascension* on 99 Records.[12] A stunning exploration of noise and guitar, the album featured future Sonic Youth member Lee Ranaldo. And it was during this period of playing with Branca that Ranaldo met Thurston Moore and Kim Gordon. And then there was hardcore.

Hardcore is a tale of two cities: Washington, DC and LA. It came from a double influence: NY punk (the New York Dolls, the Ramones, Television) and English punk (the Sex Pistols, the Buzzcocks, the Clash). When these movements ended—when the Ramones left CBGBs and the Sex Pistols imploded—the commercialization called New Wave began and hardcore retreated into its own communities. The youthful passion and sheer dedication of hardcore bands such as Minor Threat, Bad Brains,[13] Black Flag, the Germs, the Circle Jerks, and Saccharine Trust changed (or created) underground music and inspired others to form bands and start fanzines and sell their Top-40 album collections. When Kurt Cobain sold his '80s albums (Journey, Pat Benatar, Foreigner) to raise money to see a Black Flag show, he was performing a symbolic exchange that many were making and it would eventually take him to Nirvana. But before Nirvana there was Sonic Youth.

---

[12] See Tim Ross' important history of 99 Records ("Something Like a New Phenomenon") beginning on page 11.

[13] Bad Brains are a particularly potent influence on the Beasties. The Brains' mix of punk and reggae—check out the essential *Black Dots* for a 1979 recording of the band's early work—was an astonishing progression from early mixes of punk and reggae by groups such as the Clash. The Brains' stunning contribution to hardcore may be gleaned from Adam McGovern's entry on them from *Rock: The Essential Album Guide* (Gary Graff, ed. Detroit: Visible Ink Press, 1996):

> But the Brains' pioneering mix of punk with reggae also makes it an unusual giant of world music and a founder of the barrier-breaking aesthetic now spreading through all forms of art. The group's explosive sound has the creative tension of cultures actually facing each other for the first time—call it Hard World. The Brains' sensibility stems from an upbringing in the ghettos around the capital of the free world; it embodies the past shame and future promise of American multiculturalism—bassist [Darryl] Jenifer even traces his lineage from a slave-owning signer of the Constitution.

As fellow travelers through the NY music scene of the late '70s and early '80s, Sonic Youth always had links with the Beasties (thus two articles on SY included within). They grew out of the same NYC hardcore reaction. Sonic Youth is an important band historically because of their position as cultural instigators and connoisseurs: They moved in the same hardcore circles as the early Beasties and later, through the communication system set up by the hardcore circuit, SY met many of the younger bands from all over the country, including Redd Kross, Dinosaur Jr., Mudhoney, and, somewhat later, Nirvana. Their relationship with Nirvana was particularly significant because of SY's early promotion of the power trio and both their signing to Geffen/DGC. On the surface there is little in common between the music of the Beasties and what came to be called "grunge." It was just hip hop versus fuzzed-up guitar rock. However, beneath the surface there is an important connection: The first sample on the first Beasties album is John Bonham's thunder-drums from Led Zeppelin's "When the Levee Breaks." And the drummer for Nirvana played like Bonzo.

Mirror 2: My Man Jack Kerouac

I say, God bless young fighters, and now I'll take a rest and wait for my trainer's bottle, and my trainer's name is Johnnie Walker.

—*Jack Kerouac, "In the Ring"*

Cobain described the music of Nirvana as sounding "like the Knack and the Bay City Rollers being molested by Black Flag and Black Sabbath."[14] The combination of pop, punk, and metal became the sound of Nirvana, and, for a short time, it made them the biggest band in the world. An early Nirvana song pointed to this mix: "Aero Zeppelin" is a decidedly punk song celebrating the sluggishness of metal, an homage also taken up by Run-D.M.C. when they covered Aerosmith's "Walk This Way" in 1986. Run-D.M.C.'s version of "Walk" was a huge crossover hit—amplified distortion met amplified MCs from Queens—and the video for the song became MTV's first rap staple. The loud, riff-heavy, and blatantly aggressive sound of metal became the music of post-Watergate youth ("But I'm gonna set it straight,

---

[14] As Cobain told Gina Arnold, his early attempts at recorded music "sounded *exactly* like Black Flag. Totally abrasive, fast, punk music. There were some Nirvana elements, some slower songs, even then. And some heavy, Black Sabbath-influenced stuff. I can't deny Black Sabbath. Or Black Flag." See Arnold's *Route 666: The Road to Nirvana* (New York: St. Martin's Press, 1993) and *The Nirvana Companion* (John Rocco, ed. New York: Schirmer Books, 1998) for descriptions of hardcore and metal influences on Nirvana.

this Watergate"). It is easy to forget that the Beasties' first hit, "Fight for Your Right (to Party)," is a *heavy metal* song. It spoofed the entire metal mentality through metal, but few got the joke. ("No Sleep Till Brooklyn"— the song directly after "Fight" on *Licensed*—bows to the notorious speed metal band Motörhead.) But grunge is dead and the Beasties are still moving, rhyming, and growing. *Moving Pictures*: the video Nathaniel Hornblower directed for "Body Movin'" from *Hello Nasty*, points to this "moving": It references Italian Schlock Master Mario Bava's 1967 psychedelic, super-criminal extravaganza *Diabolik*. This is an interesting move on Hornblower's part, considering the fact that the archetypal metal band, Black Sabbath, took their name from a Bava cult classic starring Boris Karloff. Grunge is dead and Iron Maiden is still schlepping around the corpse of Eddie. Nirvana could not last. And this is probably the greatest shock of all the Beasties' shocks: their continuance, their transformation, their evolution.

Hip hop is a form continually renewing, reshaping, redirecting itself. This is one of its strengths and one of its weaknesses. The Beasties have grown with the form. Here's a snapshot reading of the Beasties' Effect from Jon Savage's seminal history of English punk:

> RAP: The Black Punk: aggression, politics and empowerment translated into black music after 1982. An equation made explicit by the Beastie Boys' crossover success in 1987, and by records like 'Punk Rock Rap' by the Cold Crush Brothers (Tuff City, 1984). Just consider Public Enemy. Just consider Bart Simpson, and Black Bart.[15]

Savage published these words in 1992. In 1999, the Beastie Boys appeared on *Futurama*, Matt Groening's new show about a guy who gets frozen ("Walt Disney he is FROzen") and ends up in the future. (In one thousand years from now, the Beasties will be on their seventh album.) The Beasties have not only grown with or outside hip hop, they have grown with or outside popular American culture. They have survived gangsta rap, the Parents' Music Resource Center (PMRC), grunge, techno, MTV, the swing revival, and the Spice Girls. They haven't just survived, they've thrived and built a huge fan base in the process. The Beastie Project opened an entire new world of music, and others such as Cypress Hill, the Disposable Heroes of Hiphoprisy, and Beck have followed their example. But who could have foreseen this outcome in 1987? Yes, back then they had a chart monster,

---

[15] Jon Savage, *England's Dreaming: Anarchy, Sex Pistols, Punk Rock, and Beyond*. New York: St. Martin's Press, 1992.

and yes, back then they could write dope rhymes and deliver them with a ferocious bravado. But after their break with Def Jam and Rick Mr. Slayer Rubin (and their move to LA!), who would have thought they would produce something like *Paul's Boutique*? (Robert Christgau weighs the impact of this album on the band and their audience in the most perceptive article written on early Beastie Evolution, "How Ya Like 'em Now?," on page 91.) A multilayered and THICK slice of American culture, *Paul's* is a psychedelic, bombastic, ecstatic orgy of samples and rhymes ("The Godfather of Soul in the Belly of the Beast"). Mike D: "One of the positive things about sampling is that you're incorporating a musical and cultural history into what you're doing."[16] The Beasties struck with this album at a time when other sample classics were also being born: The year before, Public Enemy had released *It Takes a Nation of Millions to Hold Us Back,* and De La Soul gave *Paul's* competition with *3 Feet High and Rising.* At the same time they were experimenting with the frontiers of sampling, the Beasties were adding brothers-in-arms to the cause; over the years many others participated in the Beastie experiment: DJ Hurricane, Run-D.M.C., the Dust Brothers, Mario Caldato Jr. (see Adam Beyda's conversation with Caldato in "Recording on the Fly"), Money Mark Nishita, and Mix Master Mike. And with their third and fourth albums, they did something else again.

Something else on the third and fourth albums: *Check Your Head* (1992) and *Ill Communication* (1994) represent the Beasties hitting the Outer Limits of their game. Funk, Punk, the ghost of the Meters, hip hop, *mad* approaches to their instruments (*instruments!*), the Biz, the game of basketball, metal, Blue Nun, NY, cannabis, LA, Q Tip, Tibetan Monks, and an evolving spirituality were mixed, freaked, composed, shot through two albums of astounding range and power. The first two Beastie albums were shocks to the system ("I've got more rhymes than Phyllis Diller!"), while the second two albums were shocks to the system, but the system—music, culture, whatever you live with—had been altered by the Beastie Boys. In a conversation with Tim Ross and Richard Allen in *Tuba Frenzy,* Nosaj from the great (and highly underrated) New Kingdom made a connection between doing shows and playing ball. The exchange that ensued encapsulated the Beasties' career and their importance for music and youth culture:

> *Richard:* It's interesting, because the Beastie Boys were at one point so into basketball that they actually arranged their shows in quarters. They

---

[16] Quoted in Hillel Schwartz, *The Culture of the Copy: Striking Likenesses, Unreasonable Facsimiles.* New York: Zone Books, 1996.

changed their setup or they did one hip-hop quarter, one instrumental quarter, one rock quarter . . . .

Nosaj: Really? That's phat, that's phat. That's why I like them a lot. Because they've been around for such a long time and the audience knows their catalog so well, but every time they still give people a little something cool, a little something different. And it always feels like the first time when you see them, because you never know how they're going to look like, how they're going to slang their shit. They true to their audience and if you're a real live fan of theirs . . . they respect their audience, they always give them dope shit, dope singles, dope remixes, dope artwork, something different. Now they got their audience thinking because it's a thinking time where you have to be a thinking person if you want to survive in the world. And their audience is this trust-fund audience and they know that, so they're like, "OK, let's get these people before they get out into the real world and make decisions. We've been having fun this whole time, let's start thinking about some serious issues." They really brought their audience up and now their audience is really looking around and thinking about shit. Whereas Rage Against the Machine just came up out of the box like that. But the Beastie Boys worked you up from drinking Budweiser to smoking pot to doing acid . . . .

Tim: 'Cause they were growing up too . . . .[17]

And the drive to have their audience "think" has proven to be the greatest Beastie shock of them all.

The early Beasties were an eruption from the Id: three white guys with mics ripping on Buds and buds and hormones. The stage show for the *Licensed* tour featured women dancing in cages (an adolescent male fantasy), giant cans of Budweiser (an adolescent male fantasy), and a giant penis rising from the stage and towering over all (an adolescent male fantasy). And they rapped about angel dust, White Castle, beer, and girls. But they were not villains, they were just "chillin' like Bob Dylan," and like Dylan, they changed. The plight of a violently oppressed Tibet became their cause. In 1994, with the help and instigation of Adam Yauch, the Milarepa Fund was established; two years later the first Tibetan Freedom Concert was given in San Francisco. Since then the Beastie interest in social activism has widened, with their latest efforts directed at relief for Kosovo refugees and a new series of Tibetan Freedom Concerts. The fifth Beastie album, *Hello Nasty*, is a return to hip hop and samplescapes—it is a fitting explo-

---

[17] "New Kingdom" in *Tuba Frenzy*, #4, 1998.

ration of the Beastie past and future at the same time that it marks the full-blown political presence of the band.[18] This turn from angel-dusted to angel-trusted surprised some, but considering the Beastie Evolution, this turn toward the social and spiritual was always there in the music. Their roots—hardcore and hip hop—are overt political forms, and thus it is not really surprising that the Beasties have developed an active and vocal politics. What has really surprised many is the spiritual turn epitomized by Yauch's embrace of Buddhism ("I took a sledge hammer and I broke my nine"). But a way of reading this turn is given early on by Adrock during *Paul's Boutique*: "while I'm reading *On the Road* by my man Jack Kerouac." Kerouac once called America "the motherland of bumdom." He meant this with reverence as the greatest compliment he could give.

What Kerouac did in *On the Road* was to write about himself and his friends—the Beats ("children of the American bop night")—in such a way as to change American culture. It's a novel embodying the great American desire to discover, experience, explore. The kind of spiritual freedom at the core of the book had a huge impact on rock: It put the BEAT in Beatles, and rock acts from the Grateful Dead and the Doors to David Bowie and R.E.M. claim it as an inspirational spark. Kerouac had two great influences on the ecstatic, *spontaneous* prose making up his novel: a guy named Neal Cassady and jazz. Both these forces never stopped moving: Cassady was the greatest driver in American history; before he was fifteen he had stolen over 500 cars, for joy(rides) and never for profit. Car Thief: He stole cars and took girls driving, driving, driving ("I smoked up a bag of elephant tranquilizer"). Later he drove Ken Kesey's Magic Bus across the country with a head packed with acid. Cassady's bottomless energy—he once drove across the country nonstop to ask Allen Ginsberg about a vision he had, and then drove back—and his endless monologues inspired Kerouac's approach to spontaneous prose, or the burst of writing he let flow from his head without checking with the internal censor. (He wrote *The Subterraneans* in three days!) Kerouac demanded from himself this unchecked rush of words: "By not revising what you've already written you simply give the reader the actual workings of your mind during the writing itself: you confess your thoughts about events in your own changeable way. . . ."[19] The key word here is "confess." Kerouac's art—and the entire Beat aesthetic—was

---

[18] See George Kaplan's search for the hip hop "unconscious" on *Hello Nasty* in his review of the album at the end of this book.

[19] Ted Berrigan, "Jack Kerouac (1968)" in *Beat Writers at Work: The Paris Review,* George Plimpton, ed. New York: The Modern Library, 1999.

based on confession. Kerouac came up with the term "Beat Generation" and he was careful to call it "no hoodlumism":

> Beat doesn't mean tired, or bushed, so much as it means *beato,* the Italian for beatific: to be in a state of beatitude, like St. Francis, trying to love all life, trying to be utterly sincere with everyone, practicing endurance, kindness, cultivating joy of heart. How can this be done in our mad modern world of multiplicities and millions?[20]

Music was one way to help with the confession.

A Kerouac anecdote about the legendary jazz club, the Five Spot (Frank O'Hara: "and I am sweating a lot now and thinking of/ leaning on the john door in the 5 SPOT"):

> Lester Young played there just before he died and used to sit in the back kitchen between sets. My buddy poet Allen Ginsberg went back and got on his knees and asked him what he would do if an atom bomb fell on New York. Lester said he would break the window in Tiffany's and get some jewels anyway. He also said, "What you doin' on your knees?" not realizing he is a great hero of the beat generation and now enshrined.[21]

The Beasties follow in this line. Inspired by black culture, Kerouac wrote without fetters: "Time being the essence in the purity of speech, sketching language in undisturbed flow from the mind of personal secret idea-words, *blowing* (as per jazz musician) on subject of image."[22] Inspired by Kerouac and the Beats and (again) black music, rock began. Inspired by Cage: "Art instead of being an object made by one person is a process set in motion by a group of people."[23] Inspired by punk. Inspired by hip hop. Inspired by postmodernism. Inspired by Chuck D ("Now they got me in a cell"). Inspired by collage. Inspired by Bad Brains. Inspired by funk. Inspired by Aerosmith and a packed cooler. Inspired by New York. Inspired by . . . , ah, hell, fuck it. I just can't wait for the Country album the Beastie Boys keep threatening to give us.

—*Queens, June 1999*

---

[20] Jack Kerouac, "Lamb, No Lion" in *Good Blonde & Others*, Donald Allen, ed. San Francisco: Grey Fox Press, 1993.

[21] Jack Kerouac, "New York Scenes," in *Lonesome Traveler*. New York: Grove Press, 1960.

[22] Jack Kerouac, "Essentials of Spontaneous Prose," in *Good Blonde & Others*, Donald Allen, ed. San Francisco: Grey Fox Press, 1993.

[23] John Cage, quoted in Richard Kostelanetz, *John Cage (ex)plained*. New York: Schirmer Books, 1996.

At Madonna's first gold record party in '85 with David Lee Roth and Sean Penn. Photo © Glen E. Friedman.

Part One

FROM WHITE CASTLE TO THE NILE

1986: SUCH SATELLITES AS HEAO-2 *WILL UNCOVER VAST, UNSUSPECTED HIGH-ENERGY PHENOMENA IN THE UNIVERSE, INDICATING THAT THERE IS SUFFICIENT MASS TO COLLAPSE THE UNIVERSE BACK WHEN IT HAS REACHED ITS EXPANSION LIMIT.*

—*Philip K. Dick, "Predictions" (1981)*

"WE'RE ALSO WORKING ON A TELEVISION PILOT THAT'S BASED ON THE CHARACTERS WE ARE NOW."

—*Mike D in 1987*

A Beasties Timeline: 1981–1987

Beastie Boys

1981 Michael Diamond, Adam Yauch, Kate Schellenbach, and John Berry form the first group called Beastie Boys.

1982 After the original lineup releases the *Polly Wog Stew* EP, John Berry leaves the band. Adam Horovitz, formally of the Young and the Useless, joins the Beastie Boys.

1983 Beastie Boys release a 12" on Rat Cage: "Cookie Puss"/ "Beastie Revolution."

1984 Beastie Boys meet Russell Simmons and Rick Rubin. Kate Schellenbach leaves the band. The band's first single on Def Jam is released: "Rock Hard"/ "Beastie Groove."

Music

1981 MTV shows its first video: "Video Killed the Radio Star." ESG release the *ESG* LP, which includes "UFO," on 99 Records. Minor Threat release their first two EPs. Black Flag put out *Damaged* while X put out *Wild Gift.*

1982 CDs are introduced. Afrika Bambaataa fashions electro-hip hop with "Planet Rock" and Grandmaster Flash and the Furious Five give the world "The Message."

1983 Minor Threat release *Out of Step* and disband. Sugar Hill Records puts out Grandmaster and Melle Mel's "White Lines (Don't Don't Do It)."

1984 Birth of Def Jam and the release of their first single: L.L. Cool J's "I Need a Beat." Run-D.M.C. release their first album. Madonna emerges out of the NYC club scene. The Minutemen release the classic *Double Nickels on the Dime.*

1985   The Beastie Boys open for Madonna on her *Like a Virgin* tour. The band appears in the film *Krush Groove.*

1985   The PMRC (Parents' Music Resource Center) begins its attack upon popular music and calls for warning labels on "explicit" albums. Sonic Youth release their trip though dark America called *Bad Moon Rising.*

1986   The Beastie Boys spend the summer touring with Run-D.M.C., L.L. Cool J, and Whodini on the *Raising Hell* tour. Late in the year, the first Beastie Boys album, *Licensed to Ill*, is released.

1986   Run-D.M.C. release the rap classic, *Raising Hell*. The Hollis rappers' version of Aerosmith's "Walk This Way" is a huge crossover hit. Public reaction against rap shows begins after a disturbance at a Run-D.M.C. show in Long Beach, CA. Bad Brains release *I Against I* on SST and Sonic Youth put out *EVOL* on the same label. Eric B. and Rakim get *Paid in Full.*

1987   *Licensed to Ill* quickly turns platinum. The Beastie Boys embark on the legendary "Together Forever" tour with Run-D.M.C. The sold-out tour is marred by confused public reaction over the growing popularity of rap; this culminates in the British tabloid war against the Beasties. In Liverpool, the home of the Beatles, a soccer crowd turns up as the audience and destroys the stage with bottles and bodies. After the show, Adam Horovitz is arrested for allegedly wounding a concert goer with a can hit back into the audience by a baseball bat. The Beasties continue on a long, worldwide tour. *Licensed to Ill* becomes the fastest-selling album in Columbia's history. The Beasties make TV history by becoming the first act ever to be censored on *American Bandstand.*

1987   Public Enemy put out their debut *Yo! Bum Rush the Show*. Kool Moe Dee releases *How Ya Like Me Now*. Inspired by sci-fi writer Philip K. Dick's obsession with the Double, Sonic Youth release *Sister*. Boogie Down Productions unleashes *Criminal Minded.*

The opening article in this book comes from a Boston rock 'zine and it captures the Beastie Boys during a transformation: Kate Schellenbach and Rick Rubin are both playing with the band. The Beastie stage show seems to reflect this very short-lived lineup. A year later, Joanne Carnegie reported on Beastie involvement with Madonna's 1985 *Like a Virgin* tour. Both of these pieces describe significant early stages in the evolution of the Beastie Boys (although some things never change; Carnegie in 1985: "You never know when to take them seriously").

In "Something Like a Phenomenon: The 99 Records Story," Tim Ross provides a valuable look into the history of 99 Records. A history of 99 Records is a history of NY experimental music in the late '70s and early '80s. From No Wave experimentation and avant-garde compositions (Glen Branca) to postpunk funk jamming (Liquid Liquid) to early funk/hip hop innovators ESG, 99 displayed some of the most volatile and vibrant music produced by the NY underground. The Beasties never appeared on 99, but the music on and "around" the label—members of Sonic Youth played with Branca—had a deep and lasting influence on NY experimental music. And 99 is the label where experimental rock and funk connected with the evolving force of hip hop (ESG's "UFO" is the one of the most heavily sampled tracks in hip hop history).

The remainder of this first section is concerned with the emergence of the pop phenomenon called the Beastie Boys. Nelson George, in his "Rhythm & Blues" column from *Billboard*, first puts the Beasties in perspective following the initial splash of *Licensed to Ill*, and Dave DiMartino reports on a canceled Beasties show. Linda Moleski then describes how *Licensed to Ill* shocked everyone in the marketplace, from the Beasties own record label to critics and consumers. (A Columbia marketing executive: "Around here we're calling it the Beastie Boys phenomenon.")

Bill Holdship and John Kordosh then go to an early Beastie show and submit an incredibly *negative* review that mirrors some of the early reaction to the "Beastie phenomenon." Bill and John both reply to their twelve-year-old review in a preface to it.

Chuck Eddy's "The Beastie Boys Take Over?" is one of the first important critical appraisals of the band and their impact on pop culture. At the beginning of this *Creem* cover story, Eddy describes how the Beastie Boys broke into his room and poured water over him as he slept. Unknown to Eddy, this scene was recorded for *The Beastie Boys Video*. Eddy later apparently sued the Beastie Boys for what the *Village Voice* described as "the initial aquatic assault and for commercial appropriation of Eddy's image."[1]

This first section ends with Nelson George describing the furor caused by a truly historic pop event, the "Together Forever" tour. I then try to define hip hop. Adam Heimlich ends this section by describing his listening to early Beastie music as well as getting lost in a brave new world.

SHEENA

THE BEASTIE BOYS: HIP HOP TO THE COOKIE PUSS SLOP

Boston Rock # 49, 1984

I toppled out of the Beastie Boys van, with 12 pages of notes—but minus a six-pack. There's no denying the full-throttle pleasure of chatting with six wiseass kids from New York City, hyped outta their rhyming minds on a weekend tour—and if Bantam Books ever needs an editor for *The Beastie Boys: The Early Years,* I've got the definite scoop.

It takes 15 minutes for them just to introduce themselves, and they have to say everything twice since someone else always talks over the first try: Okay, okay . . . there are two guys named Adam. . . .

"No, I'm Bill Hammill. That's my stage name."

"You have a *stage* name?"

"Nah, that's the name on my fake ID."

"I'm Rick, I'm the D.J."

"Just Rick, you're sure?"

"OK, put Rick Double R."

Well, if you've heard the Beastie Boys' landmark musical contribution 'n' claim-to-Fame, "Cookie Puss" (and for a while there, it was getting a tad irritating to hear it on the radio *again*), you can imagine the kind of giddy minds that produced such a masterpiece. The Beastie Boys are four kids, plus soundman Scott and DJ Rick, all hooked in on one big in-joke. Lead singer Michael Crawford[2] desperately tried to keep things on track, but only succeeded in setting up another volley of punch lines. They're kinda

---

[1] R. J. Smith, "Eddy Sues Beastie Boys," *Village Voice,* February 2, 1988.

[2] Aka Mike D.—*ed.*

know-it-all'y, but then, they've been going to nightclubs and practice spaces from an age when I was still playing with Barbies. They've got street smarts *and* school smarts, and as is often the case, the result can be obnoxious.

"Cookie Puss" is, after all, the song that's hip to everything, right? It's lampooning the groovier-than-thou Grandmaster Flash approach to the world of hip-hop, and at the same time sending all the Malcolm MacLarenized masses hungering after more cleaned-up whomping. An hour with the Beastie Boys (who get my attention by yelling "Yo, man!," wear name buckles, and refer to a vicious reviewer as "a jealous toy that mus' be stop") and I can't decide if they really wish they were black or if they're just making fun of the most stereotypical aspects of a culture.

Village Voice critic Tom Sommer apparently called "Cookie Puss" a "racist" song, although he liked the tune. Or as Adam Yauch, bass, modifies: "The impression I got was that he thought we were talentless assholes who made a good record by mistake." For all the song's snottily spoofish elements, it's as much a tribute as a caricature and vice versa. When I commented on their belt buckles Scott put the whole cult back into perspective: "I'd like to point out that I do *not* have one," he said, rolling his eyes.

Beastie Boys ("Boys Entering Anarchistic States Towards Internal Excellence") met as pubescents (13, 14) hanging out at New York's Rock Lounge, Tier 3 and the Botany House, digging the Stimulators and the Bad Brains and moving to New Order and Delta 5. Kate (drummer) and Crawford formed the Young Aborigines, a very progressive unit with two drummers that Yauch sometimes showed up and jammed with. "We were making fun of all the hardcore bands that were coming out everywhere. . . . It started as satire and NOW it's a way of life," Yauch hisses. The joke got to Kate, though, who "hated playing that stuff" ("Now I like it though"), and the band broke up. Was the world to be denied "Cookie Puss"?

Nyet. Onto the scene comes Ratcage Records maven Dave Parsons who caught the Beasties at a party and persuaded them to regroup and do a record. *Polly Wog Stew*, a likeable, but not groundbreaking, eight-song seven-inch EP came out. "We did it with the intention of breaking up," recalls Crawford, "but the record sold okay and we got gigs from it."

The Beasties' activities in the next year or so were stifled mostly due to Yauch's decision to attend college and a disagreement between Yauch and original guitarist John Barry,[3] who eventually left. He was replaced by Adam Horovitz.

---

[3] The guitarist who played with the Young Aborigines and with an early incarnation of the Beastie Boys was John Berry, not "Barry."—*ed.*

Unexpectedly, Doug (Doug who?—forget it, the B'Boys figure I know all their friends in NYC; they keep saying things like, "All this happened while we were at Judy's house. . . .") snagged them a couple of hours in a 24-track studio: "They did the soundtrack for *Star Wars* there. Diana Ross uses it, they do a lot of jazzhomofusion. . . . We didn't know what we were doing. The two songs we did as a joke were 'Beastie Revolution' and 'Cookie Puss,'" recalls Crawford. "It was just a massive creative outpouring," he winks.

"And there were all these weird instruments lying around," adds Yauch, "which is how we got all the nutty sounds for 'Beastie Revolution.'"

Ratcage/ Important put this lucky accident out and bigtime hit like a ton of bricks; 10,000 sold, a recommendation in *The Face, Rockpool,* and—most important—airplay at the hottest clubs, black and white (Danceteria, Roxy) and on radio stations from coast to coast, including KISS-FM and KROQ. *Soul Train,* someone asserts, is the next goal.

After "Cookie Puss" went massive, the Beasties needed to hire a full-time DJ to accommodate the live show. So, they nabbed Rick Double R, of Hose, a New York slaver 'n' funk outfit, with, I guess, the same lofty ideals as the B'Boys.

"We met Rick at a gig at the Kitchen—he had a bubble machine," Kate recalls. "He was working with Soul Sonic Force DJ . . . Jazzy J?"

Horovitz protests, "Rick *went out* with him for a few months, that's what"—but Rick's busy trying to make sure I get down that he's wearing *Sudden Impact* style, bullet-proof Gargoyle sunglasses. Anyway, the guy's practically related to every hot DJ in the Big Apple, which can't hardly hurt the Beasties.

For the first part of their set at the Rat, the band went at it alone and the audience was puzzled at the straight hardcorish set, expecting Rick and the bubble machine to break in any second. By all reports, I was in the minority, but I liked this part of their set. The songs were decent and the delivery better, especially "Egg Raid on Mojo" (from *Polly Wog Stew*) and "Subculture," which is thrashy, but preceded by a "Hey, y'all! What's your sign" rap from Crawford. "Don't be stuck up! Kiss some ass!" he yelled at the crowd when the bouncers started getting itchy to punch someone. Now, that's a change.

They dumped their instruments and came back to do the rap part of the evening. No "Cookie Puss," and some fuck-ups (Kate drops the rap and gets soundly booed), but it was disarming, especially after the slickness of Grandmaster Flash and other exponents of the "real" thing. Yauch is the best, looking vaguely embarrassed about delivering letter-perfect rhymes and adding a little endearing foot shuffling to his segment. Horovitz, band brat, does a little poppin' and the band blows out with the best touch of the evening—an approximate cover of "Cum On Feel the Noise," to the crowd's delight. Not too heavy/ Not too lite/ The Beastie Boys are/ Fun for nite.

JOANNE CARNEGIE

BEAUTY & THE BEASTIE BOYS

Creem, September 1985

DETROIT—We all know the story *Beauty & the Beast*. Well, there's a similar tale to tell, only the beasts *here* are boys. And the beauty? She's a girl named Madonna.

Back in 1979, these Beastie Boys were playing hardcore rock in the underground clubs of NYC. They were quite young then—13 or 14 years old; one member might've even been 12. Despite their ages, they somehow

On tour with Madonna in early 85: As close as they could get.

managed to get past the I.D. check to make what they call "hard-metal-core" music. They played a half-dozen gigs and then broke up.

In 1981, the band re-formed without Beastie Girl Kate Schellenbach and they released a seven-inch EP, *Polly Wog Stew*. Breakdancing was becoming a popular way to break your *neck*, and along with that, rapping went with the moves and the grooves. The Beasts tried it. Audiences approved. Soon came "Cookie Puss," a radio hit which sparked mild controversy over its suggestive title, but "the song was written about ice cream cookies," claims Michael Diamond. By 1984, the Beastie Boys were rapping full-time.

During this same period, DJ Mark Kamins was spinning music in NYC dance clubs. And Madonna—yes, *that* Madonna—was making rounds in these clubs pushing her demo tapes. Kamins co-produced Madonna's first LP. And her success is hot history by now. The Beasties met Kamins too, and he recorded the original tracks on their newest EP, *Beastie Boys*. Here's where the Beasties met up with the Beauty.

The Beastie Boys opened for Madonna on her recent U.S. tour. "We actually asked *her* to tour with *us*," deadpans Adam Yauch. The Beasts do a lot of that. You never know when to take them seriously. "Where's the closest White Castle?" one of the Boys muttered upon meeting me. "I'm starving!"

The Beastie Boys' rockin' rap often includes "borrowing" a riff from AC/DC or Led Zeppelin, and, surprisingly, it fits. When questioned, Adam Horovitz simply replied, "A few years back, this guy with shorts on—I think his name was Angus—came by the studio. He heard a guitar riff of mine and liked it," he explains. You almost begin to believe his story.

Didn't they get some flack for doing what is traditionally a black music style? "We got called a few names, but once people hear us, they automatically realize how great we really are," says Yauch.

And, as if rapping, rocking and being with Madonna aren't enough, two of the Beastie Boys have formed a side group, The Young & The Useless, with former Beastie Boy/girl Schellenbach. Mike Diamond, meanwhile, plays drums with Big Fat Love, which includes original Beastie, John Berry.

The Beastie Boys have also cut a soundtrack song, "She's On It," for an upcoming movie, *Krush Groove*, which includes music from Sheila E., Run-D.M.C. and Chaka Kahn. They're working on a new song titled, "Beastie Boy Toy." And, a potential title for their first full-length LP is *Don't Be a Faggot*.

"You must understand one basic fact about the Beastie Boys," Yauch states in his Brooklyn-born accent, "and that's that we do *anything* we want. Besides that we've heard the word: 'You white boys are the coolest ever.'"

TIM ROSS

SOMETHING LIKE A PHENOMENON: THE 99 RECORDS STORY

Tuba Frenzy #4, 1998

Downtown Manhattan, 1999. You're strolling around in the middle of Greenwich Village, just a few blocks south of Washington Square Park, when you take a wrong turn and walk by 99 MacDougal Street. There, directly underneath a rasta-flavored headshop and an unexciting record store (ironically called Route 66), is "the spot so hot you'll scream": a fairly indistinctive bar/restaurant called Cafe Creole. Uhh . . . big deal, right?

Not so fast, pedestrian. In the late '70s and early '80s, a very different business occupied this partially below-ground space where bohos now drink beer and eat jambalaya. The operation was 99 Records, New York's finest underground record store for many years and a key focal point of the early '80s downtown music scene. Perhaps more importantly, the 99 MacDougal space served as the base of operations for Ed Bahlman's 99 Records, a short-lived but highly influential independent record label that documented some of the era's most interesting and original sounds. Releasing classic works by New York musicians like Glenn Branca, the Bush Tetras, ESG, and Liquid Liquid, 99 was where postpunk and no wave experimentalism lived happily alongside sparsely funky percussion-heavy rhythms and reggae/dub-heavy stylings. Now all but forgotten, the label was somewhat of an American analog to Britain's seminal Rough Trade imprint, and historically, 99 Records ought to be remembered as one of the first and greatest American indie labels of the 1980s.

So freeze, rocker—don't push those Adidas so quickly towards the curb. We haven't even touched on 99's hip-hop connections yet, but don't worry, we'll get there in due time. Just take a look inside, OK?

1. ED BAHLMAN

The story of 99 (pronounced "nine nine," not "ninety-nine") begins and ends with one Ed Bahlman, a born-and-bred Brooklynite with a strong work ethic and an intense passion for music, especially new and underground music that wasn't wholly embraced by the mainstream or even punk establishments. It should be noted that not only did Bahlman refuse to be interviewed for this article, but for over a decade, the man has kept an extremely low profile and has remained completely detached from the music business and the NYC scene that he once ruled. For unspecified reasons, Ed Bahlman has refused to give up any of the 99 master tapes for any monetary price, thus infuriating many of the 99 artists who have repeatedly tried to get their out-of-print recordings reissued on other labels. Bahlman has been equally reluctant to shed any light on the many unanswered hows and whys of 99's history and demise, but by talking to many of the other key 99 figures, I was able to discover many things about the 99 years. I even learned some things about Ed Bahlman, who was born in the early 1950s and is now about 46 or 47 years of age.

During his heyday, Ed Bahlman was a devoted fan of all different sorts of music: reggae, underground rock, even early '80s German electronic music. Bahlman had a vast amount of often-obscure musical knowledge and a sharp ear for all of the distinct elements of a recording. Over the years, he became quite a capable producer/soundman and even did some DJing at New York City clubs. According to Ed's younger brother Bill, who was one of NYC's top DJs before and during the 99 years, Ed's sonic abilities are considerable.

> **Bill Bahlman:** He has a remarkable ear. I know when I listen to music with him, he picks things out that I think would pass by so many other people. Just listening to any new track that I play for him, he's very intuitive about where that sound came from or what this break in a particular song was taken from, what other artist has done the same thing before, or whatever. And I think that's one reason why some of the records that he produced were so original—because he really did stress that in the recording. He had a very keen ear for what he was doing. If you listen to the way he produced the records that he put out, he had an incredible sense of sound that came forth in the records.

Ed was also quite the workaholic.

> **Bill Bahlman:** He really did a tremendous amount of good hard work. He worked from morning 'til night, whether it was running the shop or

going to see bands in clubs, getting in and doing recording sessions, going out with the bands in the clubs and doing their sound and being there for soundcheck. Everything he was doing, he worked very hard at, around the clock.

Additionally, Ed Bahlman was quite a sharp businessman. Not only did he move surprisingly large quantities of his 99 releases, but he only sold records cash-on-delivery, meaning that he didn't have to deal with the heinous 30-60-90-days-and-beyond accounting terms that so many of today's independent labels are forced to just accept.

> **Glenn Branca:** The fact is, Ed was an unbelievably good businessman in the end. He just didn't know the business at first. But it didn't take him long to learn. And once he learned, man, pphhhh. . . . I mean, he got the distributors and he knew how to deal with them. Believe me, what he did was truly exceptional—to move 10,000 copies [of *The Ascension*]. Even with all the press we were getting, to move 10,000 copies of that record was a small miracle. You have to realize that Hüsker Dü sold 20,000 records and that was a regular, relatively commercial rock band.

Despite his many talents, Ed Bahlman had a fiercely independent ideology and a few odd personality quirks that probably prevented 99 from being even more successful than it was. Richard McGuire and Sal Principato of Liquid Liquid both remember the extremely paranoid side of Bahlman, the side that tended to distrust people or companies who didn't appear to share his integrity and devotion to the music.

> **Richard McGuire:** Ed was always paranoid of losing control. I remember Rick Rubin coming into the store, talking about his idea for Def Jam and asking advice. Ed thought it was a bad idea to have a major label act as distributor. I also remember hearing that Ed had an opportunity for ESG to play *Saturday Night Live* but that he said "no" out of fear of losing control.

> **Sal Principato:** There was a perception that he only associated with quality, down-to-earth people within the music business. Ed had a hands-on approach to his business that both enhanced and stifled opportunity. It was my impression that there were offers coming in that Ed would ignore because of, one, the control issue and, two, because he felt practically no one was to be trusted. Even distribution deals he'd shy away from, thinking it would result in some unforeseen disaster.

According to onetime 99 employee/manager Terry Tolkin, Bahlman just didn't have the ideal temperament for longtime survival in the music industry.

> **Terry Tolkin:** Ed was just a fragile guy . . . a very fragile soul. He cared too much about what he was doing.

2. GLENN BRANCA

A rock musician and devoted theater enthusiast from Harrisburg, Pennsylvania, Glenn Branca had been attending Emerson College in Boston during the early '70s when he decided to drop out of school (six credits shy of his degree) and move to London. After a year of various theater activities in London, Branca returned to Boston and joined forces with a friend who knew a lot about not only music but performance art as well. Together the two friends started the Bastard Theatre, an odd sort of avant-garde theater group that put on extremely experimental drama/music productions using just a shoestring budget, a cast of non-musician friends, and months and months of planning and rehearsal time.

Glenn Branca had long been a passionate record collector and rock fanatic, and by the mid-'70s, he had become somewhat dissatisfied with the Boston scene. The shining stars of New York's punk explosion (Patti Smith, the Ramones, etc.) held a much greater allure, so in late 1976, the 27-year-old packed up his belongings and moved to New York City. Much to Branca's chagrin, the excitement that he was pursuing wasn't exactly there anymore.

> **Glenn Branca:** Part of the reason I came to New York [was that] I wanted to come to the heart of the BEAST. The outrageous thing is I came here and the scene was *dead*. There was nobody playing anywhere. All you got is Wayne County, Cherry Vanilla, and all these kinds of half-assed bands. Patti and all the main bands had been signed. They were all off touring. They never played in New York at all. Of course there was Alan Suicide, who [was] my greatest inspiration. When I saw Alan Suicide it was like, "This is what I came to New York to see." It was at Max's so it was *loud*. Devastatingly.[4]

Not long after arriving in New York, Branca met up with a like-minded theater/music nut named Jeff Lohn; together, the two friends plotted a

---

[4] Glenn Branca interview by Howard Wuelfing, *Forced Exposure* #16, 1990.

Bastard Theatre-esque drama group before eventually deciding to form an actual band. Thus began the Theoretical Girls, a quartet consisting of Branca on guitar, Lohn on keyboards/bass, Margaret DeWys on bass/keyboards, and future producer/engineer extraordinaire Wharton Tiers on drums. In a short period of time, the T-Girls (as Branca sometimes referred to them) became very popular in both SoHo art circles and the downtown dives where unsigned New York bands could actually get gigs. Musically, the band used some of the same menacing atonality and repetitive rhythmic thud as the better-known no wave bands of the day (the Theoretical Girls were occasionally referred to as the "fifth band" on the classic four-band *No New York* compilation). But the Theoretical Girls were by no means limited to a particular style.

> **Glenn Branca:** Theoretical Girls was truly an experimental band, because every song was different. We were just trying every possible idea that came to our minds. We really didn't care at all what the fucking audience thought. And all of a sudden we had this incredible audience that was coming from the art world. When we played audition night at CBGBs, the place was totally packed. And although Hilly [Kristal, head honcho at CBGBs] *hated* us, he had to book us because we packed the place.[5]

In 1978, Branca released a well-received Theoretical Girls seven-inch on his own Theoretical label. That same year, Branca formed the Static, a trio with Branca (guitar; arty opera-tinged vocals), Branca's girlfriend Barbara Ess (bass), and Christine Hahn (drums). The Static were more focused and a bit more extreme than the Theoretical Girls, blending dramatic performance art with a uniquely tense and kinetic style of experimental rock that had many of the same qualities (strange chords and guitar sounds, frenetic tempo shifts and musical climaxes) that would later make *Confusion is Sex*-era Sonic Youth so compelling. Before breaking up in late 1979, the Static released a great seven-inch ("My Relationship" b/w "Don't Let Me Stop You"), also on Branca's Theoretical imprint. In fact, it was through the selling and distribution of his two bands' seven-inch singles that Glenn Branca first encountered Ed Bahlman and 99 Records.

3. IN THE BEGINNING

When the 99 store opened up in mid-1978, not only was Ed Bahlman not involved, but the store wasn't even a record store. 99 began as a punk

---

[5] Alex Foege, *Confusion Is Next: The Sonic Youth Story*, New York, 1994, p. 28.

clothing/accessories store run by Gina Franklyn, a British clothes designer who had moved to New York in 1970. In 1977, Franklyn had started Manic Panic (NYC's first all-punk boutique) with the infamous Tish and Snooky, two sisters who had been backup singers in an early schtick-heavy version of Blondie before forming their own joke-punk band called the Sic F*cks. Tish and Snooky were, to quote Thurston Moore, "the models of Please Kill Me-era fashion/streetwhore CBGB eleganza" and, thus, right at home at Manic Panic.

After a year at Manic Panic, Franklyn parted ways with Tish and Snooky and set up shop at 99 MacDougal Street in mid-1978. Assisted by former Manic Panic employee Sara Reyes, Franklyn continued to design and sell fashionably punk clothes and accessories similar to the type of stuff sold in London's punk boutiques. Shortly after the opening of 99, Ed Bahlman came in as a customer and met Gina. The two started dating and before long, Ed was helping out in the store and selling a small number of punk/independent singles.

> **Glenn Branca:** 99 was Gina's store. Ed was her boyfriend. And he said, "Oh, can I sell some records out of here?" And she said, "sure." It started out with just a few imported singles. I guess I started going there in '78 because I was releasing independent singles with my bands and I would go around to whatever stores. And 99 was one of the stores that would buy independent singles. All they had were singles. The store that I remember seeing was a store that had about 30 singles for sale. That was about it. It was a clothing store. [The record part] started out very small. I was just walking down MacDougal Street one day and in the window there were seven or eight independent singles, mainly from England. So I went down into the store and he had maybe twenty or thirty more that he was selling.

Despite his new ventures at 99, Ed Bahlman retained his previous full-time job until at least 1980. Even from the very beginning of things, the man was exercising an impressive round-the-clock work ethic.

> **Terry Tolkin:** Ed was working on the Upper East Side of NYC when he opened the record side of the store at Gina's. He was a super at an old co-op building. He kept that job for some time after starting the store, about two years I suppose, working the third shift in a 24-hour building. So he'd open the store at noon, work 'til 8 pm, eat, go out 'til 4 am, and then go to the building. It was a union job and he had worked there a long time so I think there were a lot of vacation and sick days used up starting the store.

Before 99 started, the primary place in New York to get punk and underground records was Bleecker Bob's, run by the notorious "Bleecker" Bob Plotnik. But with Ed's vast musical knowledge and Gina's extensive connections in Britain, 99 Records rapidly became *the* place to shop, especially for those looking for the latest, coolest postpunk sounds.

Gina Franklyn: One day I said [to Ed], "I have to go on a buying trip to England. Why don't you come with me?" And I used to know Geoff Travis at Rough Trade, and so I introduced Ed to Geoff and they hit it off. And then I said, "Gee, why don't you bring in all this so-called alternative music." The stuff that Rough Trade was putting out. No one was bringing it in then. So that's what we used to do, stuff suitcases and bring them back and drag boxes of stuff back over. I remember bringing huge cartons of *Metal Box* back with me, waiting for customs to stop me, but they didn't. If we'd waited for it to be shipped over, we wouldn't be the first in the city, so I physically brought them all back with me so that we [would be] the first to get *Metal Box*, since that was such a big deal.

Glenn Branca: Eventually [Ed] would go into serious competition with Bleecker Bob and that became sort of a war for awhile, because he was covering Bleecker Bob's territory. 99 became tremendously popular. It was *the* collector's store. All the DJs got all of their records down there. And Ed had tremendous taste. He knew *the* most obscure stuff, both in reggae and the independent rock scene. And Bleecker Bob was such a fucking asshole—and I suppose he still is—that nobody wanted to go in there if they didn't have to anyway. Ed would be perfectly willing to take out a record and play it if you wanted to hear it and, shit, he was a tremendous well of information, whereas all Bleecker Bob wanted to do was take the girls into the back room!

Branca certainly wasn't the only early 99 customer who went on to play a major role in both the label's history and the early '80s NYC scene. Devoted record collector and future Sonic Youth guitarist Thurston Moore was also an early 99 shopper.

Thurston Moore: [Before], when you came to NYC searching for punk you went to Bleecker Bob's for records. There was a record store around the corner that carried punk stuff too, but it was more of an avant-garde classical/jazz and folk place . . . oh God, if only I knew then what I know

now! One day in the midst of PiL/Slits mania, 99 Records opened up and it was way more hipper than Bleecker Bob's, which was more of a "Stiff Records rule!" kinda vibe. Ed Bahlman and Gina were selling contemporary dub and underground sounds (Rough Trade, Chiswick, etc.) and it was *the* greatest place to hang out.

Due in part to its superior record selection, extremely knowledgeable staff, ultra-hip clientele, and unique listen-before-you-buy allowances, 99 Records quickly became one of *the* central gathering points for NYC's early '80s underground music scene, as 99 recording artist Vivien Goldman attests.

> **Vivien Goldman:** The store used to function a bit like the old Rough Trade shop, where it was very much also a milieu or salon, where people would hang out and you'd have an exchange of ideas. It was a very creative atmosphere.

And an ideal launching pad for an independent record label.

4. RECORD #1

As much of a *rock* fan as he was, Glenn Branca had been extremely interested in extended musical compositions and avant-garde sounds for quite some time. Throughout his years as a devoted fan of bands like Aerosmith, Alice Cooper, and the New York Dolls, Branca's ear had been open to everything from experimental art-rock to Indonesian chanting to 20th century classical music. Henry Cow and Gustav Mahler were two of his favorite artists, period.

But for all of the experimenting that Branca had been doing with the Static and the Theoretical Girls, it wasn't until a somewhat impromptu solo gig in the spring of 1979 that Branca decided to make a radical break from the shackles of the standard rock lineup. Early in 1979, Max's Kansas City had contacted Jeff Lohn in an attempt to book the Theoretical Girls (on a bill with seminal no wave groovers the Contortions, no less). At the time of the call, Branca was on tour with the Static, and rather than speak for his band, Lohn opted to perform by himself. Upon returning to NYC, Branca chose to do the same and decided to perform a piece that he had composed for six electric guitars, bass, and drums.

> **Glenn Branca:** It was all kind of organic. The rock bands I was doing were really experimental bands and I was trying tons of different ideas. And one

of the ideas was to do something for lots of guitars. It was just another idea that was sort of sitting there. And what happened was I was invited to play at Max's Easter Festival, which was sometime in '79. Or my band was, but the guy who I was doing the band with, Jeff, wanted to do a solo gig. So I did a solo gig, too, on the program. Instead of Theoretical Girls playing, we both did our own separate things. That's when I did a piece called "Instrumental for Six Guitars," which was just another one of my ideas. And it went over incredibly well. It was just whatever friends of mine happened to be available at the time. I used Barbara and Christine from the Static and they actually both played guitars. I had a different drummer for the guitar band—Stephan Wischerth, who I'd gotten from a band called Youth In Asia who had split up. I would never have stolen him from them, but they had split, so I immediately grabbed him. As far as I was concerned, he was the best drummer on the scene, period. I kept doing both bands for awhile, but my heart was with the big guitar group. I was sort of doing it all at the same time—there was a period where I was doing the big guitar band, the Static, and the Theoretical Girls all at the same time. And then every single piece I wrote for the guitars was so fucking good, so I said, "Fuck the bands, I'm just going to do the guitars."

And "do the guitars" he did. In the months after his successful "solo" debut, Branca composed several ambitious large ensemble guitar pieces.

> Glenn Branca: That year I wrote a number of pieces very quickly. I wrote a piece called "Dissonance," which was meant to be a prototypical idea of rock music as dissonant. And I wrote a piece called "Lesson No. 1," which was very clearly a very easy piece that was meant to be a kind of rock minimalism. I wrote another piece called "The Spectacular Commodity" that was intended to be a kind of nineteenth-century classical music played by a rock band.[6]

"Dissonance" and "Lesson No. 1 for Electric Guitar" were thematically simple yet strikingly powerful pieces that didn't require the multiple guitar attack that the ambitious composer had used in the clubs. It wasn't long before Branca and a stripped-down quintet were ready to put a record out.

> Glenn Branca: I had to get a record of this stuff out. I already had more than an album's worth of material. And so I started hustling around. And

---

[6] Alex Foege, *Confusion Is Next: The Sonic Youth Story*, New York, 1994, p. 33.

I didn't know anybody and I wasn't being approached by any labels or anything like that. So one of the things I did was go into Ed's store and say, "Hey, listen man, have you ever thought about starting a record label?" And he went, "Yeah, I have thought about it, but I don't know what to do. How do you do it?" And I said, "Well, I've released two records already. I know the whole thing. I know the manufacturers, I know how to get it mastered, I know the studios, the whole deal." And he said, "Oh yeah, well how much is it going to cost?" And I came up with the lowest possible prices that I could think of, which were pretty low, and he said, "Well, yeah, I think I'd be interested." So it went from there.

In today's musical climate, with millions of labels giving damn near anything a try, it might seem odd that Branca would have any difficulty getting his music released. But in 1980, there were almost no independent record labels in New York. An inaugural 99 release seemed to be the best option Branca had.

Thurston Moore: It was funny 'cause nobody really had a label going in NYC except Charles Ball who had Lust/Unlust (which put out the initial no-wave stuff) and before that [there was] Ork, which put out Television and [Richard] Hell, and Patti's Mer label. These were way short-lived and weren't band-scene labels. I remember working in the shipping department at Masterdisk when Ed Bahlman came in to master Glenn Branca's 12-inch and I was like, "Whoa . . . you're putting a record out?" He said Glenn just came in and asked him to do it 'cause he thought it would be a good idea! Ed went for it and did it!

Released in March 1980, the powerful *Lesson No. 1* 12-inch (99-01 EP) schooled all listeners via a rock-band-plus-one-more lineup: Branca on guitar, future Knitting Factory all-star Anthony Coleman on organ/keys, F.L. Schroder on bass, Stephan Wischerth on drums, Michael Gross on guitar for "Lesson," and Harry Spitz on sledgehammer for "Dissonance." The A-side "Lesson No. 1 For Electric Guitar" was a gorgeous exercise in musical linearity, starting out with minimal pendulum-esque guitar-chime tick-tocks and following a majestic trajectory into pulsating masses of beautifully swirling harmonics. In some ways, the cut (one of Branca's "prettiest" works) has proven to be the rarely farmed middle ground between the pleasant, streamlined minimalism of the early '70s krautrock of Harmonia and Neu! and the guitar-noise density of later Branca-influenced rock outfits. The pounding pulse continued on *Lesson No. 1*'s B-side, but the much darker and aptly named "Dissonance" wove together twelve minutes of ominous clanging and churning tone clashes, all punctuated by percussive metallophone strikes and Wischerth's furious drum rolls. With its frenzied six-string brutality and tense ebb-and-flow climaxes, "Dissonance" turned out to be somewhat archetypal with regards to Branca's later larger ensemble works.

From a business standpoint, *Lesson No. 1* was quite a success. The record sold a few thousand copies and paved the way for the next releases on the young but already well-respected 99 label.

5. BUSH TETRAS AND Y PANTS

By the end of 1980, Bahlman had put out two more records—both of them seven-inches by female-dominated bands that were well-connected in the NYC music scene. Bush Tetras guitarist Pat Place had been part of the original Contortions lineup that had recorded the classic four *No New York* tracks, the *Buy* LP, and James White and the Blacks' *Off White* LP. By the middle of 1979, the tantrums of James Chance and the greedy dictator antics of Anya Phillips (Chance's girlfriend and the Contortions' so-called "manager") had become completely unbearable, and Place did as the rest of the not-Chance members did—she walked. In the months that followed, Place (renowned for her unique rhythmic style and slide guitar playing) formed the Bush Tetras with vocalist and Cleveland transplant Cynthia Sley, bassist Laura Kennedy, and drummer Dee Pop. In early 1980 the band began playing shows at Tier 3 and other downtown clubs, and before long, the Tetras were receiving lots of praise for what *Musician* magazine referred to as "arty, dissonant ultrafunk."[7] Steady gigging helped the Bush Tetras become big favorites in the local clubs, which is where Bahlman first heard the band.

Dee Pop: I met Ed in '79. I used to shop [at 99] a lot and we became sociable quickly. [Once] me and my mom went to see Black Uhuru's first ever NYC show at Hunter College and Ed was there. I introduced the two and my mother started yakking and actually invited Ed to see the Bush Tetras. Ed came to see us at Hurrah's and he liked us a lot. Ed signed the band to a one-off 45. We recorded "Too Many Creeps"/"Tropics"/"Snakes Crawl" at a jingle house in midtown NYC. We actually used equipment belonging to John Travolta's brother, who was in the midst of riding his brother's coat tails and recording an album of his own. Donny

---

[7] Yablonskaya, liner notes to Bush Tetras's *Boom in the Night* (ROIR, 1995).

Christensen of the Raybeats produced, for a lack of a better word. I don't think anyone really had a clue as to how this stuff was done.

Released in the latter part of 1980, the "Too Many Creeps" 7-inch (99-02) received significant airplay on WNEW-FM and in New York dance clubs. The hit single even reached #57 on *Billboard*'s Disco chart and went on to sell a reported 30,000 copies. An appropriately named NYC anthem, "Too Many Creeps" was highly infectious and somewhat Gang of Four-like, with Sley spilling out monotonal tired-of-the-city sentiments over a taut driving groove composed of sparse guitar plinking, undulating bass rumbles, and tight, punchy drumming. The first B-side, "Snakes Crawl" was slower, with Place exorcising queasy slide guitar demons over a start-stop bit of dub-influenced rock. "You Taste Like the Tropics" sped things back up and closed the seven-inch off with a short blast of catchy, angular postpunk.

Not unlike Place's Contortions or Gang of Four, the Bush Tetras had found a way to blend white punk abrasiveness with elements of disco, reggae, and funk. The combo's postpunk hybrid also acted as somewhat of an American analog to femme-led Rough Trade bands like the Slits, the Delta 5, and the Raincoats; thus, it was probably not surprising when the Tetras garnered a lot of underground attention in Britain. A February 1981 show at London's Rainbow Club drew rave reviews from *New Musical Express*, which boldly proclaimed, "Bush Tetras will be a New York legend. They steal/save/ARE the show."[8] It was during this particular UK tour that the Bush Tetras recorded a second seven-inch for Rod Pierce's Fetish Records. "Too Many Creeps" would prove to be the band's one and only 99 release.

> **Dee Pop:** [The first single] was the only business we had with Ed. Ed wanted to do another 45 with us but we decided to do our next record with an English label called Fetish. We actually wanted Fetish to release our stuff in Europe and Ed in the States but Ed didn't wanna share. So that ended our 99 story.

Like the Bush Tetras, Y Pants also included a scene veteran among its members. For Y Pants that veteran was Barbara Ess, Glenn Branca's girlfriend and former bassist in the Static. The Static had officially broken up in fall 1979 when drummer Christine Hahn moved to Berlin, where she

---

[8] Ibid.

became the drummer for the German band Malaria. Y Pants got started up very soon thereafter.

> **Gail Vachon:** I [had been] making films, but the soundtracks were becoming more interesting to me than the images, and I learned that anyone could make their own record . . . it wasn't that expensive. Boris Policeband was one of my inspirations. I used a lot of tape loops. I told Barbara, who lived upstairs in my building and had had more experience with this sort of thing, that I wanted to make a record. She was also interested in what she called "small music" and suggested [that] we work together. I think we had one or two sessions with just the two of us. I played a little red toy grand piano that I found on the street, whose notes corresponded only vaguely to a Western scale. I think she played thumb piano. Then I bought a toy piano with more keys and Barbara switched to a small ukelele.[9]

Glenn Branca offered the brand new band a December '79 gig opening up for his guitar group, and this provided an impetus for Y Pants to begin solidifying their ideas and lineup.

> **Barbara Ess:** I had been meeting with Gail and we [did] little music. She was playing a little keyboard and I was playing a little ukelele. And then Glenn was going to do a big guitar piece and he invited us to open for him at Tier 3, so then we had to get it together. And we called Virginia, who I had met at some jam session at an artist's place. I had also seen her play with Jeff Lohn of Theoretical Girls—once they did a piece together though she didn't play drums then. But we needed a drummer and thought that maybe she would do. She had never drummed before [but] she got so good. And then I added the bass that I had been playing before. Virginia got a small-scale regular drum set as we kept playing. We put everything through all these different [effects], especially a phase shifter that I still have.

> **Gail Vachon:** Our original idea was to play toy instruments. Verge's first drum kit was a child's Mickey Mouse set with paper heads. We used contact mikes on the toy piano and the uke, and put them through phase shifters and other kinds of filters. But we also wanted it to have more presence, so Verge put together a real, if slightly modest, drum kit, I supple-

---

[9]Gail Vachon, liner notes to Y Pants CD (Periodic Document, 1998).

mented my toy piano with a two-octave Casio keyboard, and Barbara put aside the uke on some songs for a bass guitar.[10]

Y Pants had discovered a way of making music in a rock band format while integrating a unique art/performance element that toyed around with the concept of scale. It was an unusual sight: grown women playing tiny instruments and still using big amplifiers and effects. The trio began playing regularly in New York clubs and art spaces, and eventually, Ed Bahlman came to see Y Pants, having heard positive things about the band from Glenn Branca.

> **Barbara Ess:** Ed came to see us at Irving Plaza and he liked it. I remember he said to Glenn, "I see what you mean."

Bahlman offered to do a seven-inch with the band and the four-song EP *Y Pants* (99-03) was released in 1980. The EP's most anomalous tune was a bouncy bass-led cover of "Off the Hook," a lesser-known Rolling Stones tune. The single's other three songs ("Beautiful Food," "Favorite Sweater," and "Luego Fuego") were a bit stranger, weaving a unique ghostly sound out of toy piano, heavily effected bass, passionate vocal cries, and Piersol's snappy, staccato drumming (which, stylistically, wasn't all that far from the compellingly rhythmic skin-pounding of Slits/Raincoats drummer Palmolive).

> **Gail Vachon:** The first song I remember working on was "Beautiful Food." Most of the songs were written by Barbara. Verge contributed several good ones and I seemed to excel in coming up with good cover versions. We all hashed out the arrangements together, sometimes from just a germ of an idea . . . we fit in nicely, both as a variant of a rock band and as performance art.[11]

6. ESG

Unlike their future 99 labelmates, the members of ESG weren't familiar faces in the late '70s NYC underground. When the band started, over half of its members hadn't even completed high school yet. ESG were about as detached from the downtown scene as they could possibly be, both spiritually and geographically. The band was formed by four sisters who lived

---

[10] Ibid.

[11] Ibid.

in the South Bronx and had grown up listening to James Brown, the Supremes, the Jackson 5, and Aretha Franklin.

> Renee Scroggins: [My sisters and I] lived in this project. It wasn't a nice neighborhood, and my mother didn't want us hanging out in the streets getting into trouble. And she knew we liked instruments [because] we used to watch shows like rock concerts and things like that. So she bought us the instruments we were interested in.[12]

Renee's instrument was a guitar—first an acoustic guitar but eventually an electric one. Oldest sister Marie got congas, Valerie got drums, and youngest sister Deborah got a bass. None of the girls ever took music lessons; instead they honed their skills by simply staying at home and jamming out all sorts of ideas.

> Renee Scroggins: We tried a lot of different sounds that didn't work. We didn't want to sound like anybody else. We didn't want folks to hear us and say we were copying anybody.[13]

By the end of the '70s, the group had added family friend Tito Libran on congas and abbreviated its "too feminine" name (Emerald, Sapphire, and Gold) to the shorter and more rhythmic ESG. More importantly, ESG had hit upon a unique sound that was right for them: a repetitive and skeletal percussive-funk that flat-out *scorched*, like Bronx blacktops in the oppressive August heat.

> Renee Scroggins: I grew up listening to James Brown and it was the funkiest music I could ever hear, especially when he would go to the bridge and let the funk rip. So I felt that he would always make that little funky space too short. You know, the part that made you want to really dance and get down? I wanted to do something like that but let that funky space ride![14]

Ed Bahlman discovered ESG while serving as a judge at a CBS Records-sponsored talent search. The band struck out with the rest of the judge

---

[12] Renee Scroggins interview, *Brave New Waves* radio program (Canadian Broadcasting Company, 1995).

[13] Jim Testa, "E.S.G.—Emerald, Sapphire—Solid Gold," *Discords*, summer 1981.

[14] Renee Scroggins interview, *Brave New Waves* radio program (Canadian Broadcasting Company, 1995).

panel, failing to even place in the contest, but Bahlman went nuts over the band and offered to be ESG's manager and soundman. Before long, the enterprising Scroggins girls were playing regularly at clubs like Hurrah's and Danceteria, where they wowed music critics and other unexpecting Manhattanites. One mid-1980 show at Hurrah's proved to be a particularly important one for ESG, as it introduced the band to the head honcho at influential British indie Factory Records.

> **Renee Scroggins:** We were opening for an act of [Factory's] called A Certain Ratio. And [Factory head] Tony Wilson said, "I like what you're doing! How would you like to make a record?" And I said, "Yeah, we'd like to." Ed Bahlman was our manager and he said, "We'll hook it up."[15]

Almost immediately, ESG entered the studio with noted British producer Martin Hannett—a hasty development rumored to have been made possible by the fact that Ian Curtis' May 1980 suicide had forced Joy Division to cancel previously booked studio time with Hannett.

> **Renee Scroggins:** A week later we were in the studio with [Martin Hannett]. And we went in and we played. [Hannett] was no pressure or nothing. We appreciated the fact that he did not mess up or distort our sound. He left it like it was.[16]

From these Martin Hannett sessions, Factory put together a three song ESG single ("You're No Good"/"Moody"/"UFO") for release in Britain. In turn, 99 took the three Factory songs and added three live tracks (recorded at Hurrah in December 1980) to make a six-song 12-inch EP for the States. Released in early 1981, *ESG* (99-04) was nothing short of a masterpiece: eighteen minutes of infectious and economical funk grooves, mostly percussion and bass but with vital contributions (minimal guitar plinking; high-pitched soulful vocals/chirps) from the band's unofficial mouthpiece/leader, 21-year-old Renee. Though she only played guitar on two songs, Renee shined especially brightly on the classic "UFO," on which her guitar stabbed out a sinister and repetitive *Psycho*-like motif that perfectly topped off a strange space-funk instrumental already full of stops/starts, speed changes, and awesome drum fills.

---

[15] Ibid.

[16] Ibid.

"UFO" may have been the most startling track on *ESG*, but the debut had numerous other extra-special grooves. "You're No Good" kicked the record off with sultry midtempo attitude, while "Moody," with its conga breaks and ur-house-music rhythms, was the obvious pick for dance floor action. The live side of the EP showed ESG at their sweaty and workin'-it best, tearing through the funky gotta-get-paid anthem "Earn It" and two speedy semi-instrumentals ("ESG," "Hey!") anchored by sharp precise drumming and occasional title chanting.

ESG's debut amazed critics and caught many an underground music fan completely offguard, thus prompting the occasional mischaracterization of the band as "minimalist salsa." The EP also went on to join the Bush Tetras single as one of 99's best-selling records ever. The record's most enduring legacy, however, lies with its later (and unintentional) entrance into the hip-hop arena.

7. LIQUID LIQUID

Like ESG, Liquid Liquid went through a slight moniker modification and a few sound-and-error trials before hitting upon the stripped-down rhythmic beat-funk that would become the band's trademark. Liquid Liquid developed out of Liquid Idiot, a band that Richard McGuire and Scott Hartley had formed as students at Rutgers University.

> **Richard McGuire:** In 1978 I was in school studying art and I would jam with friends in my living room. This turned into Liquid Idiot. Scott Hartley played drums. I played a beat up organ and a guitar tuned to an open chord. We had another guitar player (Ken "Man" Calderia) and a sax player (Bob Seanus). None of us really knew how to play with the exception of Scott, who had taken drum lessons. I got the name by picking random words out of a hat and it was perfect because the music sounded idiotic. We recorded all these silly jams with a mono tape recorder. Later [we] edited them down to the best parts [for] a self-produced seven-inch.

Released in early 1979, the fifteen-minute-long Liquid Idiot seven-inch had nine disorienting tracks of improv jamming, complete with lots of odd atonal noodling and lo-fi tribal grooves. It was quite an interesting record, one that could easily be passed off today as the mid-'90s practice tapes of Soul Junk, the Shadow Ring, or Thinking Fellers Union Local 282.

Around this same time, McGuire and the rest of Liquid Idiot played in a big-band version of the Idiot idea. The Idiot Orchestra contained 12 members and included all four members of the eventual Liquid Liquid quartet.

> **Richard McGuire:** The Orchestra consisted of everyone who was in the Idiot, all of Liquid Liquid, and anyone else we knew that owned an interesting instrument. The sound was big and creaky. There were two clarinets, two basses, two saxophones, a cello, a violin, a trumpet, a synth, marimbas, and drums. It was kinda like Raymond Scott, only none of us could really play.

The Idiot Orchestra also released a seven-inch single, but before long, the various Idiot experiments gave way to coarse rock simplicity.

> **Richard McGuire:** By the following year some of us had moved to New York and the band [went through] personnel changes. Sal Principato, who I've known since I was 16, was living out in San Francisco writing some songs with my brother Bill. They came to visit, we rehearsed some of the songs, wrote some new ones, and before they were scheduled to go back, I went into CBGBs and got us a show. Eventually my brother left the band, and I was playing guitar, Sal was on bass and vocals, and Scott on drums. This incarnation was . . . more like a power trio, more "rock 'n' roll," but in a very naive way. We were playing out in clubs like Tier 3 and this place called A's which was a loft on Rivington Street. We played there with Jean-Michel Basquiat's band Gray and Alan Vega from Suicide.

This version of Liquid didn't exactly set NYC locals and club owners on fire, but as the band's members became more and more excited by Jamaican reggae, British dub-influenced postpunk, and the extended grooves of Can and Fela Kuti, Liquid Idiot's punk naivete began evolving into something altogether different.

> **Richard McGuire:** The band started to gel [when] we were all living in the same place and listening to a lot of reggae . . . Bob Marley, Tapper Zukie, lots of dub. I remember finding a Fela Kuti record called *Zombie* that we all loved. We were still listening to punk bands like the Clash and we liked the Slits a lot. But we were also listening to the *Super Fly* soundtrack. I remembering hearing "Rapper's Delight" and Kurtis Blow's "The Breaks," but I remember thinking of them as novelty records. Around 1980, I made a conscious decision to streamline our set and only play what we were calling "Big Beat" songs—essentially groove songs, songs

with either a sway or an oomph. I took over the bass and dropped the guitar, we added Dennis Young who played marimba—I knew him from school. At this point we had to change the name. The word "Idiot" seemed too punk and our sound was changing.

By fall 1980 the band had re-dubbed themselves Liquid Liquid, a name that reflected the increasingly fluid and repetitively rhythmic direction in which their music was heading. The quartet was ready to shake things up with their unique brand of "body music"—music that you could dance to.

Sal Principato: Like a lot of musical performers in the early '80s, we were "searching for the perfect beat" and it came in many forms, not all of them musical. I was personally enamored by reggae music and Afro-pop. In general we were impressed by most any traditional or cultural music that we came across, also certain deconstructionist kinda rock: Can, DNA, PiL, Iggy. [But] we always felt it was important to filter the music through our own experiences and not just appropriate musical culture for opportunistic purposes.

The new Liquid Liquid brew was a smooth mix of simple yet powerful bass/drum grooves, loads of Latin/African-flavored percussion, and Sal Principato's uniquely haunted-sounding vocal cries, which often sacrificed actual intelligibility in favor of emotive and expressive musicality.

Sal Principato: I come from an almost literary tradition, meaning I always aspired to be a wordsmith not for the words' literal meaning but for their ability to evoke grand vistas by way of atmosphere, texture, and rhythm. My work with the Liquids consisted of development and discovery in public. What I discovered were utterances that first appeared in the delivery room and have been with me since. In my own convoluted way I needed to express my passion for passion. The vocal snippets found in dub reggae had a huge affect on how I approached "singing." I had this inexpensive analogue pitch control/echo unit that I would take on stage with me to twist, turn, and sweeten my utterances. There was a fairly obscure vocalist from Argentina named Yma Sumac who did some wild cross octave vocal gymnastics. I was very impressed with [her] in the early Liquid days.

Soon Liquid Liquid was really working-working and the band felt that it was ready to release a record. Richard McGuire had heard of the 99 label from Glenn Branca, a fan of the Liquids ever since he'd caught one of the three-piece Idiot gigs at A's. McGuire decided to give 99 a try.

> **Richard McGuire:** I went down to 99, met Ed, and gave him a tape. I don't think he was too impressed, so we decided to record ourselves. We recorded "Groupmegroup" and "Rubbermiro." We had some guest spots—on "Groupmegroup" we had a conga player, Bill Kleinsmith, and on "Rubbermiro" we had trumpet from Richard Edson, who later played in Sonic Youth and the Lounge Lizards and went on to act in *Stranger Than Paradise* and numerous character roles. *And* we had Al Diaz on metallophones which he had made himself out of conduit pipe. Al was already famous in graffiti circles as the other half of SAMO along with Jean-Michel Basquiat. After I played Ed this tape he was more intrigued and he set up a show for us at Tier 3 to see how we sounded live. Afterwards he agreed to release an EP with those two tracks plus some live tracks that he would record at a show that he would arrange.

Released in mid-1981, *Liquid Liquid* (99-07) included three live cuts (recorded at a February 1981 show at Hurrah's) in addition to the afore-mentioned "Groupmegroup" and "Rubbermiro." The record's standout cuts are "Rubbermiro," a swank Caribbean/Brazilian-flavored percussion jam later used as incidental music on *Miami Vice*, and "Bellhead," an insanely infectious bells-and-drums groove that ding-dong-dings around like a faster and denser version of the Bob James "Take Me to the Mardi Gras" break later made famous in Run-DMC's "Peter Piper." "Bellhead" quickly became a big dance club favorite and one of Liquid Liquid's signature tunes.

> **Sal Principato:** I remember hearing "Bellhead" around the clubs amidst the techno sounds that were so popular then as now. I thought it was funny, all the tunes with their sequenced keyboards [and] then you'd hear this crusty song with all percussion, drums, and bells. Nobody batted an eye though, 'cept maybe us.

Of the record's other tunes, "Lub Dupe" was a short and echo-laden drum-exercise with major falling-down-the-stairs-drunk vibes, while "Groupmegroup" and "New Walk" were both midtempo "groove-oriented" songs that also received play in local NYC discos. The debut was getting lots of exposure and selling quite well—several thousand copies by some estimates. Bahlman and the band moved quickly to release a followup EP.

Released in December 1981, *Successive Reflexes* (99-09) was only a slight expansion on the debut's sound. If anything, the EP was mellower and more streamlined than its predecessor. "Lock Groove (In)" and "Lock Groove (Out)" ran together for one side-long jam on a mesmerizing marimba pattern. The B-side featured "Push" (a quick and hard drum-banger), "Zero Leg" (proto-Ui bass-rooted noodlings), and "Eyes Sharp" (a super-quiet tune with a nice bass clarinet cameo from man-about-town Elliott Sharp). *Successive Reflexes* was a solid follow-up, but Liquid Liquid's third record would be the one that finally hit the perfect wave-making groove.

8. NOT JUST NEW YORK

99's initial batch of releases consisted entirely of records by local NYC musicians, but in 1981, the label released a string of records by mostly British acts whose sounds fit in well with Bahlman's increasingly more riddim/dub/reggae-focused tastes. The first of these non-NY artists was Vivien Goldman, a British music journalist with a great singing voice. To this day, Goldman is good friends with Rough Trade founder Geoff Travis, who she had first met during the years she spent attending university at Warwick. Goldman was closely involved with Rough Trade during the store/label's earliest years; these activities, along with her various music writings, helped placed her at the epicenter of Britain's booming independent label scene of the late '70s and early '80s.

> **Vivien Goldman:** It was a whole milieu at that time, part of which is reflected in the musicians on [my] record. Which is sort of what makes a lot of people still interested in it, apart from, hopefully, any virtues of the song and the performance. Because [my record] had this stellar lineup of what was a lot of the gang at that time: Robert Wyatt, people from Public Image—I think I recorded it in downtime from a Public Image Limited album, actually. I had heard of Ed [Bahlman] and I just took it around to him. I heard Ed's was a sympathetic label. I literally went in and played him the tape. He was there serving in the shop. I can't remember what format I had it on, whether it was a cassette or an early pressing or something. But I just played it for him and he said, "Oh yeah, let's do a deal." So I said, "Wow, great! Perfect. Go for it."

Already released in Britain on Goldman's own Window label, the *Dirty Laundry* 12-inch (99-05EP) came out in spring of 1981 and sported two different sides of experimental dub/postpunk fusion—"mutant reggae," as *New York Rocker* writer Michael Hill accurately called it.[17] The record's A-side ("Launderette") featured Goldman singing a goofy love-in-a-laundromat tale over top of a spritely reggae groove composed of George Levi's dub bassline and percussion from ex-Soft Machine icon Robert Wyatt. Notable contributions also came from the Raincoats' Vicky Aspinall (awesome piercing violin), renowned UK improvisor Steve Beresford (toy piano), and Public Image Limited's Keith Levene (guitar) and John Lydon (production). For the B-side ("Private Armies/P.A. Dub"), young On-U Sound studio-noodler Adrian Sherwood took over production duties and twisted sounds from the same all-star lineup into a delightfully disorienting On-U haze. Goldman's more politically charged vocals added disembodied war whoops and multitracked cries of terror (". . . blood everywhere . . .") to the mix.

> **Vivien Goldman:** In retrospect, I think of that [record] as a punk Sade, I realize that's what it is. When Sade came out, I said, "Wow!" Although I'm more into a narrative and humor thing. That was a great boon time of women in rock, in terms of the freeing up of the punk era. I used to be very closely involved with all of those groups like the Slits, the Raincoats, Lora Logic. Some of them are friends to this day.

Soon after releasing the Vivien Goldman 12-inch, 99 released a Congo/Congos 12-inch (99-06EP). The Congos had been a Jamaican roots reggae duo; their scant 1976–77 recordings (reissued in 1996 on the Blood and Fire label) remain classic representations of the vocalcentric reggae era. Unfortunately, potentially mislabeled packaging and a lack of personnel information have made it difficult for me to determine the exact story behind this record, but reportedly, Bahlman licensed it from a label connection in Jamaica.

An additional connection between 99 Records and Adrian Sherwood came with Singers and Players, a studiocentric dub/reggae project whose loose membership (typical for On-U Sound projects) included, among others, toasters Prince Far I and Bim Sherman, postpunkers Keith Levene and Arri Up (Slits), and Sherwood's On-U sidekick Lizard Logan. The band's 1981 debut was *War of Words* LP (99-002LP), an album released by 99 in the United States and by On-U Sound in the United Kingdom.

---

[17] Michael Hill, review of Vivien Goldman's *Dirty Laundry* EP, *New York Rocker*, October 1981.

Terry Tolkin: Singers and Players came from early trips to England when Ed met people like Adrian Sherwood, Tony Wilson, and Geoff Travis, amongst many others. He and Adrian Sherwood became really good friends.

The final non-NY release on 99 came about via another of Bahlman's British connections: Dick O'Dell, proprietor of the small Y Records imprint and manager of British postpunk horn-funkers Pigbag. Ed Bahlman was a big fan of Pigbag's "Papa's Got a Brand New Pigbag" single and wanted 99 to release the single domestically in the States. Bahlman's efforts helped bring about a reciprocal release agreement whereupon 99 would release Y artists in the USA and Y would provide for the British release of 99 artists like Liquid Liquid, who happened to be first in line from 99's side of the ocean. In what must have been either a precursor to or kickoff of the exchange program, Bahlman released a record by Bristol postpunkers Maximum Joy. But the Pigbag single never happened and Maximum Joy's "Stretch" (discomix and rap) b/w "Silent St." (dub) 12-inch EP (99-08EP, 1981) ended up being the only 99 release from the Y Records axis.

Terry Tolkin: As I remember the Y thing, by the time the concept came together around the Pigbag "Papa's Got a Brand New Pigbag" 45, Ed seemed to feel that so many copies had already been sold that he should just release their next single that was about due. When Ed got the tape of the second Pigbag single, he didn't really like it. Neither did Gina or I. They became alternative rock's first one hit wonders. He told Dick O'Dell that he didn't want to put it out. He only put out the Maximum Joy record to get the first Pigbag single, but alas . . . .

9. THE ASCENSION AND DISSENSION

With *Lesson No. 1* under his belt, Glenn Branca spent much of the rest of 1980 focusing his energies on a new band—one that was a little closer to the original lineup of his 1979 six-guitar-ensemble performances. The new sextet consisted of drummer Stephan Wischerth, bassist Jeffrey Glenn, and four guitarists: Branca, classically trained guitarist Ned Sublette, avant-gardist and Chinese Puzzle guitarist David Rosenbloom, and future Sonic Youth guitarist Lee Ranaldo.

Lee Ranaldo: When I first moved to New York I was living in a loft in Brooklyn and Anthony Coleman lived next door on my floor. He was playing with Glenn then. Michael Gross moved to NYC around the same time I did. [He'd] played in the Binghamton version of my first real band, the Flucts. Somehow he got to play with Glenn via Anthony, and that's how I first heard of Glenn. I went to see his Kitchen concert and was knocked out. Later I hooked up with Rhys Chatham and played his music for a couple of gigs, and around that time I heard that Glenn was looking for players. I went to see him and he hired me after a brief meeting. I used the "you might have seen me last night with Rhys at TR3" line on him, as he was in the audience that night. Whatever, it worked.

In contributing both musical and visual/performance ideas to the group, Lee Ranaldo quickly became a vital and innovative member of Branca's miniature guitar army.

Glenn Branca: [Lee] was such an incredible musician. He's still one of the only musicians who took it upon himself to really push the music when we were actually performing it.[18]

Branca, Ranaldo, and the rest of the crew worked up several pieces during 1980, and the band even went on an extensive American tour for three weeks that December. The following year, the sextet recorded the material that would become 99 Records' first full-length album. Released in summer 1981, *The Ascension* (99-001LP) was even more ambitious and out-there than *Lesson No. 1* had been. The album was a mindblowing synthesis of pulsating rock rhythms and dense four-way mazes of tonal dissonance, all shaped by bold crescendos and bombastic clashes that had rarely been heard in the world of "rock" before. Several of *The Ascension*'s pieces hinted at the otherworldly textures that Branca would later visit in depth with his symphonies, but the album's truly magnificent track is "The Spectacular Commodity," an astounding 13-minute opus that Branca had written at the same time as the two *Lesson No. 1* tracks. With its frenetic guitar parts and Wischerth's blazing drum rolls, "The Spectacular Commodity" was rock music at its most daringly dynamic—a proto-Sonic Youth track if ever there was one.

The Ascension was received incredibly well, both in the United States and abroad. The record would eventually sell 10,000 copies—quite an achievement given the difficulty of the music and the fact that 99 was using fairly nascent independent distribution channels. *The Ascension* is still thought of as a classic record by both fans and participants alike.

---

[18] Glenn Branca interview by Howard Wuelfing, *Forced Exposure* #16, 1990.

Lee Ranaldo: *The Ascension* band was to me by far his best small ensemble. We toured the USA and Europe and got so tight with that music that it was incredible. If that band had played gigs for another year or two we would have blown the lid off many peoples' scenes. But Glenn was moving fast then and he went on to the symphonic concerts.

A small-ensemble-to-orchestra transition wasn't the only drastic change Branca would make during the 1981–82 period. Frustrated by numerous business disagreements he was having with Ed Bahlman, Glenn Branca decided to start his own record label—an action that cemented the end of an increasingly rocky Branca/99 relationship.

Terry Tolkin: Ed grew to intensely dislike Glenn between when *Lesson No. 1* came out and when *The Ascension* came out. By the time *The Ascension* came out, their relationship was over.

Glenn Branca: We had had some business disagreements. I had done a recording, a dance piece for Twyla Tharp and I released that on Giorno Poetry Systems. And I don't know if Ed would have released that or not, but I just decided to go ahead. Also, he refused to license *The Ascension*. When I say it sold 10,000, that was just in the United States. It easily would have sold another 10,000 in Europe if he had been willing to license it. And he absolutely refused. The European labels couldn't believe it, that he would not allow it to be licensed! He didn't want anyone else to have a master tape. That record could have sold many more copies because at the time, the press was absolutely tremendous—it was beyond belief. But that's water under the bridge now.

The Branca/Bahlman relationship might have been able to survive such business technicalities, but Bahlman's refusal to sign Sonic Youth to 99 Records catalyzed the breaking of the camel's already weak back. Branca had long served 99 as a unofficial musical advisor, having successfully brought both Y Pants and Liquid Idiot to Bahlman's attention, but Branca's hearty recommendations of Sonic Youth were met by nothing but deaf ears.

Glenn Branca: What happened was I started working on Ed about Sonic Youth, and Thurston was a big collector, so Thurston was in the store all the time. And Ed knew him really well. And I started talking to Ed about this band. There were no other labels in New York at that time, everybody else had gone out of business. Red Star was out of business, Charles Ball's Lust/Unlust was out of business. There was nobody! There were no independent labels except for 99, so Ed was sitting on the top of the fucking mountain. He'd done the Bush Tetras single and all this shit. And I kept bugging him about Sonic Youth. And finally one day he just turned around and said to me, "Glenn, I am never going to release Sonic Youth under any circumstances. Do not bother me about this anymore." And I can only imagine that it had something to do with Thurston. I don't know, it had something to do with something personal. I don't know that, but I [couldn't] understand it.

Branca wasn't the only person who had hoped that Bahlman would release a Sonic Youth record.

Thurston Moore: We were hoping he'd release a record by us but he never bit. We didn't even have a name yet. I told him I wanted to call the band Aspirin and he thought that was appropriate. People use to think that it was weird [that] Ed didn't release a record by us 'cause we were so tied into his trip. But he never said anything about it.

With no offers from 99 on the table, Sonic Youth happily accepted a late 1981 invitation to do a record for the brand new Neutral label. Neutral Records was the brainchild of Branca and Josh Baer, a friend of Sonic Youth's who ran the White Columns art gallery. Baer and Thurston Moore had masterminded the successful nine-day "Noisefest" music festival that had taken place at White Columns in June 1981, and Baer was eager to continue being a patron of the NYC music scene.

Glenn Branca: Bizarrely enough, Josh showed interest in starting a record label and so Sonic Youth was the first thing we did. But then Ed was really, really, really mad about that. [Before], he wouldn't even go to see them. He wouldn't even listen to them. He wanted nothing to do with them. And why, I don't know. Because, fuck, man—I had already gone through this whole same process with him concerning Liquid Liquid. And I couldn't understand why he wouldn't trust my sensibility to even go see them? To even listen to them? I don't know, there had to be something personal. But who knows. See, he didn't know that I was going to get a shot at starting my own label. I think maybe if he had known that. . . . He really went through the roof when that happened. He was really pissed about that. That just made things extremely bad between us. I'm not going to go into all the details, but there's no doubt that maybe. . . . See, at that moment, Ed was the only game in town. He could bide his time, he could play with people's dicks, he could fuck around with people and shit. He was on top of the world. He probably got into a headtrip, which usually happens to people when they first start to kind of make it a bit. So maybe that's what was going on, he thought he could have Sonic Youth whenever he wanted. He knew damn well that no major label was going to come along, because nobody was getting signed. And there were no independent labels.

Or precious few at least. By releasing the five-song EP *Sonic Youth* in early 1982, Neutral joined a tiny NYC independent label club whose primary members were 99 and Labor (a small label that put out a self-titled Swans 12-inch after having initially released records from John Lee Hooker and Michael Gira's pre-Swans band Circus Mort). Neutral followed up this inaugural release by putting out a Y Pants LP, a Jules Baptiste record, and in 1983, Sonic Youth's full-length debut *Confusion Is Sex*. Meanwhile, the 99 roster had dwindled to just ESG and Liquid Liquid, the two bands that had come to define 99's signature sound of "minimalist funk."

10. THE NEXT TWO YEARS

While it's not exactly clear why 99's release schedule slowed to a snail's pace during 1982 and 1983, one can guess that perhaps Bahlman was shooting for cohesive quality over sprawled-out quantity. A March 1981 *Village Voice* article supports such a theory, as it provides evidence that Bahlman was interested in growing slowly and maintaining a distinct 99 aesthetic. Bahlman is quoted reacting to the fact that over a hundred NYC bands had inquired about the possibilities of releasing music on his label.

> **Ed Bahlman:** If we grow too fast, we'll lose our sense of identity. Bands that we choose for the label will reflect our taste in music. When personal tastes hook up, there's much better communication.[19]

A frequent 99 customer and friend of Bahlman's tells a similar story.

> **Duane Rossignol:** During the heyday there when ESG clicked, [Ed] was getting phone calls every day from rap groups, hip-hop groups wanting to put out records. That was totally outside his usual clientele. He had every-

---

[19] Barry Jacobs, "The Singles Scene Gets Some Respect," *Village Voice*, March 25, 1981.

one chasing after him to put out a record. But because of his total involvement in an act, I guess he didn't want to spread himself too thin.

One of the New York bands that would have been a logical addition to the 99 stable was Konk, a six-piece horn/percussion group that was led by Lounge Lizard Dana Vlcek and featured Sonic Youth drummer Richard Edson on trumpet. Frequently lumped in with Liquid Liquid and the jazz/percussion-oriented combo Dog Eat Dog as part of the new batch of "naive rhythm" bands, Konk had jazzy Latin-flavored party/groove elements that likened them to the aforementioned Pigbag or perhaps a horn-filled bastardization of a West African highlife band. But for whatever reason, Bahlman didn't want Konk on 99, though he did distribute Konk's self-released 1981 seven-inch, perhaps as a favor to one or more business acquaintances.

Duane Rossignol: Ken Sitz used to do publicity for the 99 label. He worked there for parts of '80 and '81 and he was usually there every day. He'd make a lot of phone calls in the back. He managed Konk or had some kind of interest in them. And besides Konk . . . there was actually a promo tape with a 99 imprint on it for Dog Eat Dog. I think Ken had an interest in them as well.

Terry Tolkin: We [distributed] the Konk stuff. Ed hated that, but he did it for Ruth Polsky 'cause that was her pet band. Ruth Polsky was probably the most important woman in the alternative music scene. She was this really dynamic person who booked Danceteria and she used to come to the store and she was really into the English bands and I was rapidly becoming [that way]. I was writing for this magazine *Rockpool* about "alternative music," and then Ruth [came] in and said, "Why don't you start booking some bands at Danceteria on Tuesday and Wednesday? 'cause there's never anybody there on the ground floor. It's not much, but I can get you $2000 to give to a band if you can get them to play. . . ." She thought she was getting a bargain and I'm calling up Redd Kross and the McDonald brothers were like, "Yeah! OK, two thousand dollars!" They did their whole first U.S. tour just because of that. And the Buttholes and Big Black and all the Touch and Go bands that I managed and signed . . . I got to know [them] just because 99 was the focal point and I was the guy who was there every day.

Another frequent 99 customer/aficionado recalls a few other bands that had business arrangements with Bahlman's label.

Jim Finnigan: There was also Heart Attack . . . and the biggest 99-related hit of all—"Lawn Chairs" by Our Daughter's Wedding. That song was a big hit in dance clubs and on new wave radio stations—it was on Design Records, exclusively distributed by 99. Our Daughter's Wedding later signed to Capitol, re-recorded a tepid version of "Lawn Chairs" and another EP, and then disappeared into the mist. And let us not forget that the first two Def Jam records were also exclusively distributed by 99—an EP and a 45 by Rick Rubin's own grunge funk band Hose, who were truly awful.

With most of its proper roster gone and no new acts actually signed to the label, 99 wound up releasing only one 12-inch record in all of 1982. ESG's "Dance to the Beat of Moody" (99-10EP) was a short 3-song platter featuring two brand new chant-a-long rumpshakers ("Dance," "The Beat") and a souped-up reworking of "Moody" that probably got the dance floor moving even faster than the original version had.

In 1983, 99 finally released an ESG full-length. In comparison to the debut EP, *Come Away With ESG* (99-003LP) was a bit synthetic-sounding—something that's mostly attributable to the group's increased tightness and Bahlman's slicker, more dance-ready production. Nonetheless, the half-hour-long *Come Away* . . . sported several excellent tunes, including "Chistelle" (a surfy "UFO"-like instrumental), "It's Alright" (peppy reassurance with great guitar and conga additions), and "Tiny Sticks" (almost all percussion and also instrumental). But not everything on *Come Away With ESG* was quite as groovin,' and on the whole, the album suffered slightly from a deficiency of the charming rawness and breathtaking unpredictability that helped make 1981's *ESG* so brilliant. *Come Away With ESG* was a fine record, but it wasn't nearly as great as the band's classic debut.

Unlike ESG, Liquid Liquid had become that much better through years of frequent gigging and craft-honing. *Optimo* (99-11EP) was the band's third EP and a truly impressive summation of the Liquids at their tightest and most polyrhythmically funky. The awesome title track kicked the record off with a powerful metallophone/cowbell statement and a furiously driving drum beat; "Cavern" maintained the energy level with an undeniably addictive bass-driven groove that was perfect as dance-floor fodder. On the flipside of the EP, "Scraper" was a subtler but equally syncopation-happy tune with prominent marimba parts. And all the strings got pulled tight with "Out," a chop-funk-suey rocker with an odd resemblance to the *Fat Albert* theme.

Soon after the *Optimo* EP was released in mid-1983, "Cavern" became a huge hit in both the dance clubs and on black radio station WBLS. The song even spent several weeks on the *Billboard* disco chart, peaking bulletlessly in the 50s among the "likes" of Midnight Star and Kajagoogoo. On the strength of "Cavern," *Optimo* went on to sell upwards of 30,000 copies, a remarkable amount by independent label standards of the day.

11. WHITE LINES

Unfortunately for Ed Bahlman, Liquid Liquid, and 99, *Optimo*'s success would turn out to be somewhat bittersweet. The record's runaway hit was a bit *too* irresistible.

> **Terry Tolkin:** They were playing that song all the time, the Liquid Liquid track "Cavern," on BLS, the biggest black station in New York at the time. And [WBLS disc jockey] Frankie Crocker loved it and Ed would go up there and he had ESG, which they loved also. And they were playing the hell out of this Liquid Liquid track for six weeks, we were selling tons, couldn't keep it in the store. And then they stopped playing it one day. And Ed called up and for like a week, no one would see him or take his call. And then out it came. Just on the radio. We heard it. We were both in the store when we turned on the radio and a few songs later it came on and we were like, "Oh, they're playing 'Cavern' again." But they weren't. It had words....

In October 1983, mere months after 99 had released Liquid Liquid's *Optimo* EP, Sugar Hill Records released Grandmaster and Melle Mel's "White Lines (Don't Don't Do It)" (Sugar Hill #465), a catchy anti-cocaine rap that borrowed/stole from "Cavern" in a major way. For the record, Liquid Liquid's song wasn't actually *sampled* in "White Lines," just extensively copied (and slightly reworked) by the Sugar Hill house band and backup singers. The obvious similarity between the two songs was the instantly recognizable bassline—the supple and snakelike two-note pattern played by Sugar Hill house bassist Doug Wimbish was almost identical to Richard McGuire's original "Cavern" line. And that wasn't all. Other Liquid Liquid elements that got cut into "White Lines" included the high-hat/drum rhythm, the conga drum flourishes, even the melody/rhythm/words of Sal Principato's vocal lines. Principato's indecipherable opening lyric was transformed into "white...lines," while his "slip in and out of phenomena" got changed into "something like a phenomenon," a now-signature hip-hop catchphrase that has been prominently used in songs like De La Soul's "Ego Trippin' (Part 2)" and L.L. Cool J's 1997 hit "Phenomenon."

In actuality, Bahlman's discovery of the "Cavern" appropriation was probably not as sudden or dramatic as Tolkin makes it out to be. According to an October 1983 *Village Voice* article, Sugar Hill actually suggested a split publishing deal to Bahlman/99 two days before "White Lines" debuted on WBLS. Bahlman apparently refused the offer, secure in the knowledge that 99 owned the complete publishing rights of "Cavern." According to the article, Bahlman hired a lawyer to "protect the writers of the song"; Sugar Hill president Sylvia Robinson is quoted as responding, "No one is trying to take anything that belongs to Bahlman. We intend to give him his full publishing share."[20]

That Robinson would speak so generously towards 99 seems completely at odds with Terry Tolkin's dramatic (and, it should be pointed out, uncorroborated) account of Sugar Hill's strongarming tactics and an epic legal tussle.

> **Terry Tolkin:** [A] lawsuit progressed with Liquid Liquid and Sugar Hill Records and Grandmaster Flash and that bled the [99] store dry over a year and a half. We spent over $60,000 just prosecuting the case and that was a real lot of money for us at the time. Ed really didn't know what he was getting into. Sugar Hill was just a mob label—all these mob people like Morris Levy and stuff. They did horrible things [to 99]. Ed wouldn't come to the store for the last year and a half. He'd moved back to Brooklyn, where he was born. He moved into his parents' house, kept the apartment in New York but didn't really go there or use it because they knew where he lived. He wouldn't come in, because on Saturday, they'd send in these people who looked like they were crazy or something. And they'd whip out a machete on our busiest day in the middle of the day and start wailing it around, screaming and yelling. And everybody would run out. And they'd just stand there and laugh at us and leave. We had two plate glass windows and once a week, I'd come to open the store and one of 'em would be broken. At eight hundred bucks a pop. Every week they did that to us. [Ed] got his life threatened constantly. I got the phone calls at work. I would have to meet him on Sunday nights at some weird place at three in the morning with the bag with all the cash from the store that week.

---

[20] Michael Hill, "Rap-Off," *Village Voice*, October 1983.

Tolkin's account of the Sugar Hill/99 events almost sounds too sensational to actually be true, and unfortunately, no one else that I talked to had heard anything at all about Sugar Hill's window-breaking or use of machetes. Gina Franklyn went so far as to suggest that Tolkin's account was a total fabrication.

Gina Franklyn: No! No, complete exaggeration! But they did threaten Ed. They said, "We know where you live."

Franklyn also confirmed that Bahlman did move back to Brooklyn during the Sugar Hill/99 events, but according to Franklyn, the move was motivated by a "mild musical nervous breakdown" and not out of a fear of Sugar Hill mobsters. In defense of Tolkin's tales, however, it should be noted that Franklyn and Bahlman had ended their romantic relationship in early 1983 and Franklyn was no longer involved with the store on a day-to-day basis. Thus, she could have easily not known everything that might have been going on with Sugar Hill. After all, even the members of Liquid Liquid were in the dark about the case.

Sal Principato: Things got murky towards the end. *Miami Vice* used "Rubbermiro" on one of their episodes and Ed said the money we earned from that would go to getting a lawyer to settle the Sugar Hill thing. We didn't receive any *Miami Vice* money or hear of a settlement. Anything I [could] conclude about Ed's dealings with Sugar Hill [would be] pure conjecture. In other words, your guess is as good as mine.

Scott Hartley: The most frustrating thing about the whole shebang is that we really don't know what happened.

Tolkin, 99's main day-to-day employee for all of 1983 and the beginning of 1984, was at the heart of the situation and was one of the only people who would have reason to know everything about the case.

Terry Tolkin: The lawsuit dragged on for fifteen months or more, and then we finally won. We won a judgement for $600,000 and a credit on the record, all that stuff. $660,000 including court costs and legal costs. Plus points retroactive to record number one. I think we had three points, maybe? See, all this was so not defined at the time. There really wasn't anything like this going on. It was something people talked about. It was very, very much underground at that point. And in the courts it was practically untested. It was in the very early days of sampling and my connections with lawyers at the time helped us get some pretty powerful people. It was a massive settlement. I remember everybody was so elated, everybody was so happy when a decision came down that day. But we never collected. Two weeks after they lost the judgement and the appeal, [Sugar Hill] declared bankruptcy. We never got anything. And the [99] store basically went bankrupt because of that. Sugar Hill went into receivership and we couldn't collect the money. Those guys sold the title and the receivership. It's so funny because I had been a bankruptcy paralegal [and] I knew exactly what they were going to do. I told Ed that they were never going to pay a penny of it. That they [would just] declare bankruptcy and go into receivership and sell themselves the name again and the catalog for nothing, at a bankruptcy auction. And basically [Sugar Hill] got bought up by Uni, I think. Uni bought up all that stuff. And that was all Morris Levy also. He owned Uni Distribution or a large part of it. [He] basically bankrupted the company [in order] to not pay that debt and a lot of other debts they owed. Millions of dollars at the time. Now the laws have changed since then. A year after this all happened, they changed the bankruptcy laws and made them much more streamlined. [And] they looked at things like this [and made it] so that you couldn't cross-sell your own catalog back to yourself at an auction. So it wouldn't have happened if the case had gone down a few years later. But you know, things happen when they happen for a reason. Whatever that might be.

I was unable to find any newspaper articles or legal records that corroborate Tolkin's statements, but one fact is clear. According to the *Los Angeles Times*, Sugar Hill Records "filed for protection under Chapter 11 of the U.S. Bankruptcy Code" on November 22, 1985, "a day after the IRS moved to seize Sugar Hill's assets for alleged non-payment of more than $200,000 in payroll taxes."[21] The money gets divided, alright.

12. END OF THE LINE

Excruciating though it was, the Sugar Hill debacle wasn't even the only difficulty that had been plaguing 99 Records. In mid-1983 (at the height of Liquid Liquid's success), Richard McGuire left the band in order to devote more time to his rapidly blossoming art career. The other three members forged on, toured Europe, and even recorded a new record called

---

[21] Wm. Knoedelseder Jr., "Record Industry Probe Examines Small N.J. Firm," *Los Angeles Times*, March 31, 1986.

Dig We Must (99-13EP). According to Principato, however, Bahlman seemed "personally hurt" by McGuire's departure, and the 99 chief's enthusiasm for Liquid Liquid melted further once it became apparent that the trio wasn't quite as compelling as the quartet had been.

> **Sal Principato:** *Dig We Must* differs from the other EPs in that it lacks that essential 4th element . . . more specifically, the glue that binds all the sounds together [and] makes it a "song." I'm not speaking structurally but emotively . . . the production on it is pretty damn good.

> **Dennis Young:** *Dig We Must* featured me on synthesizer doing the bass lines. I feel it still had the Liquid sound. After Richard left the band, we wrote and performed music as a three piece unit, involv[ing] more instruments such as keyboards and tapes. We stayed together another two years writing and performing. We broke up because there was not much creativity left.

Bahlman's dealings with the label's other core act were far more acrimonious, however. The 99/ESG relationship had soured from financial disagreements and other business disputes. To this day ESG claims that they were treated badly and that Bahlman still owes them a lot of money. Gina Franklyn, however, tells a very different tale.

> **Gina Franklyn:** Ed was disappointed in [ESG], they just turned on him and accused him of holding that money. Which he wasn't, I know that. He was busting his ass for those people. He was like a father figure to them. I'll tell you this—they wouldn't let [ESG] into England without having cash on them, so Ed called me and said "Give them a thousand dollars to walk in with and then they can give it back to me when they're in England, 'cause they won't let them in without any cash." So I went and drew out a thousand. I gave them a thousand in cash and told them to give it to Ed when they got there. And mysteriously, when they got to England, they claimed that they'd left it in the toilet . . . that they'd lost it or mislaid it. Little things like that. Ed helped them and pushed them and he was making all their costumes and things and not charging them a penny for it. And they were just [doing] petty little things like that. A lot of the bands had falling-outs with him, they disagreed on things. I think Ed was a total purist and didn't want these big labels to move in and sign them up and spoil it. And I think the bands misinterpreted his actions, thought he was up to something or trying to cheat them out of something. This is all I

know, because even though we were living together, we wouldn't talk about it.

Ed Bahlman's labor of love had become altogether unbearable. In late 1985, Bahlman decided that he'd finally had enough.

> **Gina Franklyn:** He just got tired of doing it. The musicians' temperaments became too demanding, things got too crazy, and he got in over his head. The music biz, it just got Ed disillusioned. He didn't want to do it anymore. I remember him just getting really upset and he was almost in tears. What did they want from him? All the bands, draining him dry. He said, "I can't do this anymore." So he didn't. When I split [my business] from Ed, the lease was up in a couple of months and I didn't want to renew the lease, so I let him stay there for the last two months and I moved on over to 6th Street and added an 'X' on the end.

In early 1986, 99 Records held a clearance sale before closing its doors forever. Ed Bahlman dropped out of the limelight and has kept a very low profile ever since.

13. AFTERWORD

99 didn't even release twenty records in its short lifespan, and yet the influential label left quite a legacy. At a time when major labels had no interest in signing underground bands (having learned from punk's many commercial failures), 99 provided opportunities to creative musicians who might not have had any other way to get their music heard. In an era when successful American independent labels were few and far between, 99 provided a shining example of how to put out cutting-edge records without losing one's shirt or sacrificing one's personal taste or integrity. By sheer virtue of his hard work, his vast musical knowledge, and his considerable production and business talents, Ed Bahlman deserves much credit for being the mastermind behind one of *the* great indie labels of the 1980s.

> **Sal Principato:** I'd like to say that, in my opinion, though Ed made lots of mistakes unintentional and otherwise, it was only through his insights and efforts that groups like Liquid Liquid and ESG could be recognized at all. He got us gigs when gigs were hard to come by. He put us in the studio when we weren't sure that the jam we came up with could ever be considered a song. He called "Cavern" a hit when we called it a monotonous

little groove. Though he fumbled in the end, he did affect most people he worked with in a very positive way at the start. I personally have a certain unavoidable affection towards him because he nurtured and shared some interesting experiences with us in our formative years.

Terry Tolkin: Ed cared too much about what he was doing. I respected that and have always continued that in what I've done with my No. 6 label and what I did at Elektra. It was a very sad thing to watch happen up close, to watch the whole thing fall apart like that and to have all the bands turn their back on him. I owe him so much. And every band I've ever worked with owes him indirectly because of that.

Bill Bahlman: I thought Ed did amazing stuff back then. I personally was very proud of the work he did. Because I think he worked with artists that otherwise would not have been recorded if he hadn't started his own record label and went about encouraging Glenn Branca and Liquid Liquid and ESG and others into the studio. They may have never put a record out. And I think what Ed did inspired other people to put their own music out as well. The whole music scene of the mid-to-late '70s and early '80s was about doing new and different music and also putting the music out yourself and on independent record labels. And that legacy and that ability to do that sort of thing has continued. As much as the scene has changed and Spice Girls are number one and this that and whatever else is happening in the music scene overall, [back then] there were hundreds of new bands and artists that were recording and doing music that they believed in and getting heard in clubs and on record and on the radio. Many of those artists are still recording, and a number of them are actually doing [different] music from what they were doing back then. The example of having an independent label and putting music out is something that has continued. And a lot of music that is being created today may not have had an inspiration to do what is being done now if people hadn't trailblazed what they did in the late '70s and early '80s. That legacy still lives on. . . .

14. THE MASTERS GAME

One of the great mysteries of 99 Records has been rearing its ugly head ever since the label stopped putting out vinyl records in the mid-'80s. The burning questions on many people's minds: where does Ed Bahlman have the 99 master tapes and why has he refused to allow any of the 99 releases to be reissued? The answer to the latter question apparently has nothing to do with money.

Glenn Branca: Henry Rollins wanted to do *The Ascension* on his label. This was a few years ago, maybe four years ago. And I gave his office Ed's number. I have Ed's number, it's just that Ed won't answer or return any messages. And Ed wouldn't call them back, so there's nothing they could do. And that was about the third time I've had a call from a label that wanted to reissue *The Ascension*. The difference was that in this case, there was no doubt that they had money to put up. And it was amazing to me that Ed wouldn't even pay attention to them. I can understand him not paying attention to these other labels that wanted to do it. I don't know what his problem is. Since the Rollins thing, he's absolutely refused to take any of my calls. Before then, I offered him 100% of all publishing rights to it if he would allow it to be released. I offered him 100% of all publishing and sales royalties. Just to allow it to be released! And he refused. It's this weird, bizarre situation that doesn't exist anywhere. The guy won't talk money, he won't give prices for selling it . . . as far as he's concerned, it doesn't exist.

As Duane Rossignol points out, perhaps the tapes *don't* exist.

Duane Rossignol: The master tapes? I'm not sure if he has 'em. He wasn't the most meticulously neat and orderly person in the world. God only knows if the tapes didn't end up in a dumpster somewhere. I can't say that for a fact, but it's kind of curious. Ed's not a mean person. Where are these tapes? Has anyone seen them? Maybe they don't exist anymore.

Whether or not the 99 masters exist in the physical sense, Terry Tolkin claims that Bahlman still owns the 99 recordings legally and, thus, is perfectly justified in his refusal to comply with would-be reissuers.

Terry Tolkin: Over the years I've had so many people come up to me and approach me and offer Ed something for the catalog. I don't go out of my way to bother him with this stuff because I'm his last link with this world. Look, he owns all this stuff. They don't own it. Everybody wants to reissue all of it. He doesn't want to. I don't know . . . I can understand why he doesn't want to have anything to do with it or the people in the industry that it would take to make it happen. He wanted to own his original recordings, which he does, because he paid for everything. That's just the law. That's the way it is. He owns those—the packaging and the songs in those versions. If they want to rerecord all the stuff, that's fine.

Branca argues, however, that Bahlman's ownership of the masters is now null and void.

> **Glenn Branca:** Ed Bahlman's "ownership" of the master tapes is what's considered in the business to be a "mechanical" ownership and is contingent upon his ability to pay royalties for any mechanical reproduction he makes from those tapes. Mechanical royalties are not sales royalties and must be paid by law—they're not negotiable. As far as I know, Ed has never paid one single cent of mechanical royalties on any record he's ever released. This is similar to "owning" land but not paying the land taxes. In this sense, he would no longer have any legal and certainly not moral rights to those tapes. By the way, just the mechanicals that he owes to the musicians is probably at least a quarter of a million dollars—far more money than he ever spent on all the recording costs put together.

Despite Ed Bahlman's iron-tight grip on the 99 catalog, much of the label's discography has become available once again, albeit via technically unauthorized reissues usually taken straight off of vinyl records and not from the original master tapes. Branca's two 99 releases (*Lesson No. 1* and *The Ascension*) have been reissued separately (on two different CDs) by Newtone, an Italian label also sometimes known as Robi Droli. All three songs off of the Bush Tetras' "Too Many Creeps" 7-inch appear on *Boom in the Night* (ROIR), a retrospective CD that also includes the Tetras's Fetish 7-inch, their Topper Headon-produced Stiff Records 12-inch, and a few unreleased demo tracks. And the Periodic Document label recently released a Y Pants compendium that includes all of Y Pants's "Off the Hook" 7-inch as well as the band's 1982 *Beat it Down* LP (Neutral).

ESG's 99 material is definitely among the hardest to come by these days. A long out-of-print double vinyl bootleg called *99: The Garage Years* compiled tracks from both ESG and Liquid Liquid, but these days, just about the only legitimate place where one can find any early ESG is *ESG Live!* (Nega Fulo), a predominantly awful collection of guitar-solo-drenched live 1990s recordings that, thanks to tapes made available by the generous widow of the late Martin Hannett, includes as a bonus the three studio cuts ("You're No Good," "Moody," "UFO") from ESG's classic 1981 debut.

Last summer, Liquid Liquid's first three 99 EPs were reissued along with four extra live tracks recorded during a March 1982 show at Berkeley Square. Simultaneously issued in the United States by Grand Royal and in the United Kingdom by Mo' Wax, the Liquid Liquid LP/CD is easily the most widely available of the 99-related reissues. It's also one that has not gone unnoticed by Terry Tolkin or even Ed Bahlman.

> **Terry Tolkin:** Ed called me when he started reading about this Liquid Liquid reissue. He's not even credited on the thing. They go to great lengths to not mention his name. He produced every song on here pretty much. He paid for everything. They reproduce all the bits and pieces of the artwork but not the 99 logo anywhere. [They] really should have known better than to do something like this to somebody like Ed. A guy who really can't defend himself, you know? That's so sad. It's so obvious [that] they went to Sal or Richard and took records. And [Liquid Liquid] signed a contract with Grand Royal, who paid them some amount of money. I'm sure there's a clause in that contract, like every other contract, that says [Liquid Liquid] guarantee to Grand Royal that they own the masters, so that if Grand Royal gets sued, it just falls in the band's lap. Not in the label's. They're just taking a chance on the fact that he's going to stay hidden away. But I'm encouraging [Ed] to defend himself. But I don't know. We'll see. I mean, it's just so insulting, this packaging. It's as if he didn't exist.

While Ed Bahlman may own the Liquid Liquid masters legally, it's difficult to side with him (or even feel at all sorry for him) in this particular scenario. Without any explanation whatsoever, the man has singlehandedly suppressed the music that he once worked so hard to release and promote. Limited DJ-oriented bootlegs of the Liquid material have existed for quite some time; why shouldn't the band members jump at a chance to have their music heard by a whole new generation of beat-happy rhythm freaks and people who had no idea that "White Lines" actually had an antecedent?

Regardless of who owns the masters, bootlegs of 99 releases continue to flourish. During the last year alone, bootlegs of Liquid Liquid's *Optimo* EP, ESG's self-titled debut EP and ESG's *Come Away With ESG* have surfaced around the world. It is thought that this new wave of bootlegs are German in origin, but not much else is known.

15. SAMPLE CREDITS DON'T PAY OUR BILLS

99's first and most direct contribution to (confrontation with?) the rap world may have come via Liquid Liquid's "Cavern," but the 99 track that would come to have the most widespread influence on hip-hop was ESG's "UFO." With its eerie *Psycho*-like motif and a midtempo 45rpm-slowed-to-33rpm pace, "UFO" became the break that launched a hundred hip-hop songs. Or at least that's the way it seems to those who have heard the tune sampled so many times over the years.

> **Renee Scroggins:** Sometimes I hate to turn on the rap hour, because it's a continuous thing where "UFO" is going and going and going in everybody's record. And I'm like, "Whoa! That's my song! That's my song!" And that's not a good feeling, especially when you're not getting credit. Writing original music is hard enough. I feel like this: if an artist is using our song and for some reason, per se, they win a Grammy, I want a piece of it![22]

With the help of their manager Carol Cooper, ESG has spent much of the last decade trying to get that very "piece" from artists who have used the band's songs without obtaining permission or compensating the band monetarily.

> **Carol Cooper:** They're very aggressive about protecting their copyright and they go after people as soon as they find out that the stuff is there. [Then] it gets tied up [for] however long people want to drag it out. And of course the amount of money we ask increases with the amount of time it takes for them to come to the table. We deal with it on a case-by-case basis, but we pretty much take the same attitude that Motown takes, which is that [for] any sample, whether it be one second or twenty, the minimum that we would even think about requesting would be a percentage of the publishing, which is usually a minimum of 50%, and a minimum of four grand up front . . . usually more. It depends on what it is, whether we like the song, whether we like the artist. It depends on whether they've previously tried to exploit us without permission. It depends on a million different variables.

Or at least as many variables as there are songs that sample "UFO." The list of artists who have sampled ESG (mostly "UFO," but occasionally "Moody") is quite extensive, ranging from Public Enemy (who dropped a couple of seconds of "UFO" into the middle of "Night of the Living Baseheads") to Miles Davis (whose posthumous jazz/hip-hop fusion album contained one track that prominently used "UFO"). Many of the sample-using artists eventually worked out after-the-fact agreements with Cooper and ESG, but several of the sampling cases have yet to be settled.

---

[22] Renee Scroggins interview, *Brave New Waves* radio program (Canadian Broadcasting Company, 1995).

Carol Cooper: Among those who have come to the table and worked out settlements with us include Karen White, Miles Davis, Blessed Union of Souls, Doug E. Fresh, Tupac Shakur, Big Daddy Kane, and Al B. Sure. The Beastie Boys have sampled us, the Beastie Boys have *stolen* from us—they insist that a tune called "Transitions" is their record when it's really just a rip-off of "UFO." There's "Let's Put it in Motion" by Precious, which uses Renee's voice. "Like This" by Chip E uses Renee's voice. These are the ones that we haven't been paid on yet. There's a couple of Wu-Tang Clan ones that we're still going after. There's an Afrika Bambaataa record, [L.L. Cool J's] *Mama Says Knock You Out* has our samples in it, so does Kris Kross. [A lot of records] produced by Marley Marl tended to use our stuff. There's a song on the new Tricky record that samples "Moody." It's just so frequent and so common on so many people's stuff that it's hard for us to keep track. But as we become aware of these things, we tend to notify the company.

Cooper first noticed an ESG lift in Big Daddy Kane's 1988 Marley Marl-produced hit "Ain't No Half Steppin'," but "UFO"'s history as sample fodder goes back even further than that. Alongside Liquid Liquid's "Cavern," ironically enough, "UFO" appeared on *Ultimate Breaks and Beats, Volume 9*, a DJ-geared breakbeat compilation released in the mid-1980s on Street Beat Records.

Carol Cooper: The illegal usage of the record in the *Ultimate Breaks and Beats* series was the major one that we tried to stop. That allowed people to think that the stuff was somehow public domain. But even if [*Ultimate Breaks and Beats*] had a license from us to use the record, it wouldn't mean anybody else who wanted to could use it too. 'cause each new person who wants to use the record in any way, shape, or form has to secure their own license.

In somewhat of a break from the prevailing ESG/hip-hop tradition, a couple of artists have actually secured such a license in advance.

Renee Scroggins: Some of 'em will come to us for clearance. Doug E. Fresh was using "UFO" and we cleared that. That was fine, he gave us our credit and he gave us what was due us. Also, PM Dawn used it in their tribute to Jimi Hendrix and they gave us our credit.[23]

---

[23] Ibid.

Polite and strict adherence to legal codes in these particular cases has done very little to temper ESG's overall hostility towards wealthier and more popular artists who the band members see as having profited off of their work. Wearing their dissatisfaction on their sleeve, ESG even titled a 1992 EP *Sample Credits Don't Pay Our Bills*.

> **Carol Cooper:** Renee's attitude toward all of this is the attitude of artists, people who are original, people who believe that if people can't come up with their own music, then they shouldn't be in music. I have a different attitude because I don't write songs. I think that if it's used artistically, than that's cool, that's great.

Like Cooper, the members of Liquid Liquid actually have a healthy appreciation for the ideas behind sampling, despite the fact that their biggest hit was the blatant victim of a hip-hop hit-and-run for which they didn't receive any financial compensation for over a decade.

> **Richard McGuire:** From the beginning of time, songs have grown from other songs. What I love about sampling is that it uses "memory" as another ingredient. I feel anything should be up for grabs. You're making a collage with sound. Something like "White Lines" is just straight-out robbery, but when you hear DJ Shadow or whoever, it's like chemistry, mixing DNAs. I believe in giving credit where it's due and if the contribution is significant, then a percent of the publishing should be paid out.

> **Sal Principato:** My personal feeling about the appropriation of "Cavern" is one of ambivalence. On one hand the whole of rock 'n' roll was built on a foundation of exploiting and not compensating those who developed its sound. So I felt we were a part of this long ignominious history. Also I'd come to appreciate a lot of Grandmaster Flash and the Furious Five's work, so in some ways, it was flattering that they'd see a value in something that we did. On the other hand, one needs to be acknowledged for their creations and contributions. Sugar Hill neglected to do that, but neither did Deee-Lite when they sampled "Bellhead." My take on sampling is this: if you use parts of someone's music as a sound and not as a musical statement, it's fine as long as you acknowledge the source (for example, a James Brown yelp or a hit of the snare from a Led Zeppelin song). But when you use a coherent musical statement that's easily recognized, then it is appropriation and the source should get songwriters' credit or

something comparable. Frankly, all the uses of Liquid Liquid that I've heard so far fall into this latter category.

While their catalog has not been plundered as extensively as ESG's has, Liquid Liquid have been sampled several times in hip-hop and dance music. "Cavern" has continued to be a staple building block in hip-hop music—in the past couple of years alone, the song has been sampled in a promo-only remix of the Notorious B.I.G.'s "Nasty Boy" and as well as a song from the brand new Mobb Deep full-length. For some reason, Liquid's non-"Cavern"ous bells-on-parade sounds have been more frequently used in house/techno contexts. Deee-lite's "Build a Bridge" uses the intro to "Bellhead," while the Jungle Brothers' 1987 rap/house fusion classic "I'll House You" and DJ Sneak and Carl Craig's more recent "Remake Uno" both use portions of Liquid Liquid's "Optimo." And that's not all.

> **Richard McGuire:** I have heard a Salt 'n' Pepa song use "Cavern." I was in a store recently and heard "Scraper" used in a mix and when I asked the owner, he said he just bought it from a guy selling tapes at the Roxy. A friend of mine bought a tape in India off the back of a donkey cart and he said there was a mix using "Cavern" with all these Indian guys singing on top of it. He gave this tape to David Byrne, who was putting together a world music compilation, and somehow the tape was lost!

Despite their more-curious-than-militant attitude about having their music sampled, the members of Liquid Liquid still have strong feelings about the "White Lines" appropriation and how their interests should have been protected.

> **Sal Principato:** If Ed played it right, he could have exploited the situation to our advantage and sold a ton of *Optimo*/"Cavern" records in the wake of "White Lines," without lawyers and courts and a whole lot of hassle. I think *Optimo* sold some 30,000 units but considering "Cavern"'s exposure, it could have done much better if marketed properly. It was only when Duran Duran covered "White Lines" that it became apparent that the "Cavern"/ "White Lines" dichotomy wouldn't go away and that it was time to protect our interests. When I saw Duran do the song on the Letterman show, unlike hearing Flash/Melle Mel do it for the first time, it wasn't flattering.

In the wake of Duran Duran's 1995 cover of "White Lines," Liquid Liquid sought and finally achieved a deal that awarded them partial publishing rights to "White Lines" and some amount of financial compensation. Yet again, the money gets divided.

LIFE AFTER 99

Though he co-ran the Neutral label until it ceased operating in the late 1980s, Glenn Branca has spent most of the last seventeen years writing symphonies for both rock-guitar and traditional orchestras. Recordings of many of these great works have been (re)released on the Atavistic label, which also culled together the Static's one 7-inch and several Branca-penned Theoretical Girls tunes for Branca: *Songs '77–'79*. Branca's *Symphony No. 11* (for traditional orchestra) premiered in Holland in 1998; looking into the future, Branca's "Hallucination City," a piece written for 2000 guitars, will be performed in Paris, France in the year 2000! Talk about partying like you're no longer on 99. . . .

In addition to playing in Y Pants, performing in Branca's early orchestras, and putting out Just Another Asshole (a varyingly themed music/arts publication and 1981 compilation LP), Barbara Ess became well known in the early '80s as a visual artist/photographer. After Y Pants reached an end, Ess played in a band called Listen to the Animal; much more recently, she played in Ultra Vulva, a NYC trio that evolved out of Drum Core, a drumming-focused fem-zine that Ess put out with buddies that she'd made during a stint in the Women's Action Coalition drum corps. Still together with longtime mate Branca, Barbara Ess currently teaches and continues to exhibit her work in galleries. Every year, she and the other members of Y Pants have dinner together on each of their three birthdays.

The Bush Tetras got back together in 1995 after a nearly twelve-year hiatus, and in June 1997, the band released its first ever full-length album. Unfortunately, much of Beauty Lies (Tim/Kerr) is unlistenable art-grunge that suffers from overproduction and terrible singing. Last year, the Bush Tetras served a stint as the opening act on the Fall's now-infamous April 1998 U.S. tour; Tetras drummer Dee Pop even served as the Fall's tour manager and had the unenviable job of keeping track of the cranky, soused, and violent Mark E. Smith.

ESG are also still together in a somewhat-past-their-prime state. The band played a NYC show with the Bush Tetras in summer '97 and have been shopping an in-the-can album around to record labels. In an impressive display of family solidarity, the late '90s ESG lineup includes Renee on vocals, Valerie on guitar, and two of their daughters on bass and guitar.

Liquid Liquid declined a 1996 invitation to reunite for a show in London, but most of the band's members have remained fairly active in other musical endeavors. Sal Principato's continually evolving Fist of Facts band/project was formed in 1985 and at various times over the years has included fellow Liquid members Scott Hartley and Dennis Young, among many others. Principato, Hartley, and Young have also spent time with solo projects and a number of other New York and New Jersey bands (Arebella, Avant Garbage, Bomb Release, Like Wow, Liki Outhaus). The manager of a Manhattan rehearsal/MIDI studio since 1984, Principato has also spent part of the '90s organizing and producing various NYC-area cultural events (usually multidisciplinary amalgamations of music, poetry, and dance). Though for the most part he's been musically inactive since the Liquid days, Richard McGuire has remained extremely busy as a successful graphic artist.

On top of regular appearances in the *New York Times Book Review*, McGuire's illustrations have graced the cover of the *New Yorker* on multiple occasions. Additionally, McGuire has designed a Swatch watch (the "Weightless Swatch") and several toys, including an animated solar-powered toy ("EO"). McGuire has written and illustrated several children's books and is currently designing a lot of animation for PBS. McGuire also produced the 1997 animated video for Liquid Liquid's "Cavern," which received some airplay on MTV/M2. Speaking of "Cavern," the song is slated to appear in an upcoming Sony commercial. And finally, a couple of Liquid Liquid remix twelve-inches have been released on the Mo' Wax label.

Despite abandoning her solo career, Vivien Goldman has remained quite active in the music world, as both a music journalist and a songwriter/collaborator. Goldman's writings on renowned African musician Fela Kuti have appeared in *Rolling Stone* and *Rock She Wrote*; *Women Write about Rock, Pop, and Rap* (Delta Books, 1995), and she also wrote portions of VH1's *100 Greatest Artists of Rock and Roll* series. Goldman's newest book, *The Black Chord*, traces the links between various musics of the African diaspora. On the music side of things, Goldman has written songs with Massive Attack ("Sly"), Coldcut, and Ryuichi Sakamoto (on 1998's *Sweet Revenge*), and she recently collaborated with Adriana Kaegi, former lead Coconut of Kid Creole and the Coconuts. In her spare time Vivien Goldman runs the official Ornette Coleman web site (www.harmolodic.com).

After leaving 99 in 1984, Terry Tolkin worked jobs at Dutch East, Touch and Go, Rough Trade U.S., and Caroline. While working at Caroline, he ran No. 6 Records, a label sometimes credited with igniting the tribute album explosion with 1989's *The Bridge: A Tribute to Neil Young*. In the first half of the '90s, Tolkin worked as an A&R agent for Elektra Records, where he helped ink deals with Afghan Whigs, the Breeders, Luna, and Stereolab. In late 1997, Tolkin moved away from New York City and has spent portions of the last couple of years living in Kansas, New Jersey, and Florida. His No. 6 label has recently become active again.

Gina Franklyn currently resides in upstate New York, where she designs clothes and runs Franklyn Footwear and Clothing. Franklyn still owns 99X, now located on East 10th Street in downtown Manhattan. 99X is also the current place of employment for Duane Rossignol, who spent several years in the late '80s running a hardcore-oriented record store called Some Records.

Bill Bahlman is well-known for his volunteer work as a treatment advocate for people with AIDS. It's been said that Bill's brother Ed Bahlman still lives somewhere in Brooklyn. Ironically, Ed Bahlman was spotted at Sonic Youth's 1997 performance at the Lincoln Center. Better late than never, I suppose.

A 99 RECORDS DISCOGRAPHY

Glenn Branca—*Lesson No. 1* 12-inch (99-01EP, 1980)

Bush Tetras—"Too Many Creeps" 7-inch (99-02EP, 1980)

Y Pants—self-titled 7-inch (99-03EP, 1980)

ESG—self-titled 12-inch (99-04EP, 1981)

Vivien Goldman—*Dirty Washing* 12-inch (99-05EP, 1981)

Congo—self-titled 12-inch (99-06EP, 1981)

Liquid Liquid—self-titled 12-inch (99-07EP, 1981)

Maximum Joy—"Stretch" 12-inch (99-08EP, 1981)

Glenn Branca—*The Ascension* LP (99-001LP, 1981)

Singers and Players—*War of Words* LP (99-002LP, 1981)

Liquid Liquid—*Successive Reflexes* 12-inch (99-09EP, 1981)

ESG—*ESG Says Dance to the Beat of Moody* 12-inch (99-10EP, 1982)

ESG—*Come Away With ESG* LP (99-003LP, 1983)

Liquid Liquid—"Bell Head" b/w "Push" 7-inch (99-11EP7, 1982)

Liquid Liquid—*Optimo* 12-inch (99-11EP, 1983)

Liquid Liquid—*Dig We Must* 12-inch (99-13EP, 1984)

A PARTIAL UFOGRAPHY

1988 • Big Daddy Kane—"Ain't No Half Steppin'"

1988 • Public Enemy—"Night of the Living Baseheads"

1989 • Divine Styler—"Tongue of Labyrinth"

1989 • D.J. Chuck Chillout & Kool Chip—"Time to Rhyme"

1989 • 3rd Bass—"Triple Stage Darkness"

1989 • Tone Loc—"Cutting Rhythms"

1990 • L.L. Cool J—"Mr. Goodbar," "Murdergram"

1990 • Master Ace—"The Other Side of Town"

1990 • Paris—"Scarface Groove"

1991 • Gang Starr—"Take a Rest"

1991 • Marley Marl (featuring MC Cash)—"At the Drop of a Dime"

1991 • Tim Dog—"Fuck Compton"

1992 • Das EFX—"East Coast"

1992 • EPMD—"Chill," "Scratch Bring it Back (Part 2—Mic Doc)"

1992 • Miles Davis—"Fantasy"

1993 • Afrika Bambaataa Presents Time Zone—"What's the Name of This Nation? . . . Zulu!"

1993 • Das EFX—"Freakit"

1993 • P.M. Dawn—"You Got Me Floatin'"

1994 • Beastie Boys—"Sure Shot" (Large Professor remix)

1994 • 2 Pac—"Peep Game"

1997 • Mic Geronimo featuring DMX, Fatal, Cormega, and Ja—"The Usual Suspects"

FROM "RHYTHM & BLUES"

Billboard, *January 17, 1987*

There are many so-called experts in the field of black music, folks who make their living keeping up with the trends, sounds, and attitudes of the black music listeners who are scratching their heads this new year.

Why? Just look at the top of the Top Black Albums chart. After just eight weeks, the Beastie Boys' *Licensed to Ill* is at No. 3 with a bullet. Who are the Beastie Boys, and why are black kids responding to them as if they were the second coming of Run-D.M.C.? Mikey D, Ad Rock, and MCA are three white guys who hung out and played around New York's East Village scene before discovering the joys of hip hop. Along with friend and sometime spinner Rick Rubin, they dived mouth first into the music, getting booed at the Bronx's now-defunct Disco Fever, once the unofficial home of the rap world, and befriending Run-D.M.C.'s members and their manager, Russell Simmons. With the partnership of Rubin and Simmons in Def Jam Records, the union between the punky trio and the rap world was partially complete.

The Beasties got plenty of road work and media exposure while getting booed by Madonna's fans on her tour a few years back, and they had things thrown at them at New York's Apollo Theater when they opened for Run. These guys have paid their dues. But key to their current success is a record called "Hold It, Now Hit It," released last spring on Def Jam. The record got lost at Columbia; it did well as a 12-inch, but not well enough to force black radio to play it, certainly not when there were records by Run-D.M.C., Whodini, and L.L. Cool J in the market. But the hip hop "in" crowd—the club jocks, radio mixers, and hardcore b-boys who are the heart of this music—knew "it was chill" and that for all the jokes and the on-stage beer bashes, the Beasties could deliver. So when they heard "Paul Revere," written with Run-D.M.C., and some of the other cuts on the new album—which, it should be noted, continues the musical direction started by that Profile trio—they jumped on it and spread the word. The rap-rock connection started by "Rock Box" works because it appeals to young blacks and young whites. It is nasty, obnoxious, and, maybe, a little stupid—just like the Beasties themselves. In fact, the Beasties stage show and silly rap style create the atmosphere of a really hip frat party, one that may just propel *Licensed to Ill* to multiplatinum status.

DAVE DIMARTINO

BEASTIE BOYS DENIED RIGHT TO PARTY IN SAN DIEGO

Billboard, *February 14, 1987*

LOS ANGELES—Reports of spray-painted dressing rooms and beer thrown from the stage resulted in the cancellation of a Beastie Boys concert scheduled for Sunday (8) in San Diego.

The Def Jam/Columbia group, touring with Fishbone and Murphy's Law, had its plug pulled February 3 after University of California-San Diego officials heard of troubles at Beastie Boys' venues.

Linda Stack, pop events adviser at the university, says the decision was made after hearing of damage at two of the three most recent concerts by the group. "If they were going to continue the damage and incite the crowd, we couldn't afford to have them in our gym," she says. "It's the only place on campus we have to do concerts. And if something were to happen, there's basketball season, volleyball season and all that. We just thought we had to make a decision, and we decided not to go through with it."

Bill Adler, director of publicity for Rush Productions—which manages both the Beastie Boys and tour-opener Murphy's Law—terms the Beastie Boys reported antics as "the most trivial kind of boyish, rock 'n' roll prank." Adler says the only "objectionable" behavior he has heard of from the tour came in a Bellingham, Washington, date, when opening act Murphy's Law encouraged the crowd to fight with the security guards, referring to them as "the local Gestapo." "That could develop into some real trouble," says Adler. "I can understand a promoter getting a little excited about that."

Reports about additional troubles during the band's recent appearance at Wolfgang's in San Francisco were "pretty much blown out of proportion," according to Toni Isabella, talent coordinator for the venue. Likewise overstated were rumors that Wolfgang's marquee was shot out, adds Isabella. "It was like a pellet gun—a teeny little hole in the marquee. I didn't even know about it, and I was here all night."

LINDA MOLESKI

BOOS TURN INTO BRAVOS FOR THE BEASTIE BOYS

Billboard, *January 17, 1987*

NEW YORK—When the Beastie Boys opened for Madonna on her 1985 "Virgin" tour, they were constantly booed off stage. Less than two years later, though, the white rap trio is gearing up for an extensive U.S. head-lining tour in support of its hugely successful debut Def Jam/Columbia album, *Licensed to Ill*. With nearly 500,000 copies sold in the first month of its release, the album has climbed to No. 20 on this week's Top Pop Albums chart.

"Around here we're calling it the Beastie Boys phenomenon," says Bob Sherwood, Columbia senior vice president of marketing. "It was instant explosion, and it caught a lot of people by surprise. Next to Bruce [Springsteen], it's our fastest selling reorder record."

Sherwood credits the group's success to a number of factors, including five years of audience "build-up" and invaluable exposure on Run-

On the *Licensed to Ill* Tour.

D.M.C.'s 1986 "Raising Hell" tour. Both Sherwood and the Beastie Boys agree that manager Russell Simmons—who, together with producer Rick Rubin, founded the Gotham-based Def Jam label—played a key role in the band's development.

"Russell Simmons predicted the gold album and what's happening to us now," says group member Mike D (Michael Diamond). "He had a vision that was very much in a commercial way. We were just going on making records we wanted to make, and Russell took the music and said, 'This is gonna be incredible—the biggest thing that ever happened. You're gonna be gold, then platinum.'"

Adds group member King Ad-Rock (Adam Horovitz), "Run-D.M.C. helped us out a lot, too. A lot of people opened their minds to rap music, and when 'Walk This Way' got on AOR, it made it that much easier."

Like Run-D.M.C., the Beastie Boys have successfully crossed over to a white audience, with three of the album's tracks receiving airplay on urban rock radio. A video for their rock-rap anthem "(You Gotta) Fight For Your Right (To Party!)" recently premiered on MTV.

"The album appeals to a young, broad demographic," says Sherwood. "It's one of those wonderful projects that cuts through many barriers. The music is allegedly off-center and doesn't fit in those perfect holes, but it rattles around in everything."

The Beastie Boys are set to kick off their *Licensed to Ill* tour in late January, playing 7,000-seat venues. In addition, they will be appearing in the upcoming motion picture *Tougher Than Leather*, and they are slated to begin filming their first full-length movie, *Beastie Boys Are Scared Stupid*, in March for Def Jam pictures.

"We're also working on a television pilot that's based on the characters we are now," says Mike D.

"It's something we always wanted to do," adds group member MCA (Adam Yauch). "But now we have the money to do it. Maybe we'll go straight to network TV with it. Or maybe we'll just start our own network."

BILL HOLDSHIP AND JOHN KORDOSH

HIGH SCHOOL EQUIVALENCY TEST

Creem, *June 1987*

We'd just moved to Los Angeles from Detroit with Creem *magazine, and it was cultural shock, to put it mildly. I'd never been to LA before and had pretty much learned about it from watching* Annie Hall; *Kordosh had been here once before, to do a Steve Wonder story. In Detroit, they made cars. In LA, they made . . . well, we weren't sure yet, but we'd never made so many immediate "best friends" before in our lives. ("Bill, can I ask you a question?" Kordosh deadpanned one afternoon when we were returning from yet another bout of "doing lunch"; people never took you to lunch in Detroit. "How come all these people we don't know are always kissing us?")*

So, as strange as it may sound, maybe we just came to associate the Beastie Boys with the whole concept of LA; they were, after all, our first cover story (the infamous one in which they broke into writer Chuck Eddy's room and poured ice water on him) upon Creem's *arrival in LA. And almost everyone we met in LA music circles was talking up the Beastie Boys—when they weren't kissing us—to the point of annoyance.*

On top of that, we were both in love with the Replacements, a band we'd known back in Michigan, and one we considered the "real" Beastie Boys (working class Midwest jokers) in rock 'n' roll terms—not a trio of privileged rich kids from New York City who came across as three Jerry Lewis clones when we'd seen them (circa "Cookie Puss") open for Madonna in the Motor City . . . and who were now going to be way bigger than the Replacements would ever be.

When the 'Mats showed up in LA after recording "Pleased To Meet Me" in Memphis, we drunkenly goaded them into commenting on the Beasties: "They could use a good swift kick in the groin," Tommy Stinson laughed. Later, we asked Westerberg if the Replacements had gone to Graceland. "No," said Paul. "Elvis used to live there. It was too depressing. I thought it would be in bad taste. I didn't want to go in there." Well, the Beastie Boys had gone there and made a big thing out of it when they were in Memphis.

With Gene Simmons, c. 1986.

"Yeah, but the Beastie boys are crass assholes," said Paul. "C'mon, I'll fight 'em right now, goddammit! We're classy assholes."

And that was the thing—even if you looked at their "Fight For Your Right To Party" video, all over MTV at the time, in which the Beasties basically picked on the geeks, losers, and those not fortunate enough to be as hip as their B-Boy bad selves . . . well, last time I looked, that seemed less a definition of "rock 'n' roll" than it did "asshole." Plus, the music—and that whining rapping style (like most rockcrits, we were fans of "The Message")—just didn't strike us as very good.

Whatever the case, the show truly did suck. I guess, in retrospect, the Beasties looked like rocket scientists next to Jesse Camp, while the lyrics were totally harmless when compared to Eminem. On the other hand, perhaps they paved the way for the idiocy to follow with that whole stoopid schtick. We certainly never imagined them becoming, as Sean Lennon has said, "the Beatles of their generation." We never imagined they'd release more than one or two albums—a one-hit wonder joke band. They did manage to impress me soon enough with Paul's Boutique—*much of it the Dust Brothers' doing, but it also revealed considerable growth in the lyrical department. A decade later, I think it still stands as the best thing they've done.*

But, really and truly, we thought they were horrible that night at the Hollywood Palladium in 1987 and felt a strong need to express it. Other than the fact that Tipper Gore and the PMRC would take a quote from the review and use it out of context in one of the organization's films (much to our chagrin), I still stand behind it and I'm sure Kordosh feels the same.

—Bill Holdship, 1999

For what it's worth, I've got to admit that I kind of like the Beastie Boys now. They're pretty clever guys, and even Bill would admit their rhymes are among the funniest in rap/hip-hop. (I "think" he would admit that anyway.) And Paul's Boutique *is great! In other words: Bill and I were well-intentioned, but wrong . . . too often the case in rock criticism!*

—John Kordosh to the editor via e-mail, 1999

The Beastie Boys at the Hollywood Palladium, February 7, 1987

JOHN: This was not only the worst concert I've ever seen, it was actually the worst event I've ever been to. How do you feel about that?

BILL: Well, I basically agree with you, though I don't know that I'd take it so far as to say it's the worst event . . . .

JOHN: I mean, I'm including the time I got arrested.

BILL: Well, I can think of other things that rate right up there with "worst event." But I can think of a million other things I'd have rather done that night. Wash my hair. Cut my nails. Gone to the dentist . . . .

JOHN: We should mention that we did walk out of the concert before Run-D.M.C. even came on.

BILL: Yeah, it's important because people say that's where the concert picked up, and that Run-D.M.C. were actually pretty good.

JOHN: No, it's more important that we note that the concert was so bad that we *left,* even though we kinda wanted to see Run-D.M.C. But we were so turned off by the Beasties that we left the show in total disgust.

BILL: Well, let me ask you: Why do you hate the Beastie Boys?

JOHN: I hate them because they're ugly. Not only physically ugly, they're mentally ugly—and spiritually ugly, if I can go that far. I can appreciate stupidity. I can appreciate offensiveness. But I can't appreciate a celebration of the ugliness of humanity.

BILL: The thing that should be pointed out is that both you and I grew up loving rock 'n' roll. I *know* that I like things that offend people, especially people who deserve to be offended. I know you like things that even offend you personally. This isn't the big deal. What I find offensive about the Beasties is the sheer stupidity of it. The show was just a celebration of stupidity. There was no talent displayed on that stage. A lot of people will think we're like the old fuddy-duddies who used to denounce rock 'n' roll . . . .

JOHN: Well, they're wrong. Because, no, rock 'n' roll wasn't like that. Rock 'n' roll *isn't* like that. Rock 'n' roll isn't three ugly guys standing around, shouting, displaying no grace in the physical sense—and no ability in the singing sense. At this particular show, they sang "Happy Birthday" to one of their members, and the fact is the guy *couldn't* carry a note.

BILL: He couldn't carry a tune at all! And people will think we're old fuddy-duddies when I say that we could get up there and do the same thing. But mark my word, if you gave me the money they have behind them—and they have wealthy families, not to mention a huge record company behind them—you and I could get up there. We could spit beer on the audience—which is what they did for the whole show—yell "Motherfucker" over and over again, grab our crotches to insinuate that we have penises or something—and I really think we might be able to come up with a better show. I *know* that we could come up with better music. After all, I didn't hear any music for the 40 minutes we were there.

JOHN: I think we could do better. I don't know that we'd come up with a *stupider* show. We should mention the half-naked girl dancing in the bird cage, too. That was gratuitous sexism. It didn't really offend me . . . .

BILL: No, it didn't offend me. It was just the fact that it was offensive for the sole purpose of being offensive. It was manufactured offensiveness.

JOHN: What *did* offend me were those giant cans of Budweiser they had behind them as a stage prop. I'll go on record that I find the Beastie Boys so stupid and so ugly that I will actually not buy Anheuser-Busch products because of this. And I hope somebody from Anheuser-Busch reads this and gets it through their thick heads that this is not the way it should be. I'm not saying that the Beastie Boys should be censored or boycotted or anything like that. All I'm saying is that a smart corporation should not sponsor imbecility . . . .

BILL: Are you saying this because . . . .

JOHN: Because I like Coors!

BILL: . . . because probably 90 percent of the Beastie Boys' audience is under age?

JOHN: That *is* part of it.

BILL: Because don't forget that the Who's last tour was sponsored by a beer company, complete with commercials.

JOHN: I'm down on corporate sponsorship in general, but I've never taken it to the extent that I wouldn't buy a product because of it.

BILL: It *was* pretty shameless.

JOHN: It was *incredibly* shameless. If Anheuser-Busch wants to be involved with three ugly guys standing around, spraying the audience with beer, using their microphones as dicks, that's their prerogative . . . .

BILL: When you talk about using the microphone as a dick, it's interesting to note that no one was more offensive onstage than Jim Morrison was at times. Who could offend audiences more than someone like Lou Reed did, verbally? But there was a *reason* behind their offensiveness. And people are saying that the Beasties are like Elvis in that they're taking a black thing and transforming it into a white thing. But the difference is that Elvis was an exceptionally talented person who did his thing as well as the blacks did before him. We saw Run-D.M.C. just briefly at the *American Music Awards*, and they were *much* more impressive. The Beasties don't even do it well.

JOHN: But then the argument is that that's part of the Beasties' schtick, to be stupid. And I think they're talking stoopid with two "o's."

BILL: OK, but it's definitely not the Ramones. It's not the Sex Pistols. It's not the Replacements, who really *are*—in a much more appealing manner—what the Beasties *try* to be. It's not even the Three Stooges. Part of the problem, too, is some of the Beasties' audience might not take it as a "stoopid" joke. They might buy it lock, stock and barrel as real life. I'm gonna go out, take some crack, beat up people who aren't as "cool" as me, rape some women and shoot some guy in the face. Above everything else, it's just not funny. In fact, it's extremely mean-spirited. What is the purpose of it? What is the point?

JOHN: I guess the point is rebellion, but it's the most pointless type of rebellion . . . .

BILL: I mean, let's compare Lenny Bruce to the Beastie Boys.

JOHN: Yeah, I think there's a lot of valid comparisons, but as far as I can see, almost everyone who preceded the Beastie Boys at least had something going for them. And I don't think the Beasties Boys have anything at all going for them, other than their talent for making money. As far as I'm concerned, this thing is just a massive sham, and it should be exposed as such. People are being duped.

BILL: I agree. I saw them backstage at the Grammy Awards, and they come on like they're trying to be rude smartasses. That's fine and dandy, but they're *not funny*. And that's what's gotta be stressed. Someone asked them why Michael Jackson wouldn't let them cover "I'm Down," and one of them said "Because he had a dick up his ass." That's not *funny*. It's *stupid*.

JOHN: Maybe they should be pummeled to within an inch of their lives.

BILL: Well, certainly at least slapped up [laughter]. Why do you think the critics have, for the most part, bought this group wholeheartedly? They just did extremely well in the *Village Voice* poll.

JOHN: Well, I'll answer that honestly. I haven't the faintest idea in hell. I think the critics who have embraced the Beastie Boys have actually lost their minds. They're probably psychotic, will eventually be put away in mental institutions, and—maybe after a long treatment—they'll emerge with a keener aesthetic. And a keener sense of the value of human life and human ambition.

BILL: Do you think that some of those critics are worried that they may be getting old, and therefore feel that they must embrace the Beasties because this is representative of the "young"?

JOHN: I would hate to think that's true, although I'm not a mind reader . . . .

BILL: Do you think some of the critics are embracing them because one or more of the older critics are saying that they like the Beastie Boys?

JOHN: I don't think that. I mean, it's possible. The fact is I don't really care. I just wish that they would give me explicitly good reasons, logical reasons, *any* reasons, as to why the Beastie Boys are any good at all. Because when you see them in concert, you see them for what they really are—and that is *nothing*.

CHUCK EDDY

THE BEASTIE BOYS TAKE OVER?

Creem, *May 1987*

"They took the doors off their hinges and moved them around. They flooded two floors with fire hoses. They plugged up the toilets and destroyed the furniture. They terrorized the other guests. They were just having fun."

—*Stephen Davis,* Hammer of the Gods, *1985*

At 32 minutes past two the morning of 16 January 1987, two Beastie Boys broke into my West Hollywood hotel room and dumped a wastebasketfull of extremely wet water on my head, my bed, the carpeting and my Converse All-Stars. (I'd stupidly left the chain-lock unsecured, and I suppose they bribed the night-clerk into giving them a key.) Earlier that evening, after Pee-Wee Herman had visited their dressing room and before they appeared on the Joan Rivers's show, the Beasties were tossing parsley at me, dropping ice cubes in my hair, and "dissin'" (graffiti-artist lingo for "saying bad things about") my brown socks and flannel shirt. I interpreted all of this to mean that they did not like me.

But I didn't feel alone. Just days before, they'd been evicted from the Sunset Marquis for throwing chairs out their window into the swimming pool. And that week, they'd also become the first group ever to be censored on *American Bandstand*—Dick Clark, who'd put up with Johnnies Rotten and Lydon in past episodes, apparently determined Adrock's mid-song crotch-grab was just too much. The Beasties had previously been awarded a lifetime ban from the Holiday Inn chain after they'd cut a hole in the floor of one suite to serve as a passageway to the one directly below; they'd been banned from CBS Records headquarters after allegedly ripping off a camera at a label party. And MCA brags that he punched a *Bay Area*

Music interviewer in the face not too long ago. These guys are total jerks, and they've got the fastest-selling debut album in CBS history.

MCA, real name Adam Yauch, says he's skimmed through *Hammer of the Gods,* a book that depicts Led Zeppelin's early career as one massive Satanic orgy, complete with fishing for sharks out hotel windows and sticking the prize catches on baked-bean-marinated groupies. "It happens that we are living up to that reputation, but it's not intentional," MCA tells me. "We respect what they did. They were the only band that never buckled under to their label, and they sold more records than anybody." Beastie Mike D, whose stage title is shortened from Michael Diamond, is wearing a *Houses of the Holy* T-shirt. The first noises you hear on the Boys' *Licensed to Ill* album are John Bonham's drums, lifted from Zep's megaswing classic "When the Levee Breaks." I ask Mike D what his favorite LP of 1986 was, and he answers *Led Zeppelin IV.*

> "THERE'S A FEELING I GET
>
> WHEN I LOOK TO THE WEST
>
> AND MY SPIRIT IS CRYING FOR LEAVING . . . ."

> —*Page & Plant,* Zep IV, *1971*

B-Boy stance in '85: Adrock, MCA, Mike D.

Upon arriving in Los Angeles to meet the most famous Caucasian rap trio in the history of Western Civilization, I found their record company had sent a limousine to the airport to pick me up. I'm talking one of those huge black ones where the celebrities can look out but the peons can't look in, and of course I'd never even *touched* one before, and I thought it was obscene. The driver gave me the scenic route down Sunset Boulevard, and he pointed out Rod Stewart's and Englebert Humperdinck's abodes, and we passed U.C.L.A. The driver showed me this monument made of four white columns at the top of a small hill. He said Al Jolson was buried there.

Like Gigilo Al, and like Bob Wills and Elvis Presley and the Rolling Stones and the disco Bee Gees as well, the Beastie Boys are white people making what is supposed to be black music. Like Jerry Leiber and Mike Stoller, who wrote all of the Coasters' hits and whose "Girls, Girls, Girls" MCA claims did not influence the group's very similar "Girls," and like the Dictators, whose *Go Girl Crazy* anticipated punk and whose White Castle infatuation MCA claims had no effect on his crew's own sliders-by-the-bag fetish, the Beasties are young middle-class Jewish males chronicling the dilemma of urban-American teen hooligancy. Or rather, in the Beastie Boys' case, half-Jewish: "Purely coincidentally, we each had one Jewish parent," explains MCA. Adrock and Mike D, now 17 and 19 years old respectively, grew up in Manhattan; MCA, 20, comes from Brooklyn Heights. MCA and Mike D "have been friends forever and were boys together," MCA says; Adrock, a.k.a. Adam Horovitz, met the other two in junior high school. Noted playwright Isreal Horovitz, Adrock's dad, left home when the Beastie was a baby. MCA's first criminal act was setting a print shop on fire.

"All the kids from our high school listened to Deep Purple, crap like that," Mike D says. "When you see that shit it doesn't make you want to go out and play it." Yauch, Horovitz, and Diamond opted for the (then) unpopular alternative, dying their hair orange or shaving it off, checking out the Stimulators and Sham 69 at New York clubs, and eventually starting their own hardcore squads. "Everyone we knew was in a band," Mike D says. "That's what was cool about punk." The original Beastie Boys comprised Yauch, Diamond, and two more; Horovitz's band, The Young & The Useless, would open shows. Eventually, the combos merged. After releasing the 7-inch *Polly Wog Stew* EP on the Rat Cage label in 1982, lured by a Gotham rap subculture that seemed to parallel punk in the do-it-yourself-music department, the Boys decided to expand their horizons.

"We went into the studio and recorded 10 songs, and we did the song 'Cookie Puss' as a joke," MCA remembers. "We were making fun of

Malcolm McLaren, and the whole downtown art scene that was exploiting hip hop." A poor mix caused eight tunes to be shelved, but "Cookie Puss" came out as a 12-inch single, backed with a rasta-toasting/Musical Youth parody called "Beastie Revolution." The A-side was a seemingly sexist and racist stylus-scratch rendering of a pornographic phone call to an ice-cream sandwich store, and it turned out to be 1983's funniest novelty record. Rick Rubin, a club disc jockey whose band, Hose, did grunge-metal versions of Ohio Players and Rick James numbers, heard the disc and liked it. Beastie gigs gradually evolved from "a lot of new wave Wild-Style Burner-Style music with the turntable next to the drum riser" (sez MCA) to all-the-way-live rap, and Rubin produced 1985's awesome "Rock Hard"/"Party's Gettin' Rough"/ "Beastie Groove" EP. The record kidnapped sections outright from AC/DC's "Back in Black" and Zep's "Black Dog." The Beasties chanted, "I'm a man who needs no introduction/Got a big tool of reproduction."

Furthering their ironman-funk synthesis on the "Soundtrack From the Video She's On It" single, and helped along by a distribution deal Rubin's Def Jam Records had established with CBS, the trio burst onto MTV in late '85. A year later, after a summer of opening for the suddenly huge Rubin-produced Run-D.M.C., the Beasties were bona fide stars; within six weeks of its release, *Licensed to Ill* had already sold over a million copies, and was kicking its way up the Top 20. If you go to high school or live in a college dorm, you most likely know the thing backwards and forwards by now. *Licensed to Ill* has pushed rap into the whitest corridors of America's heartland, and (along with D.M.C., Metallica, and the Rubin-produced Slayer) has made the future safe for dangerous teenage music, a form that seemed to have died. CBS, concentrating on Bruce S. and Michael J., has an unexpected blockbuster on its hands. And the Beastie Boys are playing their 15 minutes of fame to the hilt. "Five years from now I might be selling used cars on the lot," MCA says. "I really don't give a fuck, 'cause I'm having so much fun now."

For example: I'm at the hotel, as are members of the Beastie entourage, which consists of Sean, their hepcat British manager, Hurricane, a brawny deejay who carries lots of gold junk around his neck, Cey, who has known the Beasties since childhood and now serves as roadie and astrologer and all-around nice-guy, and Eloise, an overweight go-go dancer who's supposed to look "sexy" when she strips down to black lace, I guess, but mostly just comes off as gruesome. The Beasties aren't there, and the limo driver says it's time to leave for the Rivers Show. All of a sudden this luxury machine burns rubber around the corner, just missing the limo, and skids to a halt in front of the hotel gate. MCA jumps out and runs inside, and Adrock takes the wheel even though he's never driven a stick-shift before. MCA's done doing what he was doing, and the treacherous three are ready to go now, but they're not riding in the limo: they've just rented a Town Car after getting bored with a Ferrari and a Rolls, and they don't want their dollars to go to waste. "We three ride in the front, you in the back," Mike D tells me. "That's the rule."

The limousine goes first, and we follow. The auto I'm in is manned by derelicts: MCA's wearing a wrinkled long-sleeve white button-down, a black leather jacket, and a five o'clock (or five day, maybe) beard-shadow; Adrock has on an "Applachian Basketball Camp" shirt, a red Texaco baseball cap and a light-blue windbreaker; Mike D, skinnier and nerdier-looking than his cohorts, has a gold Volkswagen pendant, black horned-rim glasses, and an earring. Their jeans have holes, their Nikes lack laces (some new fad, I think), and I'm no queer but I know these are not the prettiest men I've ever seen. Anyway, we're chasing the limo, and Metallica's "Battery" is blasting from our tapedeck, and the dudes in front of me are banging heads toward the windshield as if they constituted one orgasm. They release their seatbacks so they can ride horizontally, they "accidentally" bump bumpers with the limo a few times, they shout catcalls at the usual female suspects. ("Before we were successful we used to stand on the streetcorner and yell at girls," Mike D later informs Joan Rivers. "Now we can sit in a Ferrari and do it, and it's a lot more effective.") And they doo-wop along with the cassette, which plays the Coasters, Elvis, Roxanne Shante, Marvin Gaye, ? & the Mysterians, Stevie Wonder and—as a tribute to their adolescent homeboys, I gather—Deep Purple.

"IT BECOMES HARD TO REMEMBER THAT 'SMOKE ON THE WATER' WAS NEVER A GOOD SONG AND WAS BARELY A GOOD JOKE—AND EVEN HARDER TO REMEMBER THAT OLD BROMIDE ABOUT WHAT HAPPENS TO THOSE WHO DON'T LEARN FROM THE PAST."

—*Mark Moses*, Boston Phoenix, *30 December 1986*

Afoot in our land is disillusionment the like of which has not been seen since the Watergate years. For the generation weaned on Danny Bonaduce, awakened by Haldeman and Erlichman and Dean, and enlightened by punk and its progeny, this disillusionment casts doubt and cynicism on not only our leaders, but on the mass media that stimulate our national mood. Be a sourpuss and call it premature nostalgia if you need to, but the current interest in early '70s rock is no retreat; fact is, punk promised more and then failed more miserably than any other rock 'n' roll ever has. When Redd Kross covers Kiss, when "Walk This Way" goes Top 10, when the Golden Palominos hire Jack Bruce, it's no retreat— rather, it's a necessary return to unfinished business. If the Sex Pistols had never happened, we'd probably be better off than we are now. And if the Beastie Boys don't come right out and say this, their record certainly implies it: To me, the most amazing thing about *Licensed to Ill's* success is the youth of its audience. That children of the '80s are buying it proves how universal its ideas are. Because to get all the details, you have to be a child of the '70s.

As I've said, Bonzo slapping his drum-kit kicks off the thing. But before the vinyl's been exhausted, we've also heard musical or verbal snippets from Black Sabbath's "Sweet Leaf," Zep's "The Ocean," War's "Low Rider," Steve Miller's "Fly Like an Eagle" and "Take The Money And Run" (plus they did a cool impromptu a capella "Joker" during the Joan Rivers rehearsals), Brownsville Station's "Smokin' in the Boys Room," Aerosmith's "No More No More," Creedence's "Down On the Corner," and some Barry White tune whose title eludes me. It's no accident that the record starts with a song called "Rhymin' And Stealin'"—the ouvres of Bill Haley and Bobby Fuller and Kurtis Blow and Schoolly-D are plundered, too. But *Licensed to Ill* isn't just about creative in-joke robbery; if it was, it wouldn't be worth much. All those borrowed bits and pieces are used to make connections, to outline the perimeters of the youth culture on which the Beasties' B-boy-brat stance depends. When I asked MCA about the lyric "sit around the house, get high and watch the tube," he answered, "We're not using it because it's in a Steve Miller song. We're using it because it's a good line."

So in the long run, what makes *Licensed to Ill* a great album—one of the best of the last year, and one of a mere handful of *listenable* recent ones on major labels—is that it's got great songs. First off, they *sound* great; Rubin is one of the few current producers who refuse to sell out rythym to disco-syndrum water-torture monotony, and this album's got his biggest beats ever. With him, the Beasties could get by on their cockiness alone. But what I really mean by great songs is great *songwriting*, by which I guess I just mean common sense. Wiffle-ball bats and swirlies and Phyllis Diller and Kentucky Fried Chicken and Budweiser and Rice-a-Roni and angel dust are things we live with in this world, and sometimes even things we talk about in real life, but I'll be damned if anybody else has ever written songs about them, and even if somebody has, they never wrote a couplet as unpretentiously jocular as "My pistol is loaded, I shot Betty Crocker/Deliver Colonel Sanders down to Davy Jones' locker" or "Went to the prom, bought a fly blue rental/ Got six girlies in my Lincoln Continental." It's all about specificity, I reckon. And when the words fall together into a fantastic delinquent anthem like "Fight For Your Right (to Party)" or a fantastic rock star rave-up like "No Sleep Till Brooklyn" (with glaciated guitar from Slayer's Kerry King) or a fantastic ghetto-gangster boast like "The New Style," I just can't figure why a person would resist. If being "offended" is what bugs you, you don't love rock 'n' roll.

"WHEN I WOKE UP LATE IN THE AFTERNOON

SHE'D TAKEN ALL THE THINGS FROM INSIDE

OF MY ROOM . . . ."

—Beastie Boys, "She's Crafty," 1986

There will always be party-poopers whose knees jerk whenever rap is mentioned; it takes no "talent," they say, *anybody* could do it. For all I know they're right, but I don't think it matters—if punk should have taught us anything, it's that rock is the property of ordinary people, not supergeniuses. It's not what somebody "could" do that's important; it's what they *do* do. And though when I listen to *Licensed to Ill* I wonder why nobody has ever accomplished what the Beasties accomplish here, I'm nevertheless more cynical about hip-hop than they are—to my ears it peaked around 1982, and (save for a couple of big acts who have transcended the form) it's mainly devolved into cliché-recapitulation, best exemplified by all those "Roxanne, Roxanne" answer-records and television-theme mastermixes. According to the Beasties, if I lived in New York—where "you hear it in the clubs and you hear it on the boxes in the streets," Adrock says—I'd think differently. "There's more copycat heavy metal than copycat rap," MCA opines, hitting me in my soft spot. "We hereby challenge Bon Jovi to an MC contest," taunts Mike D.

To be fair to those still skeptical about this stuff, I thought the Beastie Boys were less than brilliant live—reminded me more of a high school talent show than a rock gig, and all the somersaults and funky chickens and spastic tics didn't conceal the fact that they dance even worse than

Madonna, who they toured the country with in '85 and were scheduled to eat dinner with the evening after they doused my bed. Of course, the Rivers show may have been an atypical performance; "they told us if we f–––– up one more time on live TV, we're done," Mike D had related earlier. Maybe they were toned down, or maybe they were over-rehearsed, or maybe I just haven't seen enough rap shows to know what it is I'm supposed to watch when all that's on stage is a turntable and three kids with microphones. The interview with Joan was certainly entertaining—MCA sat in her chair, Adrock on her desk, Mike D next to her with his arm around her; they gave her an apple with a bite taken out, and told her they were working on a concerto at Julliard. When we walked into her studio that afternoon, we'd seen a picture of Run-D.M.C. on the wall between Dr. Ruth Westheimer and Vincent Price, so perhaps Joan digs this bugaloo thang enough to invite the Boys back. Don't know whether she appreciated the *Extended Sexual Orgasm* book they presented her and her hubbie backstage at the end of the night, though.

Well, you can't claim good fortune has spolied these guys—from what I've heard they've *always* been like this. But they say they enjoy the fame, even if it means meeting dimwits like Dweezil Zappa, and even though they have to put up with fools who ask them whether they're actually black. "When my mom first heard [the album] she said it sounded like it would be real successful," MCA says, and I expect an A&R department to give her a call any day now. The Beasties have run into a brick wall or two—Michael Jackson, who owns the Beatles' catalog, refused to grant them permission to include their surf-guitar/doo-wop version of "I'm Down" on the LP; and intended non-LP B-side called "The Scenario," a murder story that the group calls their best song, proved too graphic for CBS; the label also advised (but didn't demand) the Beasties not to call their album *Don't Be A Faggot*, which was its working title. But the threesome is mostly satisfied with the freedom they've been granted, and they realize it's a rare thing in the age of Tipper Gore and Muzak Top 40. Says MCA: "The unique thing about the Def Jam deal is that we get the power to do what we want to do."

The group expects to contribute "The Scenario" to a film soundtrack in the near future; another unreleased cut, "Desperado," will be included in Rubin's *Tougher Than Leather* flick, due for release this year. Meanwhile, the Beasties are barnstorming America's auditoriums with funk-wavers Fishbone and laff-core phonies Murphy's Law, spreading their decadent sex-and-drugs gospel to the initiated and the uninitiated alike. (David Lee Roth asked them to open his tour's concerts, but they wanted to headline this time.) After that, who knows? "I don't know if we'll die doing this," MCA remarks. "And I don't think we should disappoint our audience by letting them know what we've got planned."

"WHEN IN DOUBT, I WHIP IT OUT

I GOT ME A ROCK 'N' ROLL BAND

IT'S A FREE-FOR-ALL."

—*Ted Nugent, "Free For All," 1976*

NELSON GEORGE

"TOGETHER FOREVER" INCITES GOOD & ILL WILL

Billboard, *July 11, 1987*

In Seattle, the show had to be moved because the groups involved were denied access to the city's Civic Arena. City officials said they did it because of "ample predictions of real physical trouble." In Portland, Oregon, newspapers ran headlines stating "Coliseum Concert Almost Subdued" and "Rap Groups Play Before Well-Behaved Crowd," while local news shows replayed footage from a riot at a rap concert. The *Los Angeles Times* ran three stories from three different cities when the tour hit Southern California.

The groups that generated all this attention were Run-D.M.C. and the Beastie Boys, two multimillion-selling acts whose "Together Forever" tour has been viewed by some with more trepidation than anticipation. Rap has never been very popular with arbiters of taste or the functionaries of government. Like heavy metal, it's been a whipping boy for those who don't like loud aggressive youth music. Like affirmative action, it's been used as a smoke screen by racists to attack blacks. Combine those factors with the unfortunate gang riot at the Long Beach rap show headlined by Run-D.M.C. last year and the bad press the Beastie Boys generated in England recently, and you can understand why some viewed this tour as the most dangerous thing to hit the West Coast since Larry Bird's mustache.

Ticket sales were affected by this during the tour's first 10 dates, which is too bad for Rush Productions. But, much more profoundly, the

1987: The Together Forever Tour.

interracial good-will potential of the tour has been weakened. It's hard to remember a tour of two acts, one black and one white, who've sold this many albums in such a short amount of time in the rock 'n' roll era. And the crowds during the "Together Forever" tour's recent four-night stand at Los Angeles' Greek Theater, although predominately white, were an unusual blend of whites, blacks, and Hispanics. You realize just how socially segregated America still is when you see a crowd this integrated and are surprised by it.

It is not the media's job or that of city officials to help entertainers make money. But neither are they serving the audience or city residents by stoking the fires of paranoia. As for the concert itself, it was good, raunchy fun. The Beasties drank a lot of beer, invited girls on stage, and danced funny. One night Mike Tyson was brought on stage by Run. On another, Janet Jackson watched from the wings. Overall, Run-D.M.C. and Jam Master Jay showed that they've grown considerably as performers; they've shortened songs, added recurring bits of stage business, and even gave a probrotherhood speech in the middle of the set.

JOHN ROCCO

HIP HOP, FROM *THE DICTIONARY OF THE AVANT-GARDES*

HIP HOP (c. 1979)

Hip Hop has emerged as the most vibrant and powerful subculture of the late-twentieth century. Its strength lies in its continual evolution, its ever-present thrust to renew itself. The avant-garde cultural force of hip hop—and hip hop embraces many artistic forms including rap music, graffiti art, and DJ culture—began in the African-American communities of New York City and has since permeated mainstream American culture from fashion to political organization.

Hip Hop began as a form of oppositional culture in the post-civil rights era; its first practitioners took what interested them from the club scene—the positioning of the DJ as "mixer," as spinner of vinyl—and combined it with the energy of contemporary African-American music from James Brown to Gil Scott-Heron. What emerged was a communal eruption of music, competition, dance, and a new approach to creating sounds via the turntable. This combination of the Black vernacular tradition (from work songs to the blues poems of Langston Hughes) with a new use of the machines of music (the turntable, the boom box, the sampler) was powered and enhanced by its communal origins and its competitive edge. The cultural pioneers of the form were Bronx DJs: Grandmaster Flash, Kool Herc, Afrika Bambaataa, and DJ Breakout. Each of these DJs established clear territories in the Bronx and each brought something new to the form. (Grandmaster Flash developed "scratching" or playing a record back and forth against the needle; Kool Herc's Herculords—enormous speakers that gave immense power to the bass and treble tones—set the standard for sound; and Afrika Bambaataa was the first DJ to mix rock beats into his sound.) Hip hop begins with the DJ, but rap has become its most dominant force.

The first rappers were complements to the DJ: they focused his energy and directed the tempo. B-boys and B-girls—breakdancers—danced and reacted to the DJs' "breaks," or repetition of the instrumental sections (drums dominating) of the albums they were spinning. Graffiti artists added to this by representing their groups in their art work. (Jean-Michel Basquiat began as a graffiti writer, and he brought the hip hop style into his "serious" painting and thus into the work of the pop master himself, Andy Warhol, who befriended and worked with the younger artist. At the height

Two Blocks from Def Jam: Public Enemy's first publicity shot (L to r: Terminator X, Flavor Flav, Chuck D). Photo © Glen E. Friedman.

of his fame Basquiat also released several rap albums.) The rapper's relation to the music was different because his work directly confronted the audience. The rapper reacted to the DJ by countering with his lyrics, his style, his microphone. Rap is the ultimate extension of oral performance because it relies on the projection only awarded by technology. And, just as the DJs and breakdancers competed against each other—competition that often erupted in physical confrontation between rival crews—the rapper was a voice in a competitive field. Thus rap is marked by an identifying presence relying on boasting and hyperbole for effect. Moreover, as many critics of the culture have pointed out, the immediate influence on rap were the Last Poets, the group of poets/musicians/social critics who formed at a birthday celebration for Malcolm X in 1968. Continuing in the tradition of the Last Poets, rap groups such as Public Enemy have enunciated social problems and political messages within extremely popular music.

The rise of rap over the other elements of hip hop began with the commercialization of the form—record companies stepped in and used what they could put on record. But hip hop evolved and threatened to tear apart the corporate hold. In 1988, a rap crew from South Central LA calling themselves N.W.A. (Niggaz With Attitude) released an album called *Straight Out of Compton*. It was an immediate success and it immediately had the FBI's interest. It has been called the beginning of "gangsta rap" or, as Ice Cube prefers to call it, "reality rap." What it depicted was an urban nightmare of alienation, rage, and violence. The most notorious song on the album was "(Fuck) the Police," a tune in need of little explication. But the music was also powerful, thrilling, and it transformed the rap scene almost over night. There was a backlash against the content of "gangsta rap" from parent groups and politicians (George Bush went out of his way to call one rapper, Ice-T, "sick"); and in 1996 and 1997 two prominent "gangsta" rappers, Tupac Shakur (who became the only person ever to have a #1 album while incarcerated) and the Notorious B.I.G. were shot to death. These two killings brought many of the issues of hip hop back into focus. A new form of rap emerged stressing community and tagged by the press as "sensitive gangsta." But new names are not important; what is vital is that hip hop, like the *Transformers* often cited in the work of the Wu-Tang Clan, keeps moving and changing.

ADAM HEIMLICH

"IF I PLAYED GUITAR I'D BE JIMMY PAGE": ON BEING YOUNG, WHITE AND BEASTIAL IN LATE-'80S SUBURBIA

We were following a man and his pit bulls through the dark, empty streets of Passaic, NJ. The three dogs were half a block ahead of us, patrolling. The man was some sort of security guard, I think. He was as far as we were concerned. He was leading us to where Jon's car had been towed to, and that was what mattered. The first person we'd asked for help had pointed us in the opposite direction, and we'd walked that way for some blocks, until there were no more streetlights or businesses or people, only burnt-out factory buildings. The guy with the pit bulls was our savior. He came along and asked how the hell we came to be so hopelessly lost. We didn't tell him it was the first time any of us had been drunk outside of somebody's basement, but he could probably tell.

Meanwhile, backstage at the Capitol Theatre, the Beastie Boys were pouring a jar of honey onto the heads and bodies of some teenage girls. It was no big deal, really—the girls were fans, happy to be backstage and playing a part in Beastie mayhem. It ended up being a big deal for the Beastie Boys, though. The girls' parents sued them for an inordinate sum. The ensuing legal wrangle was later referred to in a line off *Paul's Boutique* ("Time and money/For girls covered with honey"), probably because the incident was filmed for the *Licensed to Ill* tour video. My friends and I bought that tape when it came out, and recognized the venue of the honey scene as Passaic. I remember watching those Jersey girls drunkenly dance under the upended jar and thinking that if what I'd been doing at that exact moment had been captured on film, my parents would have sued the Beastie Boys too.

The reason for this, and the reason why our car had been towed from outside the Beastie Boys show, and why we got lost trying to find it, and also why we'd been totally unprepared to face the Beastie's opening act, Public Enemy, is that my friends and I had damn near no urban experience whatsoever. Our parents and our parents' parents were all from New York City, but we'd grown up, by their design, sheltered. Rather, I should really say it was by their "choice," because the design that protected my pals and me is rightly credited to Henry Ford, Robert Moses and the Levits—the founding fathers of suburbia. Had anyone ever given a moment's thought to what it would "really" mean to grow up in their auto-dependent, sub-divided world? When your daughter comes home from a concert with honey in her hair, does it hit you?

Licensed to Ill meant more to me than any album ever had, and at 16 I'd been collecting albums for a decade already. I was well aware that the Beasties' grand statement, "Fight For Your Your Right (To Party)" was one of thundering stupidity. Aficionados of classic rock and punk, my friends and I dismissed pop radio as a matter of course. But somehow Kevin found out that "Party" was just the Beastie Boys' novelty song, and he clued us in to the rest of the album. There was "Rhymin' and Stealin'," built on John Bonham's massive beat from "When the Levee Breaks" and the riff from Sabbath's "Sweat Leaf"; another brilliant Led Zep sample, from "The Ocean," in "She's Crafty"; "No Sleep 'Till Brooklyn" was as tough as Schooly D, but as heavy as "Iron Man"; that "Mr. Ed" snippet in "Time to Get Ill" cracked us up; as did the intentionally grating rhymes and manic beats of "Girls" and "Brass Monkey." Above all, we were floored by the willingness, and the ability, to chop rock 'n' roll to pieces—to leave it behind and replace it with hip-hop technique, hip-hop language. We loved Run-DMC, but we wanted to "be" Jimmy Page. Suddenly, Jimmy and his Gibson were starting to look a little funny, and a little foreign.

My high school had a tradition called a "slave dance." The day of the dance, seniors would be auctioned off to the highest bidder (the money went to charity, or something) and the "owners" would get to dress their "slaves" for the dance. (So I don't have to tell you how white my school was.) It was a costume thing—a lot of jocks attired as cheerleaders, pretending this was against their will. Anyway, in 1987, not long after our Passaic experience, me and the guys pooled our funds for a trio of real cheerleader-types, and we dressed them as the Beastie Boys. We were only sophomores, so the whole thing had a disturbing sort of "Weird Science" ring to it—until, on the way to the dance, we got them to drink the sixes of Budweiser we'd brought along as props. They arrived very much in character. The girl dressed as MCA ended up telling a teacher to suck her dick! It's one of my fondest high school memories.

Understand, *Licensed to Ill* didn't just hit close to home—it hit us "exactly" where we lived. We'd been born into one side of a microcosmic culture war—the split between Boomer liberals who stayed radical and urban after college, and those like our parents, who tried to subsume their good intentions in private-sector jobs and, to a greater extent, their suburban-bred children. Every one of my elementary school chums was a child of New York, Jewish liberals. Our ethical education was a steady diet of anti-racism, anti-sexism, anti-greed—I believe the idea was to wipe all those out in one generation. From our point of view, it was working pretty well. At 16, I'd never witnessed even a single example of the racism I'd been warned about.

The unforeseen by-product of our having been incessantly cautioned against invisible evils was a fascination, deep and undeniable, for anything that called itself evil—and the louder it did so, the better. The effect of the arrival of Black Sabbath, Led Zeppelin and later KISS and AC/DC was, I imagine, like that of hip-thrusting Elvis or leather-clad Jim Morrison, exaggerated ab adsurdim. We would confront our parents' fears and win. By the '70s, though, The Darkside didn't need to be hinted at or flirted with. But, by design, we'd missed it. Our sheltered lives had made us fearless.

If you don't believe this rift existed, go back and read *Rolling Stone*'s reviews of *Paranoid*, *Led Zeppelin II* and *Dirty Deeds Done Dirt Cheap*. You'll find that "anti-establishment" critics were disturbed by this music, and downright spooked that every time those bands came to town, the commuter trains would be packed with white kids who'd never heard the true blues, never marched for high ideals, never been mugged, never been called a wop or a kike, never had to fight for "any" right—in essence, who never knew anything besides power, and loved it.

The Beastie Boys knew first-hand the effects of this surfeit of freedom. And though it'd be many years until they'd come around to the causes of civil rights and feminism, there's evidence that even in '87 the Boys were loath to take their birthrights for granted. Living in the city makes it harder to do that. New York is particularly difficult—it must have been particularly strange, there, to be told by the '70s establishment that you could be whoever you want to be, accomplish anything you set your mind to. They put in work, alright. By the time they got to Passaic, the Beastie Boys' act was extremely well-rehearsed.

I was inspired. During "Rhymin' and Stealin'" I set my mind to kissing some girl across the aisle, but it didn't go over all that well. And after the show, when we finally got to the towing lot, my pals and I were short of cash, and Jon ended up having to trade his boombox for his car. Then at school the next day, we all got in trouble for wearing our Beastie Boys tour t-shirts, because on the back they said "Get Off My Dick." The vice-principal who called us to his office seemed genuinely disappointed that college-prep students wanted to dress like Jersey rednecks from the vocational classes. "Get Off My Dick" must not have seemed different than Metallica's slogan, "Metal Up Your Ass." It was, in fact—from the vice principal's point of view—far worse. We'd done the class-transgression thing already, and it was but an appetizer.

The same year I saw the Beasties in Passaic, U2 came to Madison Square Garden. I don't remember their performance, but I can very clearly recall Bono taking time between songs to slight my beloved Beastie Boys. "You gotta foyght fer yer royght to parr-tee," he said, shaking his head, while the band tuned up for another number about Belfast or Central America. "Yeah," he sniffed, "you rilly gotta foyght."

"Shit," I thought, "Bono doesn't get it."

Maybe in the '90s, during one of U2's countless, pathetic attempts to leap aboard the techno-rave bandwagon, it finally hit him.

The Beasties downplay their Jewishness, but it's hard to otherwise explain their feat of inter-cultural translation. Who, besides outsiders to both, could have so accurately pegged the links between the power-language of burnouts and that of black, urban youth? The message of the medium was a celebration of minority America, as seen by double-agents (*Licensed to Ill*) brought up among the majority. The Boys had talent, but to follow their lead all it really took, apparently, was a heaping measure of disrespect.

So it was pure ecstasy to be drunk on Budweiser, oogling the caged go-go dancers and rhyming along with the Beastie Boys as their huge, penile stage prop emerged from the Passaic stage. And it wasn't just stupid and decadent. I knew at 16 that my upper-middle-class, sheltered, Jewish-assimilationist background wasn't worthy of respect, and in some ways I was correct. Soon, Public Enemy would explain more. Not long after their tour with the Beasties, P.E. even wrote a song called "Party For Your Right to Fight."

Since '87, hip-hop has become the major integrationist force in this country. To the arbiters of hip-hop history, the extent of my and the Beasties participation in this story is marginal. It's simply not about white folks. African-American rap critics, in 1999, look to the sounds and images of Afrika Bambaataa, Grandmaster Flash and Eric B. and Rakim—artists who addressed urban black kids as loudly and clearly as the Beastie Boys spoke to me—and see a completely different musical movement.

But it's one that was nipped in the bud. *Licensed to Ill* was the best-selling rap album ever, and the influence of white, suburban power on hip-hop culture never went away. It's tempting to wonder what might have been, but realistically, black artists couldn't have kept their music away from the likes of me even if the Beastie Boys hadn't had built their honey-coated bridge. I was white, male and free to be curious, and so bound to wander into a ghetto sooner or later. Looking back, I can see I was lucky, and also destructive, but at least I found that out. If there's anything from my early education that my experiences with hip-hop have ultimately confirmed, it's that it's crucial to understand and be proud of who you are and where you come from. So I don't really see anything to apologize for.

Part Two

YOUR CRYSTAL BALL
AIN'T SO CRYSTAL CLEAR

"1993: An artificial life form will be created in a lab,

probably in the USSR, thus reducing our interest

in locating life forms on other planets."

—Philip K. Dick, "Predictions" (1981)

"But if you don't have a pitch control, don't buy an

album that was made after 1974."

—Adam Horovitz in 1994

A Beasties Timeline: 1987–1994

Beastie Boys

1987–88 Beastie Boys move to LA and meet the Dust Brothers.

1989 After a legal battle with Def Jam, the Beastie Boys release their second album, *Paul's Boutique*, on Capitol.

1989–92 The Lost Years. During this period a rumor grew that the Beasties were playing *instruments*.

Music

1988 Public Enemy release one of the greatest albums in any genre: *It Takes a Nation of Millions to Hold Us Back*. In the age of Reagan-Bush, Sonic Youth release the aptly titled *Daydream Nation*, a classic and their last on an independent. The rise of the gangsta: N.W.A. release *Straight Outta Compton*.

1989 De La Soul debut with *3 Feet High and Rising*. It came from Seattle: Soundgarden release *Louder Than Love* and Nirvana spend $606.17 on their first album, *Bleach*.

1990 Public Enemy continue their politics by other means with *Fear of a Black Planet*. Sonic Youth release their major label debut, *Goo*, which features Chuck D on "Kool Thing." Ice Cube punches *AmeriKKKa's Most Wanted* through the national consciousness.

1991 A Tribe Called Quest release *The Low End Theory*. Biz Markie's *I Need a Haircut* is dragged into

Your Crystal Ball Ain't So Crystal Clear

court and becomes the subject of one of the first hip-hop "sample" cases. Biz loses and strikes back the following year with *All Samples Cleared*. Nirvana release *Nevermind*. Tupac Shakur's first album appears and Ice T becomes *OG: Original Gangster*.

1992   Combining funk, punk, dunks, and hip hop, the Beasties produce the genre-bending *Check Your Head*.

1992   *Nevermind* tops the charts and the "grunge" movement is thrown into high gear. Ice T and his hardcore band Body Count produce "Cop Killer," a song that attracts the attention of President George Bush and Moses (Charlton Heston). Warner removes the track from circulation. In LA, riots erupt after a not-guilty verdict is delivered in the Rodney King case.

1993   The Beastie Boys move back to NYC to work on their fourth album.

1993   The Wu-Tang Clan begin their assault upon the wall of pop culture in *Enter the Wu-Tang (36 Chambers)*. Nirvana release *In Utero*. Luscious Jackson's first album, *In Search of Manny*, appears on the Grand Royal label. Cyprus Hill goes ganja blessed on *Black Sunday* ("The original drafts of the Declaration of Independence were written on hemp paper"). KRS-One drops *Return of the Boom Bap*.

1994   The Beasties continue to culture munch the entire twentieth century on *Ill Communication*. The band headlines Lollapalooza. The Milarepa Fund is established. A collection of vault material from the early incarnation of the Beastie Boys called *Some Old Bullshit* is released.

1994   Kurt Cobain is found dead, the result of a self-inflicted gunshot wound. Beck, the man who wrote a song called "MTV Makes Me Want to Smoke Crack," releases his first album, called *Mellow Yellow*. Nas goes *Illmatic*.

We begin with the story of the first great Beastie *comeback* album—all the Beastie albums after *Licensed to Ill* come back at something: *Paul's Boutique* strikes back at the success of *Licensed to Ill* and the lingering questions over Beastie growth after their break with Def Jam; *Check Your Head* comes back at ya and responds to the relative (extremely relative) commercial failure of *Paul's* and brings in instrumentation and hardcore; *Ill Communication* responds to the mix of the latter by mixing more and in different directions; and *Hello Nasty* reacts to the hardcore of its two predecessors (and *Aglio E Olio*) and the current old-school pull in hip hop.

Chris Morris describes the "Building" of *Paul's Boutique* before Robert Christgau reviews the album and restructures the hip-hop hierarchy at the same time ("But this time they know the difference between bad and evil"). Then Bill Holdship, coauthor of one of the worst concert reviews ever written on the Beasties, visits them for a conversation about the break with Def Jam, L.A., cookie parties, and *Paul's*. Adam Heimlich then *really* listens to *Paul's* and visits another brave new world.

Then the emerging-hardcore middle period: Havelock Nelson describes the mix of *Check Your Head* while Frank Owen talks to the band about it. Craig Rosen then announces the appearance of *Ill Communicaton*. Larry Kay raps with the Beasties about their fascination with funk and their plans for Lollapalooza. In an illuminating, if tech-heavy, description of Beastie working methods, Adam Beyda enters G-Son and talks to the band and Mario Caldato. Kim France then puts the Beasties in their place again, while Matt Diehl examines their links with Sonic Youth. I end this section with a definition of Sonic Youth, for some reason (just go listen to them).

CHRIS MORRIS

BUILDING THE PERFECT BEASTIE ALBUM

Billboard, *September 9, 1989*

LOS ANGELES—Will the Beastie Boys' new Capitol album, *Paul's Boutique*—currently No. 14 on *Billboard*'s Top Pop Albums chart—change the public's mind about the bad boys of rap?

"Not until we have a boxed set are people's minds really going to change," says Mike Diamond, aka Mike D, who is partnered with Adam Yauch (MCA), and Adam Horovitz (King Ad-Rock) in the wise-guy rap trio.

The group's reputation as unpredictable rap brats was solidified three years ago by well-reported hijinks on a lengthy nation-wide tour, which followed the multiplatinum success of the band's Def Jam debut, *Licensed to Ill*.

Diamond views the band's past indiscretions somewhat ruefully, but without any great remorse.

"We were just making music that we liked, stuff that was funny to us, and then all of a sudden it became this big controversial thing. It's almost like we don't feel responsible for it, because to a larger extent we're not."

The Boys continue to court controversy with the new album; it's unexpurgated lyrical content is flagged by a lyric advisory sticker.

"We tried to keep it off," Diamond says of the sticker. "It's really weak. It was really wack.

"It's even wacker to me when people take [new] songs like 'High Plains Drifter' or 'Looking Down the Barrel of a Gun' and [talk about] 'the Boys' violent tendencies.' They don't understand. That's a character narrative. Why is that any different than [William Burroughs's acclaimed novel] *Naked Lunch*? If that came out in this day and age, it would probably have an explicit sticker on it."

To create the dizzyingly sampled, almost psychedelic textures of *Paul's Boutique*, the Beastie Boys used the production team of Matt Dike, John King, and Mike Simpson, known collectively as the Dust Brothers. The group had known Simpson from New York's Roxy hip-hop scene, and had played Dike's L.A. club Power Tools.

"They played us a tape of what they had down, and that's what we wanted our stuff to sound like," Diamond says. "You could use the word, maybe, 'stew,' or 'pot luck dinner.' Or 'casserole,' those type of terms. What you're talking about is you're combining a lot of different things, a lot of different seasonings."

Paul's Boutique was released despite suits and countersuits between the band and Def Jam Records, which put out *Licensed to Ill*. The Beastie Boys contend that they weren't paid more than $2 million in royalties owed them from *Licensed to Ill*, while Def Jam has sued both the band and Capitol for breach of contract and plans its own new Beastie Boys album of previously unreleased tracks.

"It really boils down very simply. We got ripped off, and it sucks," Diamond says. "It's a story that's been repeated over and over again. What's really sad about it is that it's not like some unique, first-time situation. You read about it all through music history. It's a shame that people still haven't learned from this."

Def Jam disputes Diamond's characterization. The label has maintained it withheld royalties after the group members claimed they were disbanding.

Having learned from the mistakes made on their first, lengthy headlining tour, the Boys will support *Paul's Boutique* with a short two-month American swing, beginning in November.

"Since people are really terrified of going to rap shows now," Diamond says wryly, "we're going to bill it as a reunion tour, because this is a reunion for us, and [those tours] are the ones that are doing the big business. You know, the Stones, the Who, the Ringo Starr tour. Even though we never broke up, we're going to bill it as a reunion thing, and hop on that whole bandwagon."

And who will open the shows? Says Diamond: "We're thinking of maybe like Charo, Buck Owens, and the Jungle Brothers."

ROBERT CHRISTGAU
HOW YA LIKE 'EM NOW?
Village Voice, August 15, 1989

On the rap report card Kool Moe Dee stuck into *How Ya Like Me Now* back in '87, the old-schooler proved an easy marker—only two of 25 fell below Public Enemy at 80 B. The token nonentity Boogie Boys got 7 or 8 in teach's 10 categories for a 77 C+, and way below that were the perpetrators of history's best-selling rap album, the Beastie Boys, with a 10 in sticking to themes, an 8 in records and stage presence, and a 6 or 7 in vocabulary, voice, versatility, articulation, creativity, originality, and innovating rhythms. Total: 70, barely a C.

You can laugh off these grades, but with Moe Dee's archrival L.L. Cool J tied for fifth at 90 A, they did represent his sincere attempt to formalize the values of his fading artistic generation—values up-ended by Public Enemy and the Beasties. A career nondropout who earned a communications B.A. while leading the Treacherous Three, Moe Dee idealized upright manliness; having come up in a vital performance community, he didn't consider records important enough to mark for hooks, mixing, sampling, pacing, innovating textures, and what have you. Like most rock pioneers, he couldn't comprehend the upheaval he'd helped instigate: a music composed in the studio by copycats so in love with rap that they thought nothing of stretching it, mocking it, wrecking it, exploiting it—going too far, taking it up and over and out and around, making it better.

First Trip to Malibu, c. '85 Photo © Glen E. Friedman, reprinted with permission from the Burning Flags book, *Fuck You Heroes*.

If Public Enemy was a threat—collegians with a radical program, arrogantly burying their pleasures deep—the Beasties were an insult: they dissed everything Moe Dee stood for. Sons of the artistic upper-middle class (architect, art dealer, playwright), they laughed at the education Chuck D made something of and Moe Dee stood for (two years at Bard, a term at Vassar, two hours at Manhattan Community). Like millions of bohos before them, they were anything but upright, boys not men for as long as they could get away with it. As born aesthetes, they grabbed onto rap's musical quality and potential: as reflective rebels, they celebrated its unacceptability in the punk subculture and the world outside. And of course, they were white in a genre invented by and for black teenagers whose racial consciousness ran deep and would soon get large.

The way the Beasties tapped the hip-hop audience says plenty for the smarts and openness of their black manager and the black kids he steered them toward, but also testified to their own instinct and flair. From Anthrax to Maroon, those few white imitators who aren't merely horren-dous don't come close to the Beasties' street credibility. We were probably right to credit Rick Rubin with all what-have-you that as of late 1986 made *Licensed to Ill* history's greatest rap album, but in retrospect one recalls the once-fashionable fallacy that George Martin was the fifth Beatle. Certainly the Beasties unduplicable personas and perfect timing were what Rubin's expansive metal-rap was selling, and most likely a fair share of the music was their idea. We didn't think they could top themselves not because they were stupid or untalented—except for a few cretins in the Brit tabloids, nobody really believed that—but because their achievement was untoppable by definition. Outrage gets old fast, and rap eats its kings like no pop subgenre ever.

Lots of things have changed since late 1986. The Beasties' street credibility dimmed as "Fight for Your Right" went pop and Public Enemy turned hip hop to black nationalism. Due partly to the Beasties and mostly to how good the shit was, *Yo! MTV Raps* brought black rap to a white audience. History's biggest-selling rap single (and first number-one black rap album) was recorded in L.A. by a former repo man. After feuding with his black partner, Rick Rubin transmuted into a metal producer, and after feuding with their black manager, the Beasties became Capitol's first East Coast rap signing since the Boogie Boys. Chuck D and Hank Shocklee undertook to mix up a since aborted album of the Beasties' Def Jam outakes. And if the Beasties' *Paul's Boutique* doesn't top *Licensed to Ill*, though in some ways it does, it's up there with De La Soul in a year when L.L. Cool J is holding his crown and Kool Moe Dee is showing his age.

Avant-garde rap, *Licensed to Ill* was pop metal, foregrounding riffs and attitude any hedonist could love while eliminating wack solos and dumb-ass posturing (just like Kool Moe Dee, metal fans think David Coverdale has more "voice" than Johnny Thunders). *Paul's Boutique* isn't as user-friendly—I don't hear a rock anthem like "Fight for Your Right," or street beats like "Hold It, Now Hit It"'s either. But give it three plays and half a j's concentration and it will amaze and delight you with its high-speed volubility and riffs from nowhere. It's a generous tour de force—an absolutely unpretentious and unsententious affirmation of cultural diversity, of where they came from and where they went from there.

For versatility, or at least variety, they drop names: Cezanne, Houdini, Newton, Salinger, Ponce de Leon, Sahaharu Oh, Phil Rizzuto, Joe Blow, Bob Dylan, Jelly Roll Morton, Jerry Lee Swaggart, Jerry Lee Falwell. Or the samples they exploit less as hooks than as tags: Funky Four Plus One (twice), Johnny Cash, Charlie Daniels, Public Enemy, Wailers, Eek-a-Mouse (I think), Jean Knight, Ricky Skaggs (I think). For innovating rhythms, there are countless funk and metal artists I can't ID even when I recognize them. For vocabulary, start with "I'm Adam and I'm adamant about living large," or maybe "Expressing my aggression through my schizophrenic verse words" (rhymes with cursewords), then ponder these pairings: snifter-shoplifter, selfish-shellfish, homeless-phoneless, cellular-hell you were, fuck this-Butkus. Not what Moe Dee had in mind, of course. But definitely what all avatars of information overload have in mind, or some of it: "If I had a penny for my thoughts I'd be a millionaire."

These Beasties aren't as stoopid or stupid as the ones Rick Rubin gave the world (or as Rick Rubin). In fact, one of the impressive things about *Paul's Boutique* is what can only be called its moral tone. The Beasties are still bad—they get laid, they do drugs, they break laws, they laze around. But this time they know the difference between bad and evil. Crack and cocaine and woman-beaters and stickup kids get theirs; one song goes out to a homeless rockabilly wino, another ends, "Racism is schism on the serious tip." For violence in the street we have the amazing "Egg Man," in which they pelt various straights, fall guys, and miscreants with "a symbol of life": "Not like the crack you put in a pipe/ But the crack on your forehead here's/ A towel now wipe." Hostile? Why not? Destructive? Not if they can help it without trying too hard. They're not buying.

Just to dis Def Jam—check "Car Thief," which also takes on the presidency—the Beasties couldn't have picked more apposite collaborators than L.A.'s Dust Brothers, one of whom coproduced the aforementioned number-one rap album. But where *Loc-ed After Dark* is simplistic, its beats and hooks marched out one at a time, *Paul's Boutique* is jammed-soaked, frenetic, stark. It doesn't groove with the affirmative swagger of Kool Moe Dee or L.L. Cool J, and its catholicity is very much in-your-face—as is its unspoken avowal that the music of a nascent Afrocentrism can still be stretched (mocked? wrecked?) by sons of the white artistic upper-middle class. Having gotten rich off rap, the Beasties now presume to adapt it to *their* roots, to make *Paul's Boutique* a triumph of postmodern "art." Their sampling comes down on the side of dissociation, not synthesis—of a subculture happily at the end of its tether rather than nascent anything. It impossibly demonstrates that privileged wise guys can repossess the media options Moe Dee was battling for back when they were still punks in prep school. After all, this deliberately difficult piece of product will outsell *Knowledge Is King*. One can only hope Moe Dee is race man enough to take satisfaction in its failure to overtake *Walking with a Panther*, or *Loc-ed After Dark*.

BILL HOLDSHIP

THE GOOD, THE BAD
AND THE UGLY

Revolution, *November 1989*

Nestled deep in the Hollywood Hills is what you might call the Beastie Pad. Adam "Ad-Rock" Horovitz's mansion is the same type of palatial structure once reserved for Hollywood's elite— we're talking Charlie Chaplin and Zeppelin here—but then the Beastie Boys are still soaking up the financial splendor that fell their way when Licensed to Ill, *released in 1986, became the biggest best-selling debut LP in the history of CBS Records.*

Inside, there's a party in progress. This is not surprising, since neighbors say the mansion is pretty much the scene of a perpetual party. In the main room, Adam "MCA" Yauch and Mike D (Diamond) are wearing the standard B-Boys gear—the baseball caps, the medallions, the stupid Jerry Lewis expressions—as they alternately spit beer at their guests and simulate masturbation by spraying cans of beer from between their legs.

In short, they're the same jerks in real life that they always appeared to be on stage.

Nonetheless, nubile young girls who don't know any better are lying around the mansion in various states of undress, allowing themselves to be sprayed with beer, food, and other fluids that might happen to splash their way. Heavy metal music is blasting.

In another room, a group of black men—all of whom resemble Schoolly D and tote big boom boxes—are getting high. In yet another room, Ad-Rock is holding court among his Hollywood brat pack friends. Dweezil Zappa and Molly Ringwald are there, as are young starlets like Meredith Salenger, Katie Wagner, and Susanna Hoffs.

Fame and fortune. Money and power. These are the things that matter in Tinseltown, the place these New York exiles now call home. The Beastie Boys have it all . . . .

As Jerry Lee Lewis scrawled over the script for *Great Balls of Fire*: "Lies! Lies! Lies!" But the scenario above makes for a nice Beastie Boys fantasy.

Some of it is true; a lot of it, though, is the worst possible fantasy the press—and probably the Beasties themselves—could imagine. Back when they were making their first big media splash, the Beasties were accused of being everything from homophobes to racists. And you didn't have to look much further than *Licensed to Ill*—which I thought was a total scam—and their live show to see that they were total jerks.

It's been three years since the Beasties were the hottest musical sensation in the U. S. of A. The official word last year was that they had broken up, going the way of all one-hit wonder novelty acts. It only reinforced a report that MCA had, almost in tears, told his cohorts, "I don't want to do this anymore!" at an L.A. hotel pool near the end of 1987's Run-D.M.C./ Beastie Boys tour.

So it came as a bit of a surprise when the Beasties announced they'd jumped labels, leaving Def Jam behind, not to mention producer Rick Rubin and label president/group manager Russell Simmons, who many considered the Svengalis behind the group.

There are lawsuits, of course. Simmons claims the Beasties are still under contract to him, and that they owe the label many more records. (Def Jam just released its own unauthorized Beastie Boys LP, *White House*, from unreleased tapes.) The Beasties counter that Def Jam paid them less than $100,000 during the last three years, and owes them millions of dollars in back royalties. Both parties are screaming breach of contract. Add to the mess the various copyright lawsuits the Beasties say they're facing for samples on *Licensed to Ill*, and the fantasy looks more like a nightmare.

So *Paul's Boutique*, the new Beastie Boys LP that Capitol released in July, comes as a big surprise. From the brilliant title to the stuff in its grooves, *Paul's Boutique* is a better record than *Licensed to Ill*. The Beasties make a real rap record this time out—well, *sort* of. There probably aren't too many rap records you can think of that sample the Eagles, Sweet, Loggins & Messina, Johnny Cash, bluegrass, the Isley Brothers, *Sgt. Pepper*, and *Abbey Road*, just to name a few.

The Beasties aren't too eager to discuss the sampling that went into *Boutique*. In fact, MCA doesn't even like the term. "I don't look at it as sampling, because we're just taking bits and pieces that we like and putting them together in a new way," he says. "We're creating something new. It's an art form, in that sense."

They won't even admit that *Paul's Boutique* is a better or even more mature record than *Licensed to Ill*. "Everyone's been trying to say that it's more mature," says MCA, "so it may very well be, since that seems to be everyone's opinion. But we weren't really aware of it until everyone said it. As far as we're concerned, we're just making shit, you know? As far as the social community goes, it's just stuff that we felt like writing about at the time."

"I wonder if that's everyone's opinion based on what they hear or based on three years going by [between albums]?" asks Mike D. "They're just thinking, 'Oh, these guys must have grown up.' To a degree, we're still the same, but to a degree, we've changed. That's just sort of the nature of time, right?"

Ad-Rock lives in a relatively modest apartment on a residential side street just off Hollywood Boulevard. Mike D comes down the steps to let me in, and says the other Beasties are just finishing up another interview.

"Oh, you bought your own soda," he says, observing my Diet Coke. "We would have given you a soda!"

This is my first indication that Mr. D is more like a kindly Jewish uncle than a Beastie; in fact, as the interview progresses, the distinct Beastie personalities come into focus. MCA makes it apparent that he's the serious Beastie. He's generally the first to answer a question with a straight answer, and his new beard (it looks like a billy goat's, according to Ad-Rock) makes him look all the more intense. Ad-Rock is the standoffish member of the trio. He doesn't have as much to say as the other two, and sometimes mutters smartass comments in response to a question.

They haven't been tolerant of people who aren't as cool as they are, especially smartass journalists who are always in their faces. During the last tour, in fact, they took great pride in making a female reporter break down in tears. Following another infamous interview, they poured a bucket of water on *Creem* journalist Chuck Eddy as he slept, filming the incident for a home video compilation. (Their special love for media types was enhanced when Eddy subsequently sued them.) They seemed to take even greater pleasure in a circulating story that MCA had punched a *BAM* reporter in the face.

But these days, at least, it's safe to say that the Beastie Boys don't have an evil bone among them—even Ad-Rock's smartass comments don't have a sense of real meanspiritedness. And despite their differences in temperament, all three of them are adept at suddenly shifting into high gear with a series of non sequiturs; the nonsense can be triggered by everything from an observation about Deep Purple to beer-company corporate sponsorship. And the bullshitting works for them. During the course of the interview, they came up with ideas for new songs—Ad-Rock, in particular, devised new beats for both Billy Joel's "A Matter of Trust" and Gary Lewis & the Playboys' "This Diamond Ring" ("That was a def song," says Mike D).

The Beasties' conversation soon turns to decadent subjects, though, like putting sealer on the patio floor ("They're not only looking for style and function in apartments, Adam," Mike D tells Ad-Rock. "They're looking for longevity.") and the cookie party Ad-Rock had for his friends several days before. *Cookie Party?* That's right. He invited his friends over to his apartment to *bake cookies.* And what about this apartment? It's extravagant if you happen to be a rock journalist or something like that, but for a rich rock star living in Hollywood? A lot of people would have thought the Beasties were millionaires many, many times over after the success of *Licensed to Ill.*

"A lot of people would have thought?" MCA asks. All three Beasties laugh. They estimate Def Jam owes them at least $5 million, but "it's probably more at this point," says Mike D. "The meter runs at every record sold, right?"

So do they think they're ever going to see this money?

"Oh, we see it," says Ad-Rock. "We see Rick [Rubin's] big house. We see Russell [Simmons's] apartment. We see it."

But Mike D is philosophical, at least. "We see how they've spent our money, but what can we do? We can look at the upside and be content that we're in a happier situation than we would have been if we'd stayed with them."

"In the long run, we're real lucky to be away from them," MCA says.

For the past several weeks, Simmons has been talking about the Beasties to the press, claiming he created the trio's act—right down to the clothes they wear—and that he's offered to pay the Beasties their money many times if they'd make another record for him. He also claims that the group was jealous of Rubin being touted as the true wizard behind the band.

"Yeah, well, the jealousy thing really was there," says Ad-Rock, "because I wanted to look like Rick."

"What you've got to understand," explains MCA, "is that Russell is one of the fastest talkers in the business, and he will always try to say a lot of shit to muddy the waters. If someone offered to pay you the money they owed you if you promised to do some other work, then you'd probably say, 'Well, pay me for the work I've already done because that's what we agreed upon.'"

What about the statement by Def Jam that the band was defunct?

"That's what they said," says Mike D. "That's their side of the story."

"That's their excuse for not paying us," adds MCA.

Mike D explains that, at the time, the Beasties had been on tour for six months, and were supposed to go out for another three-month tour. To say the least, they weren't exactly thrilled about it.

"Being on tour is a lot of wear and tear on a person," says MCA. "I mean, it's a lot of fun. It's sort of like being drunk is a lot of fun, but if you're drunk every day, it's going to wear on you."

So the band was basically exhausted? "We were," says MCA, "and we wanted to take some time off." I mention that someone told me they'd heard MCA saying, near the end of the last tour, that he didn't want to be in the Beasties anymore. "That's possible," MCA says of the alleged comment. "Any one of us may have said that at any time. We're human beings and we get upset. I mean, if you can find me a band that's never said that . . . ."

Mike D is more blunt. "Fuck the band. Find me a single person who hasn't sat at his desk doing his job, and then, during a moment of reflection, said, 'Fuck this. Am I really supposed to be doing this?' There's a lot of people sitting at their desks, writing nothing but curse words."

Was part of the problem that, after all the hype, the media blitz, the touring, they felt compelled to constantly play the image of the Beastie Boys they had created?

"Well, if everyone expects you to be an asshole," says MCA. Mike D continues, "At a certain point people expect a certain thing out of you, so no matter what you do, you're going to live up to that expectation, so they can say, 'Oh, those boring Beasties,' and be immensely disappointed. Or, you're going to do something they perceive as obnoxious, so they can say, 'Oh, those Beasties blew through our town.' So it's really a no-win situation."

"Or an all-win situation," Ad-Rock says.

So the Beastie Boys may be difficult. They may be obnoxious. But are they the racists and homophobes they've been made out to be? Since we're discussing perceptions of the band, I admit to the Beasties that I perceived the band as something to hate. The Beasties are intrigued.

"It's interesting to me to see why people hate us, you know what I mean?" says Mike D. "It's like you said, there's all this stuff over and over about the Beastie Boys being homophobic. They're racists. And it's like what did we do to start all that?"

"Rap music is like all bragging and boasting and talking all kinds of shit," Ad-Rock says. "And I don't know why people think that because we say it it's any different than what any other MC says. Why do they take it seriously?"

Earlier in the interview, they had expressed serious dismay about how scary all the current anti-Semitism in America is, and they mentioned an American Nazi leader whose name they asked me not to print. ("There's too much media coverage of him as it is," Mike D says.)

But there was an added dimension to the racist issue, since the interview took place two days after the anti-Semitic comments recently made by Public Enemy's Professor Griff hit the national media. The Beasties address that situation as "very sad" and "very scary." So, I ask, when people accuse the Beasties of being homophobes, racists, or sexists, doesn't that run along the same lines of the P.E. fiasco?

"Like how do you mean?" asks Mike D.

"He means it's sort of the same thing," Ad-Rock replies.

"I think that's because we use certain words," says MCA. "We'll say that someone is a homo geek poseur, but . . . ."

"Yeah," Ad-Rock cuts in. "Because in Manhattan, just because you call someone a homo or a faggot doesn't mean that he actually sleeps with men."

"[But] on a realistic basis, another person's sexual preference is not our concern," MCA says.

"The thing that baffles me is where does the racist thing come in?" asks Mike D. "Why are we racists? What's it based on? I can see where they derive some of those other accusations. If that's what they want to derive, so be it. The racist thing has always kind of bothered me, though. It seems unfounded."

"Well, I can understand it," MCA answers. "I mean, [we're] white kids playing what people consider black music, whatever. So people are going to find ways to think that."

"So we hate black people? What the fuck?" says Mike D. "I mean, that's just retarded."

"People should be fighting for human rights," says MCA, "not fighting for one specific race or against any other race."

"Why dis people?" asks Ad-Rock. "You don't have to dis people."

So what's the state of the Beasties in 1989? Perhaps the answer belongs to Mike D who describes a book on pop music trivia facts he plans to write someday.

"It will be interesting facts," he explains. "None of it will necessarily be true. But you know, there's a saying I have—it's actually an old saying from centuries ago—that goes, 'Often wrong, but never in doubt.' I think that's pretty important to what we do."

ADAM HEIMLICH

"SPACE CAKE COOKIE, I DISCOVER WHO I AM": SPIRITUAL SHOPPING WITH *PAUL'S BOUTIQUE*

The most intense experience I ever had listening to recorded music took place on a bus traveling from Dharmsala, India to New Delhi. It was supposed to be an all-day drive, but turned out to be an overnight run along the unlit, poorly-paved "highway" connecting Delhi and points Himalayan. We couldn't leave in the morning, as planned, because our driver had been still drunk from the night before. We waited all day for him to sober up. This was fine by me and the rest of my Tibetan Studies class. The healthiest among us were hung over from the farewell parties our homestay parents had thrown for us, and several of us—myself included—also had food poisoning, again. So no one was anxious to put their stomach in the care of our bus driver, who liked to play "chicken" with elephants. Those of us who needed to spend the entire day within eight steps of a squat hole were particularly grateful for his excess.

We'd spent six weeks at this particular Tibetan refugee enclave—McLeod Gange, located 6000 feet of treacherous switchbacks above the sea-level city of Dharmsala—and were now headed for another, in Nepal. The place we were leaving was well known as the home of the Dalai Lama, but, ironically, he was in the States while we were there. We'd made a few powerful friends in town, though, and some of my classmates took the opportunity presented by our delayed departure to pay a final visit to one of them. The baker at the Moon Cafe could whip up a mean space cookie—so thick with hash it was bitter, and powerful enough to keep you as high as you've ever been for the better part of a day. It cost the equivalent of a dollar, and even appeared on the menu. Dave and John had him make a whole cake to share among the class. We were all adventurous college students, 20 or 21 years old. The year was 1990. Almost all of us had cake.

But our baker friend had outdone himself this time. The confection that was passed down the bus aisle as we rolled out of Dharmsala was way too potent. Two hours later, everybody who ate more than a nibble of space cake was unconscious. Lucky me—lingering nausea from my bout with "Delhi belly" precluded an overdose. I'd had three bites and could eat no more. So while everybody else's eyes grew heavy and lidded, my open sockets were confronted with swirling colors everywhere—slow explosions of red, yellow and green filling the darkness of the bus and the rural Indian landscape outside. I could have sworn, at one point, that we were riding through an airport twice the size of JFK. I knew I was really far gone, so I pulled out my walkman and *Paul's Boutique.*

The nomadic nature of our program demanded that every student in my class play a non-hypothetical version of the bar game "Desert Island Disks" while packing—we could bring no more than a handful of cassettes for the whole semester. There was no anguish in my first choice, though. The Beastie Boys' second album was impossible to tire of. The previous year, my pal Kevin had called it "the soundtrack to our lives," and he was barely exaggerating. It was deep enough to accommodate any mood. I'd brought along Coltrane and Dylan for the meditative state I'd imagined would surface after a heavy dose of Buddhism; and Minutemen and Mudhoney to keep me in the moment. But confused, stoned, alone and in dangerous transit, I reached for the obvious choice.

Complete and total synesthesia occurred during "Car Thief." It's one of the thickest mixes on *Paul's Boutique*—probably over a dozen sample loops running simultaneously, over a ridiculously complex beat that's scratched on a wah-wah-peddled turntable in the intro. I saw it all that night: The impossible slickness of the DJ's action, and how it fit into the bubbling bass pattern, interlocking with the ghostly ooh girls and that bit of the break Funkadelic's "Red Hot Mama" that the Boys slowed down and elongated in order to weave it up the middle. And I saw Horovitz, Yauch and Diamond rap, though I felt a bit self-conscious about witnessing their visages so clearly there in the dark. But there they were, like it or not, Jewish faces forming an equilateral triangle—an animated version of the covers of the dozens of magazines that Kevin kept in our "Beastie Boys library"—switching lines not in regular order but in deference to the melody of the collaborative vocal. Ad-Rock, the trickster treble, MCA the baddass bass and Mike D the midrange master-of-ceremonies were the conduit for something truly perfect, I realized, and I was finally apprehending it in glorious totality. It was bigger than music, and I was more than a fan.

The drug wore off, leaving an epic headache in its wake. But nearly 10 years later, the clarity of that memory outdoes nearly all others from my semester abroad. A few weeks later we crossed the Himalayan border for a rare foray into Tibet (the Chinese government had only just opened the occupied region to tourists). Our teachers advised us to leave our headsets behind—to give in to full cultural immersion—but I ignored them and was glad for it. There were a lot of long bus rides. In one little village, we were even able to procure some pot. We traded some photographs of the Dalai Lama for a handful of buds—their contraband for ours.

Tibetan Buddhism was outlawed in Tibet for three decades. My class toured monasteries that had been leveled by tanks, and we met old monks who'd been recently released from prison, where they'd been since 1959. The Tibetans there, we found, behaved very differently than the people we knew from exile communities in India and Nepal. Exiled Tibetans were almost always more worldly than their Hindu neighbors. These urban-Tibetan Tibetans, particularly the kids who'd grown up under occupation, were ghetto people of the most pitiable and dangerous kind—aggressively begging outcasts with no culture of their own. Confronting what we saw in Tibet, and combining the evidence with what we knew about Western genocides, made our minds reel.

There seemed one hope. Having come so far from home largely out of disgust with what I saw as an American culture of complicity, it was easy to view the ways of the exiled Tibetans as saintly. The Dalai Lama leads a campaign of non-violent resistance, and his religion is founded on techniques said to unlock the limitless potential of human compassion. My classmates and I flocked to it like puppies in a dog-food-commercial taste-test. We sought the healthy alternative.

Most of my class ended up converting to Tibetan Buddhism. I didn't quite grasp what was holding me back, at the time. Though I'd noted a few pathologies in the culture—particularly with regard to its interface with the West—and so knew it wasn't perfect, it certainly seemed an improvement. I came to believe fervently in the tenets of the Tibetan faith—meditation, the cultivation of compassion, even reincarnation and theocracy—but still couldn't adopt it as my own. To my teachers and classmates, I was a disappointment—the un-immersed, wearing a walkman in the shadow of Everest.

Now, my reasons seem as undeniable as synesthesia. I simply didn't need to traverse the globe to acquire spirituality. I was born into a rich, rewarding culture, with a profound mystic tradition. It's got some pathologies, for certain, but taking an oath and donning beads wouldn't have cleansed me of them. No way. My cultural fiber is too dense and deeply stained. A thousand reincarnations from now, "Car Thief" will still sound good to me.

HAVELOCK NELSON

BEASTIE BOYS CHECK IN WITH HYBRID SET

Billboard, *April 18, 1992*

NEW YORK—Seven years after dropping punk rock for hip hop, the Beastie Boys are heading into "the next stage" of their career with a punk-rap hybrid on *Check Your Head*, their new Capitol Records album, in stores April 21.

The album, co-produced by recording engineer Mario Caldato, was recorded at G-Son Studios, the Beasties' new 24-track facility in Attwater Village, California, where Mike Diamond (Mike D), Adam Horovitz (King Adrock), and Adam Yauch (MCA) reembraced their hardcore roots, playing instruments on 70% of the tracks, according to Yauch.

"Some of the songs are all live," says Diamond. "Others are a combination of live and [borrowed sounds]." One short cut, "The Biz Vs. The Nuge," features vocals from Cold Chillin' artist Biz Markie.

The first white crew to break rap's color barrier, the Beastie Boys recorded *Licensed to Ill* in 1986 with producer Rick Rubin. Bolstered by the single "Fight For Your Right to Party," that Def Jam release became the fastest selling album in Columbia Records' history. Moving more than 4 million units, the Beastie Boys became pop stars. When a dispute with Def Jam erupted over unpaid royalties, they switched labels.

Paul's Boutique, from 1989, was the trio's Capitol debut album. It was a critical success, but without a novelty anthem like "Fight," it sold just more than gold. Now, the Beastie Boys are back.

"After the multiplatinum success of *Licensed to Ill*, there was perhaps an overanticipation of what *Paul's Boutique* would do in the market," says Capitol A&R VP Tim Devine, who oversaw the *Check Your Head* project. "As a result, on this album, we've decided to saturate the street and the underground and let the awareness build organically, rather than from the top 40 down." Describing Capitol's strategy for the album as being "aggressively patient," Devine adds, "You have to allow music like this time to sink in."

The album's first single, "Pass the Mic," was released March 16 with an accompanying video by Nate Hornblower, who directed two previous Beastie Boys clips. According to Cathy Lincoln, Capitol's director of artist development and alternative music marketing, early responses to the track at retail radio and video outlets have "just been phenomenal. People are

G: You Know Where, '91. Photo © Glen E. Friedman.

starting to call like crazy asking about it," she says. "We seem to be in a really good setup place for 'Pass the Mic.'"

Capitol has been priming the marketplace for the Beastie Boys' return from as far back as November. The group played gigs during both the CMJ Music Marathon and Gavin conventions last fall. The shows required hard tickets; one did not automatically get in with a badge. Says Lincoln, "We wanted to make sure the public got in there, that kids could see the Beastie Boys there and start a buzz among themselves."

The group also played the Marquee in London in February to ignite an international buzz on the new album.

On February 24, to further warm up the streets, the label serviced the album cut "Professor Booty" to college radio and DJs. "It got put on almost immediately," Lincoln says. WNWK New Jersey, WBAU New York, and KUSF San Francisco are among the stations that got behind "Professor Booty."

Now that "Pass the Mic" is out, the game plan is "to go for the hip-hop tip—mix shows and rap stations," says Lincoln. Capitol is also seeking support from alternative radio and shoring up support at metal radio for the Beastie Boys. It recently serviced a Beastie Boys metal-radio sampler that includes "So Whatcha Want," "Something's Got To Give," "Time For Livin'" and "Gratitude."

In addition to Capitol's promotion and marketing efforts, a new sports and music magazine named *Blast* has agreed to include "Pass the Mic" cassette singles inside 5,000 polybag-wrapped dealer issues when it debuts in late April.

The Beasties, who did not tour behind *Paul's Boutique*, will open a road run to support the new album May 2 in Buffalo, NY. A 37-minute home video called *The Skills to Pay the Bills* is set for a May 19 in-store date. The video, which features performances from the group's career from the beginning to now, will retail for $12.98 on Capitol Video. Promotional clips for "So Whatcha Want" and "Pass the Mic" will be included in the set.

The Beastie Boys have always had a diverse audience blend, and at this point, Capitol wants to maximize all of the band's support bases. As Lincoln puts it, "We're working this Beastie Boys project like no Beastie Boys project has ever been worked."

FRANK OWEN

BEASTIE BOYZ II MEN

Newsday, *April 12, 1992*

"For people who are into music rather than politics, it's really not an issue anymore," says Adam Yauch, a.k.a. MCA, lounging in his publicist's office, clearly bored after a day of press interviews. Yauch is one of the trio of nice upper-middle-class Jewish young men who make up the infamous rap group the Beastie Boys, and he's talking about the "White Negro" question that has dogged the group ever since as teenagers in Manhattan they made the smart decision to abandon their instruments and take up rapping, turning a hardcore punk group with few prospects into a multi-million-selling hip-hop act.

With the release of *Check Your Head* (Capitol)—the group's third album and the eagerly awaited follow-up to the hectic funk montage of 1989's *Paul's Boutique*—the Beastie Boys have returned to their roots. They now augment the usual sampled sounds with live instrumentation: Mike Diamond (Mike D) on drums, Adam Horovitz (King Ad-Rock) on guitar, and Yauch on bass (with Mark Ramos Nishita on keyboards). The

Beasties and instruments in '91. Photo © Glen E. Friedman.

densely funky progressive rock and rap of *Check Your Head* is a feast of sound with a vibe more Lollapalooza! than South-Central L.A.

Nonetheless, recently the Beastie Boys turned up in the *Village Voice's* letters page, in the unlikely company of collagen lip implants and Bo Derek's cornrows, and as an example of the "bastardization and exploitation" of African-American culture. Rather than "exploiting" black culture, the Beastie Boys are an example of what academic and writer Cornel West calls "the Afro-Americanization of American youth."

White kids sporting leather Africa medallions. Black youths wearing Doc Martens. Rappers fronting hardcore bands. We live in times when white youths, knowing their parents' culture is bankrupt, are increasingly turning to their black counterparts for advice on everything from fashion to politics. Public Enemy rapper Chuck D expresses surprise at the depth of knowledge that many white teenagers he meets have about figures like Malcolm X.

It's unlikely that frat party anthems like "Fight for Your Right to Party" and "No Sleep Till Brooklyn"—still the Beastie Boys' best-known singles—turned many white kids into Black Muslims, but they did introduce rap to hard rock's mass audience.

Thanks in part to the groundbreaking work done by the Beastie Boys, it's now possible to talk of a "new whiteness" developing in young America. Not Norman Mailer's old "White Negro" journeying to the heart of the ghetto in search of the exotic and erotic, but a new sensibility that is born not out of racial self-hatred, but of the belief that black culture has something to teach whites. As Janis Joplin once said: "Being black for a while teaches me to be a better white."

At Ice Cube's recent show at the Apollo, Mike D was amazed to see homeboys at the front of the audience executing a version of the punk dance the pogo. "You've got people slamdancing to house music," says Diamond. "You've got hardcore kids wearing homeboy clothes. And now this, the b-boy pogo. The next thing you know rap DJs will be cutting up the Ramones and the Sex Pistols."

"Attitude-wise, hardcore and rap are remarkably similar," continues Diamond. "The energy is the same. And you can express yourself without having had to study music for 15 years. I used to say that the only difference was that with punk rock you have funny haircuts, whereas with rap you have funny hats."

The most remarkable thing about *Check Your Head* is the way the album brilliantly illustrates the dialogue between black and white music that is so much a part of today's pop scene. Exhibiting influences as diverse as '70s funk, acid rock, old-school rap, punk, and grunge metal, *Check Your Head* is a bold and innovative work replete with '90s multi-culti-possibilities. It comes as no surprise to learn that the album was initially intended as an instrumental, since the emphasis is on the music and not the raps. The Beasties Boys have never been the most gifted rappers; a little of their whiny voices goes a long way. The group has sidestepped this problem by heavily distorting many of the vocals. On "Whatcha Want," when Mike D raps "I think I'm losing my mind this time/I think I'm losing my mind," he sounds like he's speaking through a malfunctioning megaphone.

In marked contrast to *Licensed to Ill*—the Beastie Boys' quadruple-platinum debut effort—*Check Your Head* is not at all bratty. Gone are the boisterous high jinks and teenage fantasies of misbehavior that made their early incarnation such a hoot. In the last six years, the Beastie Boys have matured; call them the Beastie Men. On "Namaste," listening to Yauch recite a druggy poem with lines like "A butterfly floats on the breeze of a sunlit sky/As I feel this reality gently fade away" over musical backing reminiscent of the Doors, it's difficult to remember that this is the group who once supposedly drilled a hole between two hotel rooms one above the other (they'd asked for adjoining rooms) and climbed up and down on a rope between the rooms, that sealed and filled up a shower in an L.A. hotel room for an orgy, and that told a visiting British journalist that the steam emanating from New York gutters was the result of "alligator farts."

But what *Check Your Head* lacks in humor, it makes up for in beat-heavy musical freshness. Recorded at the band's own studio in L.A.—built after they fled New York's Def Jam records, using money earned from *Licensed to Ill—Check Your Head* boasts a uniquely opaque and ramshackle sound ("phat" is Mike D's preferred adjective) far removed from the perfection that comes out of most contemporary studios.

"Nowadays everybody wants the real hype digital equipment," explains Mike D, "but we outfitted our studio with all this really cheap but great sounding secondhand equipment, like clavinets, old drum kits, fuzz basses and wah-wah pedals."

The album is culled from a series of lengthy jam sessions that took place over a year and produced 100 hours of audio tape. "We wanted to make it like a break-beats record," explains Mike D. "The same way as when you sample you take the best bit of a song, we wanted each song to contain the best bits from our jam sessions."

Refuting those who say sampling de-skills musicians, Diamond says that sampling actually spurred the band to take up live instruments again: "When you sample the type of music we do, you come to respect the incredible musicianship that went into the original. And you want to be able to play like that."

To those who see hip hop as a medium whose purity needs to be defended, the musical schizophrenia of *Check Your Head* will be taken as more evidence that the Beastie Boys are no longer a legitimate rap group. To those who, like Adam Yauch, are more interested in music than politics, *Check Your Head* will be recognized as an instant rock and rap classic.

CRAIG ROSEN

BEASTIES RENEW THEIR LICENSE TO ILL

Billboard, *April 23, 1994*

LOS ANGELES—In 1986, the Beastie Boys became the first rap act to top the album chart with *Licensed to Ill*, which went on to sell more than 4 million copies.

Paul's Boutique, the group's 1989 follow-up, was hailed by critics but failed to match the commercial knockout of the debut album. *Check Your Head*, released in 1992, struck a chord with both critics and consumers and has sold more than 1 million copies to date, according to SoundScan.

Now, with *Ill Communication*, which comes out May 31 on Grand Royal/Capitol, and a high-profile spot on this summer's Lollapalooza tour, retailers, radio programmers, Capitol, and the Beastie Boys all say the time is right for the group to score again.

Ill Communication features the punks-turned-rappers (and back again) dabbling in everything from hardcore and hip-hop to funk jams.

Says Capitol president/CEO Gary Gersh, "The climate is perfect for the Beastie Boys right now. It's exactly the right time, and they're exactly where they should be."

A number of retailers and radio programmers confirm that the demand for the Beastie Boys is still there.

"*Check Your Head* was huge, and it's still selling extremely well on both configurations," says Al Wilson, head buyer for the 143-store, Milford, Massachusetts–based Strawberries chain. "The rerelease ['Some Old Bull-shit,' which collects the group's early hardcore recordings and first foray into rap] sold like a new release the first week out. That, to me, indicated that there is a real, inherent, pent-up demand for Beastie Boys product."

San Diego modern rock station XTRA (91X) PD Mike Halloran con-curs. "This new record is going to do phenomenal," he says. "I heard a couple of things, and it rocks a lot harder and hops a lot higher."

Marco Collins, MD at KNDD (The End) Seattle, notes that the band has been able to maintain a healthy fan base. "It's amazing how they continue to reinvent themselves with each album without losing their fol-lowing."

The Beasties' Mike D (Mike Diamond) notes that the musical climate has changed to the group's advantage. "Increasingly, there are a number of bands that incorporate different styles into what they do," he says. "There's an audience for everything from hip-hop to the rare-groove funky shit to hardcore."

The Beastie Boys, who also include MCA (Adam Yauch) and Ad-Rock (Adam Horovitz), recorded *Ill Communication* quickly. "Seven months is a world's record for us," says Mike D. "We worked on *Check Your Head* for a long time and we learned how to make records, and touring taught us a lot about playing together."

Like *Check Your Head*, *Ill Communication* features a mix of samples and live instrumentation.

On the live-instrument tip, the Middle Eastern–flavored track "Eugene's Lament" features Beasties pal Eugene Gore on violin. Other tracks feature keyboardist Money Mark and percussionist Eric Bobo, for whom the track "Bobo on the Corner" is named.

Mike D says, "When we started playing instruments for *Check Your Head*, a lot of that was based on the music that inspired it [like] the Meters or [James Brown's band], it was the stuff that we had been sampling. As soon as we started to do that, we realized we could still play hardcore, too. With this album, it was just a matter of getting even more out there."

Sticking with the spirit of the music, Capitol will support the album with a loose marketing plan. "Chaos is the theme of the campaign," says Capitol GM/senior VP of marketing Bruce Kirkland. The label issued a white-label 12-inch of "Get It Together," which features guest appearances by Biz Markie and Q-Tip of A Tribe Called Quest, to clubs in early April. It will be worked on the party and club circuit by a special street promotion team.

"The track has major commercial potential down the line," Kirkland says. "But we're going to build it from the street up."

A second track, "Sabotage," goes to college and modern rock radio in May.

"We are going to break every rule we know in terms of marketing this record," Kirkland says.

The Beasties are high on the recent changes at Capitol and the support from Gersh. Although the group has "complete artistic freedom," Gersh often listened to tracks while the Beasties were working on the album, Mike D says. "It's the first time that we have had access to someone in that kind of position," he says.

The Beasties' relationship with Gersh also led to Capitol signing a joint venture with the group's Grand Royal imprint, whose roster includes Luscious Jackson, and DJ Hurricane. The group also publishes *Grand Royal* magazine.

The Beasties will hit the road in early summer for some European warm-up dates, and later on Lollapalooza. Says Mike D, "We'll definitely be mixing it up and do some stuff we've never done before."

LARRY KAY

BEASTIE BOYS

Magnet, *June 1994*

"Can I say one prediction for the June issue here?" asked Beastie Boys drummer and vocalist Mike Diamond. "On the record, Birkenstocks are gonna be blowin' up on the East Coast. 'Cause they've been big on the West Coast already and they're gonna start crossing over."

"Can I just comment ahead of time," bassist, guitarist and vocalist Adam (MCA) Yauch interrupts, "that no matter how big they get, they're still wack?"

Not to be outdone, Adam (Ad Rock) Horovitz chimes in, "My man Yauchman is goin' on the Lollapalooza tour and he's gonna make platform Birkenstocks and sell 'em to all the ravers, and he's gonna make mad money."

"Yeah," Diamond adds, "he's gonna sell 'em to the Human Beatbox's little punk rock brother."

Huh?

"Did you hear about my new band, Human Beatbox's Little Punk Rock Brother?"

Of course not, I'm not Kreskin.

"Right now it's just me," he explains. "I haven't got the lineup finalized yet. I'm looking for members."

And so it goes. Try interviewing any three people at once and you're asking for confusion, especially when it comes time to transcribe the tape. Try interviewing the Beastie Boys and you might as well hire a cryptologist to decipher the stream of consciousness bound to ensue. It's not that the Beastie Boys take an attitude. They're by no means aloof. Or high and mighty.

They're just nuts—three modern-day musical sages with a license to thrill and the budget to do *anything*. The band's latest transmission to the masses, *Ill Communication*, is, simply, a 20-track global musical party.

Clocking in at just under an hour, *Ill Communication* embraces all the usual hip hop and hardcore punk trappings you've come to expect from Brooklyn's finest, along with doses of Latin swing, Asian/Middle Eastern raga-like rhythms, loads of distorted vocals, early-'70s grooves that recall Hubert Laws and Stanley Turrentine and interlude scenes from numerous Blaxploitation movies and even the renowned chants of the Buddhist monks of Tibet—a true melange that makes perfect musical sense. From the flute hook of the album-opening (and perfectly titled) "Sure Shot" to the end of the final cut, "Transitions" (the last of the album's seven instrumentals), *Ill Communication* is the Beastie Boys' most comprehensive musical statement.

The band has hit upon a definite groove, making this album in a quarter of the time to create *Check Your Head*.

"It took us six months to make this album," says Yauch, "which is the least amount of time, by far. It usually takes us a couple years. . . . We write while we record, we go in with nothing and just make it up as we go along.

We don't believe in preproduction." Diamond and Horovitz chuckle in agreement.

"Part of it might be getting easier," says Diamond, "but I also look at it like we had a lot less bullshit time, too. Where we used to go in and play music for a little bit, then play a lot of basketball. [This time around] there was a lot less R and R time. Last time we did, say, six months of music over the course of a couple years. This time it was like real time."

The trio may have spent less time on the court, but by no means have they been inactive in the time between the *Check Your Head* tours and recording *Ill Communication*. Grand Royal, the band's label, finally started releasing records by groups other than the Beastie Boys; first came Luscious Jackson's excellent debut EP, *In Search of Manny*, and more recently releases by D.F.L. (Dead Fucking Last, a fairly sloppy hardcore band with one Adam Horovitz on bass) and Moistboyz, a noisy, almost industrial outfit. The band has also published the first issue of *Grand Royal*, a magazine devoted to everything the band deems worthy of editorial coverage. From the hilarious *Ebony* parody cover in the style of Blaxploitation/karate movie posters and the most thorough Bruce Lee retrospective I've ever seen, to articles on the "Gap Conspiracy" and Kiss and interviews with Q-Tip and the Pharcyde, the magazine has it all—even Yauch's political dissertation on the Dalai Lama and Tibetan independence. If they ever stop making music, this would seem a natural second calling—except for Yauch, who prefers to spend as much time as possible snowboarding in Utah.

Making real sense of anything in the Beastie Boys' world is a challenge—it's all too appropriate the word "Ill" figures prominently in two of their album titles, as that's exactly what these guys are. But even though the lunacy manifests itself from one record to the next, don't look for any hidden meanings or interrelations between one LP and the next.

"I think it's like an illogical progression," says Diamond, "cause you're doing what you do at any moment, and those times that we made *Paul's Boutique* or *Check Your Head*, or even this one. . . . When we finish a record we just think people are gonna think we're out of our minds, probably."

"I don't know if it really comes down to logic," adds Yauch. "We make whatever we make, and then it's done, and we put it out. And it's easy to look back at it afterwards and take a musicologist's perspective and say, 'Well, this fits in with this, and it's a progression from this,' but when we're doing it, we're just playing some shit and it's whatever seems right at the time."

If *Ill Communication* just happened to be whatever seems right, then the Beastie Boys have one hell of a collective sense of intuition. When *Check Your Head* was about to be released, some people—especially music critics—were predicting failure, saying the band could never match its "flash-in-the-pan," platinum-selling debut because its brilliant follow-up, *Paul's Boutique*, had no tour support and had alienated audiences by being too sample-heavy. How wrong they were. The album was at the top of most year-end polls, the tours were a resounding success and the three proved once and for all that they *really could play*. The band's fascination with most things from the '70s that began to emerge on *Check Your Head*, especially in keyboard parts and the instrumentals, has exploded into a full-blown trip down memory lane on *Ill Communication*. The particular focus is 1970–74 and the soulful jazz-funk (not fusion!) that came out of that era. Yauch offers the B-Boy line on the subject. "A lot of musicians are trying to get away from that period's sound. We're trying to get into it."

"Most people look at that as a blemish, but *we* look at it as the learning years," echoes Diamond. "Honest."

"They were, actually, growin' up, those were the learning years, culturally," Horovitz adds.

Yes, the pre-disco '70s, a land where polyester was king, the synthesizer was a rudimentary toy and musicians played, not programmed, their instruments. On "Sure Shot," "Flute Loop" and a couple of other tunes, flute is featured prominently as part of the hook, which leads one to wonder whether the Boys had sampled Hubert Laws, the leading (and perhaps only) funky jazz flautist from that time. I should have known that the door had been swung open far wide with that, and the roundabout response is typical of what happens when you try and pin these guys down on one thing.

Remember, the question is, "Did you sample Hubert Laws?"

"No," says Diamond, "but . . . I've bought a lot of Hubert Laws records in the 99-cent bin, and a lot of times he's got [album] covers where it looks like he's gonna be the man, and I've bought a lot of Herbie Mann records . . . well, it's mostly Herbie Mann that I'm really talking about, but Hubert Laws to some extent, too, and I'm mad at both of them right now. Hubert Laws, I'm sure there's some good stuff I don't know about. But Herbie Mann, he's got all these album covers, you think they're gonna be good, but he *sucks*. He's the leader of the misleading. One of the rules, I don't mean to go back to the misleading thing, but . . . when you're digging through the bins, '70–'74—prime years. After '74, questionable, 'cause then the groove changed up to disco."

"Synthesizers started goin' outta control," Yauch adds.

And the drum beats started changing a lot, too. The live drummer was often replaced by a rudimentary machine.

"Yeah," agrees Diamond, "the beat changed from a real funky James Gadsen, 'Ain't No Sunshine' type of thing to . . . ."

Giorgio Moroder?

"Yeah, tempos got way up, and so after '70–'74 it's very questionable," Diamond continues. "But '70–'74, you see a record with a good cover, the label seems right, the musicians on there seem right, in that pocket, '70–'74, I'd say make the investment. That's my advice."

"I think," offers Yauch, "it's that from there, people had their instruments pretty set, you know, guitar, bass, organ and stuff. And everybody was trying to see how dope they could get with those instruments, and then after the synthesizer thing kicked in, people were trying to see if they could do some other shit."

"When it first came out it was cool," comments Diamond, "'cause people were still experimenting with it."

"People didn't know what it fuckin' was," offers Yauch. "Now they come out with the fuckin' keyboards that can sample every instrument."

Diamond agrees, preferring the older instrument. "The Moog, in a way, was the ultimate punk rock instrument. 'Cause the shit's just so fucked up . . . while we're on the '70–'74 thing—I don't want to go off on a tangent—you've gotta acknowledge three things: No. 1, Kool & the Gang; No. 2, Ohio Players. I just wanna point them out. They're very underrated funk bands. I mean people who know, know. But, I mean, think how many dope records Kool & the Gang had between '70 and '74. The third thing is you also had rock bands that had the funk breaks. Foghat, for instance. They had a beat. 'Slow Ride,' from *Live*. That's a beat."

"Every rock band started using the funky beats," adds Horovitz.

"Just like they are now," Yauch relates.

"Every rock band is using samples and substitution and shit," Horovitz says. "It's the same thing in the '70s, 'cause that shit was big. Everybody was trying to play funky drums. They were all trying to come off like Rare Earth, trying to come off like Bonzo [Bonham]. But if you don't have a pitch control, don't buy a record that was made after 1974."

"Even if you do have a pitch control," says Diamond, bringing the topic to a close, "I don't know if I would buy it."

So there's no sampled flute, got that? A month after *Ill Communication's* release, the Beastie Boys will begin their "summer vacation" as one of the three Main Stage headliners at Lollapalooza. In the past, the band's stage props—like a giant inflatable penis—have evoked the wrath of God-fearing towns and straight-laced promoters. This time, however, the Beastie Boys are sensitive to their ever-increasing audience. "We've got all new outfits planned," says Horovitz. "And new dance routines that Michael and I have been working on."

Yauch picks up the ball, adding, "I got my own dance steps that I'm working on, 'cause these guys are working on their routines and I don't want to bother them. And I have a couple of dancers that are backing me up . . . . I'm gonna be wearing the whole Barney outfit."

"Barney is large, you'll get over with that," interjects Diamond, beginning a fashion tangent. "You go to K-Mart. I like to shop at K-Mart, 'cause the best thing they've got is like for fashion—any shit that kind of went out and is already cool again. They still have it at K-Mart . . . like Members Only."

"Anything that used to be wack, they still have," says Yauch.

"What was the question again?" Horovitz asks.

Touring.

"Last tour was more like the cannon and the tightrope," offers Yauch, "getting shot out of a cannon and landing on a tightrope."

"This year it's 'Those Three Barneys,'" Diamond says, adding this thought that ties into the band's fans, "I forget the title, but I'm coming out with some solo shit real soon. . . . I'm gonna be comin' out like Teddy Pendergrass, T. P. You know, I need to branch out, I'm getting a little older, I've to be realistic about my prospects. I don't mean on a sexual level, I mean audience. . . . We've got the little kids that come for the Barney aspect, the grandmas that come for the T. P. aspect. I mean you can't get any broader than that. And then you've got all the people in the middle that come for 'Blue Nun.'"

"Some people come for different songs," says Yauch.

"And then they hear that song and they leave!" counters Diamond.

Yauch outlines the comprehensive Lollapalooza game plan. "Our objective is to have more fun than anybody else."

"We're gonna have a good time this summer," offers Diamond. "We've decided that, so it's a done deal. Now, that might even be at the expense of some of the other bands on this tour, but we are going to have a good time. That's what it comes down to."

"I'm already planned," continues Yauch. "I've got stuff packed for the trip. And I'm bringing, like, Twister, so we can play naked Twister in the dark, and I'm bringing that thing that you slip and slide on—put it on the ground and spray the hose on it. But if the other bands aren't going to be bringing their own fuckin' toys . . . ."

"The helmets with the beers on the side and the straws," Diamond says.

"If they don't have shit they wanna share," Yauch finishes, "that's just gonna be their own downfall."

Now the truth begins to emerge, as Diamond explains, "Actually, we've been working with a group of M.I.T. professors, and we've actually figured out how to make a very, very portable and very affordable water slide that we're gonna be marketing. But before we market the water slide, we're gonna be bringing it on tour with us, and I know some of the bands are going to want to use the water slide, and I don't know if it's going to be available. I would not be surprised if you're going to see jealousy from some of these other bands because of this stuff that'll be going on."

The sodium pentathol must be kicking in as Yauch decides to reveal the band's real master plan: "Do you guys mind if I tell him what we're really doing this summer? Can we come clean with this? It's been a few years in the working. We've talked about it before. The scientists have completed their work on the waterproof microphones and the waterproof monitors. We have a whole setup that we're doing for Lollapalooza. We're going to have actual plexiglass in front of the stage, and it'll be a swimming pool . . . we're actually filling the stage about four-feet deep with water. We're gonna have diving boards, fuckin' water polo, seals, dolphins, the whole fuckin' schmegegge."

"We're talkin' Aqua-World here," Diamond proudly states.

"Big water slides that you've gotta climb all fuckin' day," Yauch adds.

"We're still gonna have some of the stuff people have come to expect and associate with us," elaborates Diamond. "We're still gonna have the cannon, but we're gonna add a new twist. The Biz [Markie] is gonna shoot out of the cannon and do a big cannonball right into the water tank and send the water splashing everywhere! Biz is gonna do the first ever underwater human beatbox . . . . I'm gonna have the first water-proof drum set. I have to actually train right now, 'cause the water offers all that resistance, so actually, I have to have like eight times the strength. That's why I'm getting fake arms before the tour."

"We're gonna do some songs, too," Horovitz says, "but . . . ."

ADAM BEYDA

RECORDING ON THE FLY

Mix, *June 1994*

It's been a strange road for the Beastie Boys—beginning in New York in the early '80s as a punk band, continuing with their first album, 1986's Rick Rubin-produced hip hop smash *Licensed to Ill* (quadruple Platinum), then jump-cutting three years later into more experimental, uncharted (okay, Gold) territory with their second LP, *Paul's Boutique*. That record upped the ante on the Beastie method of constructing wicked pastiches of bass-heavy beats, replete with out-there samples. But for 1992's *Check Your Head*, the trio of rappers set out on a whole new tangent, picking up their instruments again to resuscitate and incorporate their punk roots.

They've reinvented themselves a few times, but if the persistence of wild eclecticism in their music can be called stable, they may have found a more stable voice with their new joint, *Ill Communication*. From the opening dog yelp to the closing lordly drum reverberations, the new LP gets funky on the experimental tip. The album encompasses an amazing range of styles, mixing up old-school punk, cool-hard funk, and strident and jazzy hip-hop jams. Though it's crammed with fresh ideas and sounds, the new album bears a strong formal resemblance to *Check Your Head*. This is due, at least in part, to the similarity of the circumstances in which the two LPs were recorded, including similar methods, locale and personnel.

Way up front in the Beastie personnel file is Mario Caldato Jr., who engineered *Paul's Boutique* and co-produced and engineered *Check Your Head* and *Ill Communication*. Caldato first crossed paths with the Beasties in the mid-'80s when the band played a fateful show at LA club Power Tools. Says rapper/drummer/bon vivant Mike D, "The club didn't have a professional sound man, so we blew out the whole bottom end of the P. A. after the first three bars of one song. So Mario [who was in the audience] went up to [club owner] Matt Dike and said, 'You guys should really get a professional in here.'"

"I got the job the following week," adds Caldato, who in addition to his studio work, mixes house for the Beasties on tour. And when Dike, with John King and Mike Simpson (under the *nom de produce* the Dust Brothers), went on to album work with Tone Loc, Young MC, then the Beasties, Caldato was on board as engineer.

While Caldato became a fixture on the Beastie team, the band was busy indulging in some conspicuous nest building, starting its own record label, Grand Royal, and constructing a studio in time to record *Check Your Head*. G-Son Studios, set up in Grand Royal Headquarters in LA, is the casual if not trashy digs where the Beasties do their many things. Despite some jazz they were handing out about their "finely tuned" control room, what they have is not a high-end facility but a comfortable, effective place to work, an on-call spot for laying down the bits of fanciful whim and bone-crushin' funk that make up a B-boys album. Based around a 32-channel Neotek Elan console and a Tascam 2-inch, 24-track ATR-80, with Auratone Cubes and Tannoy 15 monitoring, the studio comprises a control room, a large room for live jamming and a pre-production/magazine-publishing room.

The studio is essential to the Beasties, because they don't write songs per se, instead constructing them out of all kinds of bits and pieces—accretion, pasting and cutting are the operative principles. Their current M.O. includes laying down dozens of hours of instrumental jams, recording a multitude of vocal parts, assorted sound effects and funky samples in no particular order, then combining and recombining these elements on the fly, making a variety of mixes. Having their own studio allows them the latitude to experiment. "That's the purpose of having our own place." Mike D says. "If we were at a place where we had to pay $1,500-a-day lock-out, we couldn't come in with a vague idea in our heads and say let's go for it."

But go for it they do—not from a particular starting point, instead employing a variety of approaches, as the mood strikes them. Some songs start with just a sample. In fact, a huge range of sampled sounds found their way onto the new album in one form or another: The hypnotic soul of "Bodhisattva Vow" mixes chanting Buddhist monks with an echo-drenched Beastie vocal; "Root Down" is based on a sweet Jimmy Smith groove, in tribute to that master of the Hammond organ.

Each of the Boys has a sampler at home, which they put to good use. Mike D, who uses an Akai MPC-60, says, "We'll have something that one of us will have done at our house, and everyone will hear it on a cassette. Then we'll come in here and start laying it down and play a bunch of stuff over it or play some beats or whatever." Although the Beasties get a lot of their raw material by sample hunting and gathering, they creatively respond to material they use, making it their own in surprising and inventive ways. "We're all huge music fans and listeners and collectors," says Mike D. "That just finds its way into what we do, whether it's through sampling or inspiration or misinterpretation."

Their sampling mania extends even to their own jams, which they will mine for interesting morsels. And because live jamming figures heavily into their work, they have to sift through hours of tapes: For *Check Your Head*, they laid down 90 hours of jams on their Panasonic SV-3700 DAT. "A lot of times, we try to get the multitrack going," Caldato says, "but when it's not quite together, we just roll the DAT."

When they go back and listen to DATs, they'll compare notes, and if they find something they want to use, they might sample it, dump it right onto the multitrack or do some digital editing. They used Sound Tools for the first time on the new album, and also liked editing on an ADAT.

Caldato says that DAT jams loom large on *Ill Communication*, particularly in several of the shorter songs: "'Eugene's Lament' was just a one-minute jam on the DAT, then we repeated a couple of sections of it and had Eugene Gore overdub violins. The rest of the music was straight to DAT. That's why it sounds kind of screwed up, but it came out nice."

If this approach seems a little cavalier, it's important to understand that for Caldato and the Beasties, it's not about going for a pristine performance or a clean sound; it's about inspiration, imagination, feeling and experimentation. At root, they're 4-track-cassette kind of guys. "I'm definitely more impressed with people who can make records on a cassette 4-track than on a digital machine," Caldato says. "I give 'em way more props, and it generally sounds better to me." Mike D wryly adds, "People underestimate cassette compression: Cassette compression is where it's at."

Distorted sound is a vital part of their aesthetic—they like funky, dirty grooves and gritty sounds. (When asked about using SR on the 2-inch, Mike D goofs, "No 'Doubly' here—I don't know why you'd want to reduce the noise.")

They do all manner of messin' around to find sounds that interest and move them. For example, they get beats from old drum machines, toy key chain sound chips—you name it. On live albums, Mike D says, "We've recorded in practically every place on this building you could possible do it. We throw a bed sheet over the entire kit and play it that way." ("Or tape $100 bills on all the heads," adds Caldato.)

Miking also provides plenty of hijinks. The way some people appreciate the fine sonic qualities of vintage tube mics, the Beastie Boys and Caldato appreciate the distortion offered by cheap, bizarre or broken mics. An old, broken Webster carbon mic comes in handy, and a $10 Radio Shack mic set on the floor somewhere near the drum kit gives an interesting drum sound. Though they'll use Shure 58s a lot (and sometimes an SM7) for rappin' and squawkin,' they have a proclivity for decidedly non-professional vocal mics. A secret weapon? The $35 Sony Karaoke Variety mic. Caldato says he saw a demo one day in Little Tokyo and liked what he heard. "I got one and bought it back to the studio and tested it. Everybody liked it, so I bought them all one for Christmas."

"Most of the distortion on the vocals comes from the mic," Caldato adds, "because they usually cup the mic or yell into it or whatever. Then some of the time it gets distorted a little more at the mic preamp, and sometimes out of the compressors, too—I just slam the compressors [dbx 160 and 165] and crank the outputs, then add some effects."

In terms of effects, Caldato employs a limited palette. "I just use the old rack-mount Ibanez HD1500 and DM 2000; they've been my right and left hand for the last two records. That's all I use—two echoes and two reverbs. The REV7 was the first reverb I bought, and I just use the shit out of it. And the SPX. And it sounds alright." A newly acquired EMT plate also got a good workout on the album.

As you might expect, they mixed the new album the way they recorded it—on the fly. "Since we've got our own studio," says Mike D, "it's not like we do a bunch of songs then mix a bunch of songs. The songs we have we'll mix, gradually through time. Maybe we'll do eight or ten different mixes of a song by the time we get to the end. And each time we do something, we add a couple of things, eliminate things, do overdubs or whatever. So, each time it changes. A lot of times, we'll do a mix and completely change the hook or the verse."

They ended up with ten two-hour DAT's worth of mixes of *Ill Communication* material. What actually made it onto the LP includes some material mixed during their earliest sessions. The Beasties began laying down basic instrumental tracks for the album at New York's Tin Pan Alley Studios, and while there they threw together some mixes. "I had these rough mixes on the album—mixes that had no EQ; just pan, volume and a reverb send. Like 'Rickey's Theme.' That's basically the rough mix coming off the monitor section of this old board."

When it comes down to it, Caldato says, "We've got 24 tracks, so we lay it all down, and then in the mix we weed through it and try stuff. We make mixes and listen to 'em, live with 'em. We try a lot of shit, and if it works, it works. There are a lot of ideas in the group, and I throw in some, too. A lot of times, we end up going with our gut feelings, like using rough mixes. The stuff that we spend more time on doesn't come out as hype. It's weird. If it's there, it's there—it comes out by itself."

KIM FRANCE

THE BEAUTY OF THE BEASTIES

New York Magazine, *May 30, 1994*

On a gray Saturday afternoon during the tail end of fashion week, an aggressively casual cluster of young hipsters slouches about on lower Wooster Street. Photographer Michael Lavine—the Annie Leibovitz of the alternative-rock crowd—jokes with friends in front of Gourmet Garage; *Spin*-magazine cover girl Juliana Hatfield sits quietly on some gray concrete steps. Then waifish celebutantes Zoe Cassavetes and Donovan Leitch Jr. show up, plus guitar hero J. Mascis of Dinosaur Jr. and dozens of record-company A&R and publicity types. Soon, there are ski caps, old-school suede Pumas, corduroy jackets, skateboards, and midriff tops as far as the eye can see. They're all here for a "guerrilla" sidewalk fashion show for X-Girl, the line of clothing designed by Kim Gordon of the band Sonic Youth and stylist Daisy von Furth.

X-Girl is a spinoff of X-Large, the popular line of extra-baggy jeans, T-shirts, and jackets for men that is co-owned by Mike Diamond (a.k.a. Mike D) of the Beastie Boys. Though the other two thirds of the Beasties—Adam Yauch (a.k.a. MCA) and Adam Horovitz (a.k.a. Adrock)—are not involved in X-Large, the line is in every way the physical manifestation of Beastie attitude. Von Furth and Gordon have no small amount of downtown cachet, but it is their association with the Beastie Boys and all the young, attractive, and talented people luxuriating in refracted bits of Beastie aura that makes this gathering seem so very ground-zero hip.

"The Beastie Boys popularized knit caps, nylon coach jackets, and baggy chinos, and they pretty much single-handedly brought back old-school Pumas and Adidas," says a reverential Von Furth, who pays way too much attention to this sort of thing. "And Adam Horovitz pioneered that early-seventies poly-nylon Mean Streets shirt."

The Beasties' whole crew is here: Sofia Coppola—who has taken a break from her hectic schedule of partygoing and getting photographed by Steven Meisel to help organize the show—is stalking about with a clipboard looking serious. Proud father Francis Ford has dropped by, seemingly to applaud her incipient work ethic. Photographer/video director Spike Jonze is passing out photocopied fanzine-like programs. Ricky Powell, longtime hanger-on and host of the popular public-access-cable show "Rappin' with the Rickster," is skittering about, camera in hand.

With Rob Lowe, 1985.

The Marc Jacobs show being held across the street lets out, and curious fashion types like Linda Evangelista and Kyle MacLachlan, Steven Meisel, Anna Sui, and Bill Cunningham descend to find a happening in their midst. The X-Girl show itself lasts a mere fifteen minutes. Actress Ione Skye (who is married to Horovitz) strides bashfully down the runway in a mini-miniskirt. The show ends with an X-Girl bride and groom shaking a bottle of champagne and inadvertently spraying some well-dressed fashion vultures. Suzy Menkes of the *International Herald Tribune* flees in schoolmarmish disgust.

⌒

Which is somehow appropriate. Since these three New York natives got together about a decade ago, the Beastie Boys have become pop music's premier brats. They remain endlessly annoying to those too old—or too uncool—to get the joke. But for a generation of kids who see Spinal Tap as more of a defining cultural moment than Woodstock, the Beasties reign as supreme ironists, mining rock and hip-hop culture for every ounce of their inherent absurdity.

Nirvana, three kids who began in a deadbeat lumber town near Seattle, may have been the barely articulated if authentic scream of Generation X. The Beasties, three errant and marginally talented spawn of New York's cultural elite, have made a joke of the entire rock-star trip. But almost accidentally, they became really, really good musicians along the way. Came to jeer, stayed to cheer. Sort of.

"I don't want to be compared to, like, Guns N' Roses," Diamond insists one day over breakfast in New York, referring to the increasingly self-important metal group, "because Guns N' Roses don't have any sense of irony. Axl Rose doesn't say, 'I want to be under water and swim with the dolphins in my video; it'll be really funny,' even though I think it's the funniest shit I've ever seen."

The Beasties may not be as big as Guns N' Roses, but they are much more interesting. Musically, they have forged a style that deftly mixes hardcore, hip-hop, and funk into an unlikely mix that somehow makes perfect sense; call it cultural trash-compacting. A new album, *Ill Communication*, out this week, is already being hailed as a breakthrough, and they will get their most widespread exposure yet this summer when they tour as headliners of the fourth annual Lollapalooza fiesta of alternative music and really neat T-shirts.

The Beastie Boys have come to personify an entire generational aesthetic: jiving, jokey, resolutely (if fashionably) scruffy, and contemptuous of traditional racial boundaries. "The Beastie Boys always took their musical taste from lots of different sensibilities," black rap impresario Russell Simmons, who discovered the group in 1984, says from his car phone. "Their music is a reflection of who they are. Most rap stars—while they may be creative—are commercially in a vacuum. But the Beasties are more open-minded. They've always been ahead of their time."

"Our little self-sufficient fantasy world," Mike D cracks of Grand Royal headquarters, the Beastie Boys' alternative Neverland in Los Angeles. It's an unprepossessing studio and office, notable only for a half-basketball court and skateboard ramp. But the warren of rooms has the comfortable, cluttered anti-glamour of a college newspaper. A recent afternoon finds the Beasties in situ, shooting hoops and reliving their thrilling encounter with Sofia Coppola's dad back in New York. "Francis was chillin' with his multicolored scarf!" Horovitz says, only half joking (they are, in fact, always precisely half joking). "He was running things. Come on, you've got to give props to anyone who could show up with the old-school blazer and the multicolored scarf. That was genius."

"He was goin' for the professor look," says Yauch. "I'll bet he drove a Saab there."

"We're lucky," says Diamond later. "One of the most enjoyable things in life is when you can be around like-minded creative people. Good things are always going to come from that."

"The fact is," says Horovitz, "anyone could do the shit that we do."

⟿

Or so they would have you believe. At Adam Yauch's apartment in Los Angeles—where he lives alone in a funky, old Deco-style residential hotel—the Beasties are together to try on costumes and plan a video shoot for *Ill Communication*'s second single, "Sabotage," which is to be directed by Spike Jonze. It's a takeoff on plain-clothes-cop shows from the seventies like *The Streets of San Francisco* and *Starsky and Hutch*. Everyone seems to be sporting a beeper, a portable phone, or both.

A black girl with dyed platinum-blonde hair, camouflage T-shirt, and a British accent is fitting the band members in an ever more ridiculous series of seventies outfits and wigs. The Boys are watching old *Streets* episodes on videotape, trying to ape Karl Malden's hand gestures, figuring out which L.A. street is hilly enough to approximate an actual street of San Francisco, and who should sit where in the car for maximum parodic authenticity.

"The captain wouldn't be driving," Mike D thinks out loud. "He has to ride shotgun so he can jump out fast. And the rookie has to sit in back so he can jump out and get us coffee and shit."

The next day they start shooting the video in various locations around East L.A., winding up around lunchtime in front of Yauch's building to shoot a scene where Yauch, Diamond, and Horovitz jump out of the car in hot pursuit of a perp. Usually, video shoots for major-label bands are grandiose affairs, with countless hair and makeup types, personal assistants, and flunkies. But the "Sabotage" crew is so bare-bones that an unsuspecting passerby might mistake it for a student film. Except for the part when Ione Skye shows up for lunch.

With its mix of self-conscious superficiality, low-culture slumming, and artless hip, the Beastie scene could be understood—if one feels the need to interpret all subsequent youth culture through the prism of the sixties—as an updated take on Andy Warhol's Factory. One must, of course, remove the wanton drug use, the high-art pretensions, voyeurism, and Andy. But back in the sixties, everyone who was young, beautiful or creative showed up at the Factory at some point. And today, it often appears as though everyone under 35 who is doing anything creative in New York or L.A. is at some point sucked into the Beasties' vortex.

When they're in New York, the Beasties do time with the noise artistes of Sonic Youth [see "When Will These Old Guys Shut Up?", next in this volume] and Stephen Malkmus from the band Pavement. Out west, their hub is older, Hispanic parts of L.A., neighborhoods like Silver Lake and Los Feliz that have become popular among artists, musicians, and slackers.

Diamond and his wife, filmmaker/video director Tamra Davis (her "Gun Crazy" was an underappreciated ode to estrogen-charged ultraviolence), live in a large, well-appointed house with a pool in the Silver Lake hills. Yauch is nearby in Los Feliz. Horovitz, by far the most conventionally L.A. of the three, lives with Skye in the Hollywood Hills. Earlier this spring, at a Hollywood house party where Horovitz's former hardcore band, DFL (Dead Fucking Last), played, Drew Barrymore held court on a sofa, reeking of patchouli.

———

Those who remember the early Beasties may have a hard time believing that the band is still going, much less thriving. Not too long ago, the Beastie Boys were regarded as nothing more than a novelty act. Their debut album, *Licensed to Ill*, made them the first rap artists to top the charts and to receive coverage in the mainstream press. But they were vilified by much of the rap community, accused of perpetrating nothing more than an updated version of blackface; notorious homophobes—they wanted their debut album to be called "Don't Be a Faggot"—they performed with go-go dancers in cages, giant inflatable Budweiser cans, even a huge hydraulic penis.

When you grow up in the cradle of New York Jewish intellectual middle-class bohemia, this sort of boorishness is regarded as, you know, goyish. But that was exactly the point. When the Beasties met in the early eighties, they were three precocious wiseacres bent on meeting the not inconsiderable challenge of rebelling against rebellion-proof parents. Yauch, the son of an architect and a social worker, grew up in a Brooklyn Heights brownstone. He left the touchy-feely Friends school and enrolled himself in Brooklyn's decidedly rougher Edward R. Murrow high. As a youth, he built bombs at home. Horovitz, the son of playwright Israel Horovitz, was living with his mom, now deceased, on 11th Street in the West Village. Mike Diamond, the son of an (also deceased) art-dealer father and interior-decorator mother, grew up in a duplex on Central Park

West full of museum-quality art and graduated from artsy St. Ann's in Brooklyn Heights. As a teenager, he shaved his head bald, wore four earrings in one ear, read Charles Bukowski, and was no doubt seen as just charming by his parents' friends.

They met at long-gone downtown nightclubs like Tier 3, the Rock Lounge, and the Mudd Club, where they went to see second-wave punk bands like the Bad Brains and Minor Threat. They formed the Beastie Boys in 1981 as a half-serious hardcore band with Kate Schellenbach, who was part of a gang of girls they spent time with. (Horovitz joined two years later.) "Suburban kids were coming to shows and slam-dancing and we were mad that it was ruining the scene," says Schellenbach. "So we were like, ha-ha-ha, we can make a hardcore song too! We'll call it . . . 'Bodega!'"

Then, in 1983, hip-hop started moving downtown. Rap pioneers Run-D.M.C. had just had a big hit with their first twelve-inch; one couldn't walk a block without seeing a break dancer; and graffiti artists were demi-celebrities. The Beasties and their friends bought into the entire vibe, wearing fat shoelaces, spraying graffiti, and venturing up to 167th Street in the Bronx to a rap club called Disco Fever.

"There were, like, twenty of us guys going through a momentary confusion as to the fact that we were white," says a longtime friend of the band, musician Tom Cushman. "I remember nights we'd stay out late tagging [spray-painting graffiti], then we'd go back to Diamond's house and collapse on the sofa in front of a huge Leger mural."

The early incarnation of the Beastie Boys approached rap music with the same semi-serious, goof-off attitude it brought to hardcore. They recorded "Cooky Puss," a crank call to Carvel ice cream's 800 number—the Boys talking in fake black accents—over a hip-hop beat. While "Cooky Puss" offended some, it became a hit on college radio.

If "Cooky Puss" planted the first seeds of Howard Stern-ish controversy around the band, it also gave them the idea that they could succeed as white hip-hoppers. But as much as they liked to rap—Horovitz in particular displayed a natural ability—they knew close to nothing about how to D.J. Fortuitously, they met Rick Rubin, a heavy-metal nerd from Long Island who had started the Def Jam record label from his New York University dorm room. Rubin's business partner was Russell Simmons, the brother of Joe "Run" Simmons of Run-D.M.C. Rubin saw white boys rapping and smelled high-concept pay dirt. Envisioning a way to bring hip-hop to the suburban masses, he and Simmons played Svengali. They edged out Schellenbach (who had shown little affinity for hip-hop and was, ick, a girl), and Rubin, a talented D.J., insinuated himself in.

Then Yauch went upstate to Bard and Diamond to Vassar, but both eventually dropped out and moved back to New York. They recorded a couple of twelve-inches on Def Jam, but also played in a number of other rock and hardcore bands.

"All of these bands plus a couple of others were rehearsing at this place on Chrystie Street where Adam Yauch and Mike were living," says Cushman. "It was above a Chinese whorehouse, and it was below a number of sweatshops that went night and day. Water dripped from the ceiling and rats were everywhere, but the good thing was you could play music there whenever you wanted. Every now and then the landlord would come in and bring his business partners. They'd stand around and laugh, and think it was the funniest thing they'd ever seen."

Distracted by their other projects, the Beastie Boys were going through a dormant phase when Simmons called to say they'd been booked to open for Madonna on her *Like a Virgin* tour. The tour was a disaster. The Beasties were booed offstage every night by bewildered 13-year-old girls, and made even less of a splash with Madonna's gay fans. They returned to New York and recorded *Licensed to Ill*, an album unlike any other on the market, which featured a mix of hard-rock riffs and hip-hop beats with bratty, puerile lyrics. They prepared for their first tour by treating it as one big cross-country goof.

"We were sitting in this office," Diamond remembers, "and we had this tour guy saying, 'Okay, what do you guys want to have onstage? You can have anything you want.'"

"Anything!" Horovitz breaks in.

"'Magic tricks! You can disappear in the crowd and come back onstage!'"

"Then he said, 'Sting had big, giant blow-up zebras,'" Yauch interjects, "and one of us said, 'Can we have a giant blow-up dick?'"

The *Licensed to Ill* tour coincided with the runaway success of their single "Fight for Your Right (to Party)," an all-out parody of heavy-metal anthems of the day. The song nonetheless became a huge hit on the frat-boy circuit and attracted thick-necked, red-faced keg-party guys to the Beasties' shows. It was an early lesson in the limits of irony.

"That song was a complete goof on the same people who ended up in the front row, totally identifying," says Yauch. "We'd think, 'Whoa, if they'd seen us when we were punk rockers, they probably would have wanted to beat us up.'"

But the Boys were having an excellent time, handling quick success just as gracelessly as most rock stars do. They brought friends on tour, and Cushman remembers several shows where it was his job to stand just off-stage and throw beers at the guys. One friend was designated "Trim Coordinator," and it was his responsibility to scope out local shopping malls, issuing backstage passes to cute local girls, and to find volunteers to go-go dance in the cage every night.

"There was one scene at a hotel," says Cushman. "A man showed with a state trooper looking for his 16-year-old daughter."

There's a telling Spinal Tap-ish scene near the end of the Beastie Boys' *Licensed to Ill* tour video: The band members are in a backstage dressing room, drunk out of their minds after a show. Yauch picks up a can of beer, hurls it into the bathroom and breaks a mirror. Not to be outdone, Horovitz heaves a whole six-pack. Then the groupies arrive, and the boys spray them with beer and aerosol cans of whipped cream. Finally the cops show up and haul them off to jail.

"It's a fine line," says Diamond, unwittingly echoing a memorable phrase from Spinal Tap. "At first it's really funny and totally sarcastic. And the whole idea that you were even doing it is totally ridiculous. And then it becomes a reality. And then you become part of that reality."

By the end of the tour, the band's relationship with Rubin and Simmons was becoming increasingly frayed (the band, after much legal wrangling, broke off with Def Jam). "But we weren't only falling out with Rick and Russell, we were falling out with each other," says Diamond. "We'd been through this really strange, almost alienating, experience that was the *Licensed to Ill* tour."

Yauch was particularly unhappy, and told friends he wanted out. He formed another band, Brooklyn, and spent a hefty sum of his own money recording a demo album. Horovitz was dating Molly Ringwald, and was spending more and more time in L.A. A movie project for the band, *Scared Stupid*, bit the dust, rumor has it, after Ringwald read the script and told Horovitz it would ruin any chances he might have of a Hollywood career.

At some point Yauch, Horovitz, and Diamond drifted back together and flew to L.A. to record an album. "We rented this house together off Mulholland Drive [christened The G Spot]," says Yauch. "And by the time we were done with the album we'd all fallen in love, so we left the house and got our own places. It didn't make sense to be paying rent in New York, so we moved out."

The Beasties signed to Capitol Records, and released two albums, *Paul's Boutique*, in 1989, and *Check Your Head* three years later. The latter was an adept and musicianly effort, melding rap, a bit of hardcore, and long jams reminiscent of the Meters and Booker T. and the MG's. It was all so legit. And not a pose. The band had passed beyond particularly flagrant lifestyle crimes, though Diamond and Horovitz today smoke enough pot to give everyone in their direct vicinity a contact high. Yauch went through the most radical transformation of all, studying Buddhism and trekking in Tibet. "The East Coast in general has a real skeptical view of spirituality," he says. "When we grew up, spirituality was really unfashionable in terms of raising your kids. Being here, I've been more able to open up to that stuff." Formerly depraved stars turning to Eastern religions is one of the more hackneyed rock cliches going, but Yauch seems so sincere that it would be ungenerous to begrudge him.

Mike D is galumphing around his cluttered office at Grand Royal, picking up stray bits of Beastiana from the floor. He happily opens a big crate of sneakers from Converse. As he tries on the different pairs, Adam Horovitz bursts in with a Subway sandwich and a big bag of barbecue-flavored potato chips and flops down on the floor. Yauch peeks his head in; he's just back from San Francisco, where he saw the Dalai Lama.

Grand Royal is not only a kind of overgrown playpen; it's the base from which the Beastie Boys are pursuing what rock stars used to call their outside "projects." Like supermodels preparing for their imminent lean years by lining up exercise-video contracts, the Beastie Boys have been wise enough to diversify. Mike D has X-Large, the Los Angeles clothing store that opened a branch in the East Village last year. They have their own record label, Grand Royal, which has a distribution deal with Capitol. Aside from controlling most aspects of their own albums, Grand Royal puts out a handful of albums by other bands. The label's most promising act is Luscious Jackson—a surpassingly hip all-female funk group composed of friends from the Beasties' high-school days (including original Beastie Kate Schellenbach), and whose underproduced but winning EP, "In Search of Manny," topped this year's *Village Voice* critics' poll. A full-length album is due out this summer.

Then there's *Grand Royal*, the magazine, produced by the Beasties and a tight circle of friends. The first issue provides an interesting glimpse into Beastie life: There are an interview with the rap group Pharcyde and an editorial by Yauch saying he disapproves of the gun one member of Pharcyde is holding in a photograph accompanying said piece; a story on the political situation in Tibet; tips on "de-reeking" after smoking pot; and a fashion story showing Horovitz modeling Joey Buttafuoco-inspired leisure wear.

As he appraises a pair of sneakers, Diamond regales his band mates with a story about a Pearl Jam concert—featuring that most tortured and whiny of rock stars, Eddie Vedder—that he saw in New York. Pearl Jam has zero credibility among in-the-know music types, and Horovitz and Yauch rib Diamond for going to such a hopelessly lame show. But Diamond has brought it up to make a point, and he forges ahead.

"Eddie was giving a speech, and he kept saying something like 'fuck,' and all these rock people are going 'yeah!' And Eddie gets to the point where he goes, 'I could probably just say 'fuck' and you guys would all clap.' And I thought, man, that's kind of depressing. We could get up there and say 'fuck' and people would clap. But then I realized, you know what? I can't ever really worry about that. Because they're Pearl Jam. And we're not."

"What people don't realize is that it's the rock star who gets the short end of the stick," Yauch says.

Horovitz chimes in: "Everyone thinks it's fun and games. And we're getting fucked! It's really tough to get out there and do what we do, you know?

"Like, we've slugged it out in clubs all our lives! And people are really down on us. They don't understand. It takes a lot of courage to get up onstage and be a rock star every night."

They're kidding, of course.

MATT DIEHL

WHEN WILL THESE OLD GUYS SHUT UP?

New York Magazine, *May 30, 1994*

Sonic Youth, New York's "other" legendary offering to the gods of alternative rock, is a band rife with appealing contradictions. When Thurston Moore opens the door to the sprawling SoHo loft he shares with Kim Gordon, his wife and musical cohort, he's wearing not the grunge rags you'd expect but a spiffy Polo shirt, a button-down with wide blue stripes. Their apartment is just like their music: a perfect combination of total trash and sweet shine, the teetering stacks of used paperbacks in the living room

Kim Gordon of Sonic Youth. Photo by Tommy Drazic.

set off by a sparkling white-tiled bathroom where Chanel bottles perch on a marble sink. As a workman cranks up a drill, Moore apologizes for the mess—they're building a nursery for the child he and Gordon are expecting in late June (Moore is 35, Gordon is 41), a girl who will be named Coco. "All I know is we need to buy diapers," says Moore, "so I'm going to make some records, and all the yuppies in the world can feed me with money."

A certain type of smart, hipster yuppie, perhaps, given the abrasive guitar-feedback assaults that Sonic Youth traffics in. Furthermore, Gordon's advanced pregnancy leaves the band unable to tour behind its new record—the perfectly titled *Experimental Jet Set, Trash, and No Star*.

Gordon herself eventually wanders into the living room, as pregnant as billed, along with 31-year-old drummer Steve Shelley. (Lee Ranaldo, 36, the band's fourth member, is in Europe doing a solo tour.) Somehow, the three of them look far more benign than the people you would imagine were responsible for *Experimental*, one of this year's darkest, most disturbing—and most powerful—records.

But that's what makes Sonic Youth so "echt" New York. Like a long string of gangly, affectless, noise-mongering downtown intellectuals—cf. Jim Carroll, Richard Hell, Lou Reed, John Cale, Tom Verlaine—Gordon and Moore seem more like oldsters who've bothered to strap on guitars only as a break from their close textual readings of Baudelaire. New York-school noise isn't a scream of anger; it's a carefully considered artistic choice. But the band comes by its New York-school anomie naturally; it has been, after all, thirteen years since Sonic Youth committed its first sonic transgressions. Along the way, the band has managed to influence nearly every aspect of nascent "alternative" rock, becoming mentors to everyone from Nirvana to Dinosaur Jr. "It never occurred to us to stop," says Gordon, "as we didn't have anything better to do."

Right now, they're debating where to eat lunch. Moore wants to try Zoe; Gordon is set on T Salon, the genteel tea emporium underneath the downtown Guggenheim. Shelley couldn't care less.

On the way to T, the members of Sonic Youth receive a sign that, despite their advancing age, the Zeitgeist is still with them: A skateboard shop on Lafayette Street is blasting *Experimental* at a disconcerting volume.

They're completely at home inside the rarefied precincts of T Salon. Moore keeps his sunglasses on and, fully reinforcing his eager-to-be-adolescent reputation, talks about how impossible it is to find clotted cream in New York anymore; how cramped New York recording studios are; and how obsessed he is with New York's mayor. "We have Giuliani's son singing on our next single," he says deadpan. "It's a new song we're doing for this film—it's a series, you know, about police. . . ."

"Police Academy!" offers Shelley.

"Yeah, Police Academy 6: The Spaz," says Moore. "It's about the son of, like, a kind of cop/mayor of a big metropolis. It's about his son joining a punk-rock band. He's the vocalist." Moore scrunches up his face and blurts out an uncanny imitation of Andrew Giuliani as a punk singer.

Moore and the others manage to get serious long enough to talk about making *Experimental*. "One review said it was obvious that with this record, we were really trying to disassociate ourselves from the current pack of alternative major-label rock, which is sort of what we get lumped into—Smashing Pumpkins, Soundgarden, Alice in Chains," says Moore. "Maybe they're right. This record has no aspirations to be part of that world. I think the Beastie Boys have come to the same conclusion we have—the most radical recordings are done by kids who just go in and plug into a light socket, blow out an amp, and call it a song."

As on earlier Sonic Youth albums, there's a ghost of personal catastrophe lingering over *Experimental*. Songs like "Winner's Blues" and "Self-Obsessed and Sexxee" will have an awful lot of people thinking about Kurt Cobain and Courtney Love—an association furthered by the fact that Sonic Youth helped arrange the marriages of both Nirvana and Hole, Love's band, to Geffen Records. "Of course, people you really do know come into your lyrics," says Moore, "but it's not about any one individual."

What is the record about, then? Personal politics, mostly. "Bull in the Heather," Gordon explains, deals with "using passiveness as a form of rebellion—like, 'I'm not going to participate in your male-dominated culture, so I'm just going to be passive.'"

Thanks to Gordon's pregnancy, everyone in Sonic Youth is getting some time to him- or herself. Shelley and Moore are each putting out several records on the independent labels they run (Smells Like Record and Ecstatic Peace, respectively). Ranaldo is publishing a book of poetry and finishing up a solo record. And Gordon has helped launch the fashion line X-Girl [see the previous "The Beauty of the Beasties"].

Their entrepreneurial zeal is understandable: Compared with friends like Nirvana, Sonic Youth hasn't sold all that many records—although *Dirty* did a respectable 500,000 copies worldwide. Even on its home turf, the members of Sonic Youth are constantly reminded of how their resolutely noisy records keep the band out of the mainstream. Indeed, they carp about their verge-of-celebrity status. "Thurston and I went to the Knicks' playoff game—we were given front-row, courtside tickets for my birthday," says Gordon. "They were, you know, naming off all the celebrities who were there—John McEnroe, Brooke Shields, Tony Bennett, Ethan Hawke, Spike Lee . . . but no Kim and Thurston."

What if, by some fluke, *Experimental Jet Set, Trash and No Star* goes platinum? "It'll be just another day," says Shelley almost convincingly. "And there'll be a day after it that we don't have a platinum record." Gordon allows herself to be a bit more starry-eyed, albeit with a characteristic weirdo edge: "Our baby will have silver teeth."

JOHN ROCCO

SONIC YOUTH, FROM A DICTIONARY OF THE AVANT-GARDES (1999)

SONIC YOUTH (1981)

Born against the dawn of the age of Reagan, Sonic Youth lived in New York City and created a sound that pushed rock music through the avant-garde wringer. Their sound was post-Beat, post-Warhol , post-punk , post-hardcore ("Black Flag growing their hair out"), post-No Wave. Their music was different because they were different; schooled in the aesthetics of pop music and art, Sonic Youth combined their punk education with an intense experimentation that changed everything from the instruments they played to the people who heard them. In the liner notes to the reissue of their first album, *Confusion Is Sex*, the critic Greil Marcus had this to say: "In 1983, Sonic Youth was going to extremes most other bands didn't know existed; in a certain way, they were issuing a challenge to the rest of pop music. As things turned out, they pretty much had to answer it themselves." And these "extremes" continue.

In many ways, the story of Sonic Youth begins with a man who made John Cage shake in his boots. His name was Glenn Branca. After hearing a piece Branca composed for ten guitars, Cage remarked: "I found myself responding in ways that brought me back to my ego. My feelings were disturbed. . . . I found in myself the willingness to connect the music with evil—with power. I don't want such a power in my life." Such an invocation of frightening power was Branca's aim. Influenced by Krzysztof Penderecki, Olivier Messiaen, and the rumor of war that had been New York punk, Branca came to Manhattan in 1976. He borrowed instruments and formed a band called Theoretical Girls who almost immediately tied themselves into the SoHo art scene by "playing" before a performance piece by Dan Graham. Theoretical Girls became the basis for the SoHo side of No Wave, the short-lived ('78–'79) but intensely influential post-punk movement that combined the punk ethos with a vibrant and often disturbing energy. (Brian Eno is credited with killing the scene by attempting to capture it on the infamous compilation *No New York* [1978].) After No Wave dissolved Branca began forming revolving "bands" or "guitar armies" with himself as composer and conductor. The guitars they used were modified junk set to odd tunings.

Thurston Moore of Sonic Youth. Photo by Brian Rocco.

Branca's experiments with the electric guitar pushed his music between blatant critiques of rock culture and an embrace of the untapped power of the instrument.

It was this mix of art and rock, No Wave and performance art, punk and Cage, Branca and Graham that was the background for the emergence of Sonic Youth. Art-school graduate Kim Gordon worked with Graham and met Branca through him. She played bass in Sonic Youth but, more importantly, she brought her interest in the avant-garde to the music. Lee Ranaldo played with Branca before bringing his guitar to Sonic Youth and Thurston Moore, the band's other guitarist, brought to the new music an extensive knowledge of the punk subculture. The band went through several drummers before Steve Shelley permanently kept the polyphonic beat: they came upon him in a hardcore band called the Crucifucks during the Dead Kennedys' Rock Against Reagan tour in 1985.

Sonic Youth's first recordings were stunning affairs combining energy, inventiveness, an interest in dark Americana, and subtle humor. But the most striking feature of the music was the sound of their guitars. Extending Branca's fascination with the power of the electric guitar, Sonic Youth compiled an arsenal of junk-shop guitars and set them to bizarre tunings. These "prepared guitars" opened a whole new world of noise and broke with the traditional sound and, more importantly, the traditional limits of rock. Like good Dadaists, bad children, and Sun Ra, Sonic Youth broke their toys to make new toys. Not since Jimi Hendrix repositioned the guitar in relation to his amplifiers and his audience—not since Hendrix *reinvented* the electric guitar—has there been such a revolution in the approach to the standard tool of rock. However, their revaluation of the guitar was just the beginning of their experiments. They played their instruments *hard* and invoked Henry Cowell's banging, shattering tone clusters. (Moore and Ranaldo often use egg beaters, screwdrivers, and other hardware against their strings.) Their later albums and performances are marked by improvisation inspired by free jazz. (Moore has played with Cecil Taylor and Milford Graves.) In 1997, Sonic Youth played a night of music at Avery Fisher Hall under the title "Guitar Futurism." The title and their performance that night was a gesture toward their avant-garde background; Luigi Russolo's *The Art of Noise* (1913): "It is necessary to break this restricted circle of pure sounds and conquer the infinite variety of noise-sounds." But before Avery Fisher Hall, Sonic Youth followed Warhol into pop.

After a trilogy of extraordinary albums—*EVOL* (1986), *Sister* (1987), *Daydream Nation* (1988)—on the influential independent label SST, Sonic Youth signed with a major label, Geffen/DGC, in 1990. Since that time they have released six albums that have stretched and redefined popular music. (They were also instrumental in having Geffen sign Nirvana, the band that conquered the mainstream and effectively ended punk.) This redefinition has always been Sonic Youth's goal and their ability to achieve this has always come from their knowledge of the avant-garde tradition. Their latest album is called *A Thousand Leaves* (1998) and on it is a song called "Hits of Sunshine." It is dedicated to Allen Ginsberg and it extends Sonic Youth's experiments in noise and song structure. It is also an acknowledgment of the Beat influence on their music; Ginsberg: "The person lives in us and then we perish. What perishes is an embodiment of the person, who never dies. He is like time—the present dies, becomes past, but Time never dies in the continuum." "Hits of Sunshine" is Sonic Youth's *Lycidas*: it is an elegy pointing to pastures new.

Part Three

SMARTER THAN SPOCK

Live Long and Prosper: The Beasties and Billy Idol.

"2010: Using tachyons (particles that move backward in time) as a carrier, the Soviet Union will attempt to alter the past with scientific information."

—Philip K. Dick, "Predictions" (1981)

"Once we become incarnate in this world our actions, or lack thereof, affect it, and we are all thereby responsible."

—Adam Yauch in 1996

A Beasties Timeline: 1995–1999

Beastie Boys

1995 The Beasties release two important EPs: the hip-hop *Root Down* and the hardcore *Aglio E Olio*. The Beastie "hardcore tour" follows.

1996 The Euro Funk instrumental EP entitled *The In Sound From Way Out!* appears. The first Tibetan Freedom Concert is held in San Francisco.

1997 The Second Tibetan Freedom Concert takes place on Randall's Island in NYC. *The Tibetan Freedom Concert* live album is released.

1998 *Hello Nasty* is released. The Third Tibetan Freedom Concert takes place in Washington, D.C. The Beasties embark on a world tour.

Music

1995 While in Rikers, Tupac Shakur releases *Me Against the World*. Sonic Youth operate *Washing Machine*.

1996 Beck hooks up with the Dust Brothers and delivers *Odelay*. The Fugees enter with *The Score* while Chuck D writes his *Autobiography of Mistachuck*. Tupac Shakur dies of gunshot wounds received in Las Vegas.

1997 Allen Ginsberg and William S. Burroughs die. The Wu-Tang Clan reemerge with *Wu-Tang Forever*. Mike Watt releases the apex of rock operas on *Contemplating the Engine Room*. Notorious B.I.G. is killed in a drive-by shooting.

1998 Lauryn Hill's *The Miseducation of Lauryn Hill* becomes the most critically lauded album of the year. Sonic Youth release the stunning *A Thousand Leaves*.

1999 For the first time, the Tibetan Freedom Concert is spread out over four cities across the globe: Amsterdam, Tokyo, Sydney, and East Troy, Wisconsin.

1999 DeForest Kelley, aka Dr. Leonard "Bones" McCoy, dies at 79. The Roots pick up instruments on *Things Fall Apart*.

Jon Pareles begins this section by going to a Beastie Boys show on Strong Island to listen to "*Star Trek* bleeps [mixed] with the deep drone and low trumpets of Tibetan Buddhist chants." Then Adam Yauch has a conversation with Akiba Lerner and Mark LeVine about Tibet, religion, social responsibility, and spirituality.

Ann Powers goes to the Tibetan Freedom Concert on Randall's Island and files a report filled with her usual acumen; she gives us the entire two days. Adam Heimlich follows with a critique of Beastie politics while Princess Superstar encounters Mike D, that "special individual," in her gym.

This book ends with three conversations about the past and future Beasties: Everett True shoots words with Jon Slade and Stephen Sweet via e-mail; Neil Strauss talks about the Beasties as listeners, as "collector-musicians"; and George Kaplan ends it all by being kidnapped by space monsters.

JON PARELES

THEY PLAY LIKE AMATEURS, AND THEY'RE DARNED PROUD OF IT

New York Times, *May 13, 1995*

The Beastie Boys have been making records since 1981, and making hits since 1986. They still sound like amateurs, and that's the best and worst thing that can be said about them. At the Nassau Coliseum in Uniondale, Long Island, on Thursday night, they had an arena full of teen-agers jumping, slamdancing and shouting along to low-fi sounds that could have been made in someone's basement.

Over the last decade, the Beasties have staked out the psychic and sonic territories of high-school cutups across America. They started as a hardcore band, blasting fast guitar chords and whining tales of petty vandalism and complaint; then, in the mid-1980s, they switched to rapping, using hard-rock power chords and funk samples with equal brashness.

The Beasties evaded most of the racial tensions inherent in white hip hop by never pretending to have ghetto roots. They were always clowns, evoking suburban mischief rather than urban anger or desperation, in voices of pure slapstick: MCA's hoarse muttering, Mike D's high whine, Ad-Rock's screech. Through the decade, the Beastie Boys have devoted most of their lyrics to boasting about all the fun they're having: driving around, smoking pot, getting girls, making records.

On their 1994 album, *Ill Communication* (Grand Royal/Capitol), they switch off between rap and hardcore, presenting them as two guises for the same insolence. Onstage, they have dropped their old hunkering gestures; now, they jump around like punk rockers.

Compared with most rappers, the Beasties are no great shakes. Their rhythms are simple, their rhymes hit or miss, despite a knack for off-the-wall analogies. And while they brag about their technique, they know better than to improve it. Any more virtuosity would separate them from their fans, and it would drain the goofy pleasures from their music. The Beastie Boys' gift is that their music sounds as if it's just thrown together: a guitar snippet, a staticky drumbeat, some percussion and the tag-team vocals. It has too much momentum to be genuinely random, but it doesn't sound calculated.

Blown up to arena-scale wattage, some of their material took on an anarchic glee. Their opening noise mixed *Star Trek* bleeps with the deep drone of low trumpets of Tibetan Buddhist chants, then bounced them around the room with quadraphonic speakers, which added to the band's joke. Quadraphonic sound at concerts had been the mark of audio perfectionists like Pink Floyd. But the Beasties simply used it as a high-tech joy buzzer, making people turn their heads to see where the electronic hoots came from.

While the show started with an adrenaline burst, its momentum grew fitful. Every so often, the Beastie Boys would pick up instruments (Ad-Rock on guitar, MCA on bass, Mike D on drums, with backup musicians) and play midtempo funk vamps, perhaps to rest their voices and calm the moshing. Each time, the funk sounded like filler, pointlessly padding the set. The Beastie Boys have a problem common to both middling hip hop and hardcore; there's no dynamic variation, so songs can either maintain their opening energy or sag. Yet fans didn't mind a few ups and downs. With the Beastie Boys, they saw living proof that brattiness can be a way of life.

The Beastie Boys will be at Madison Square Garden on May 24.

AKIBA LERNER AND MARK LEVINE

AN INTERVIEW WITH ADAM YAUCH

Tikkun: A Bimonthly Jewish Critique of Politics, Culture & Society,
11 (6) (November/December 1996)

LeVine: Adam, you are mostly known for your involvement in the rap group the Beastie Boys, but in recent years you've also been focusing your energies on freeing Tibet from Chinese domination. Would you tell us a little bit about what's going on in the Free Tibet movement and in particular, tell us more about the Tibetan Freedom Concert you orchestrated this past summer?

Yauch: Many people were involved in organizing the concert; its primary purpose was to raise awareness about Tibet, the Chinese occupation and human rights abuses there, but we were also trying to raise awareness about human rights abuses within China itself. Both the Tibetans and the Chinese people share the same problem: the repressive Chinese regime. So the concert was also to support the Chinese democracy movement. But its main purpose was to help people realize how much we as individuals, even in the West, are constantly influencing these situations on the governmental, corporate, and personal levels.

For example, every time we go shopping, we are casting a vote for or against human rights. If we purchase Chinese-made products, there is a good chance they may have been made by forced prison labor. These prisoners are usually guilty of exercising what in America are considered their basic human rights—freedom of speech or freedom of religion. We must think about this when we spend our money.

The concert was promoting an ongoing boycott of all goods marked "Made In China." The A.F.L.-C.I.O. has endorsed this boycott, along with 130 other organizations.

The cornerstone of the problem is that our corporations are lobbying our government to separate human rights issues from trade. These multinational corporations are motivated by greed. The case of South Africa proves that financial sanctions do have an effect on human rights.

LeVine: Talk to us about the plight of Tibet.

Yauch: The Chinese invaded and overtook Tibet in 1950, taking complete control in 1959, when the Dalai Lama, the country's spiritual and politi-

Early '85 in LA: Yauch is flying. Photo © Glen E. Friedman, reprinted with permission from the Burning Flags Press book, *Fuck You Too*.

cal leader, fled into exile. Approximately 1.2 million Tibetans have been killed as a direct result of the occupation. They have no freedom of speech or of religion. China is giving financial incentives to Chinese citizens to move into Tibet. This ongoing population transfer has overwhelmed the Tibetan people, making them a minority in their own country. The Dalai Lama lives in India, where he leads their government in exile in a nonviolent struggle for freedom.

I think that the nonviolent aspect of their struggle is the most significant thing about it. The contrast between the hatred that is projected by the Chinese authorities and the compassion sent back by Tibetans is like night and day. If a change does not come in the next few years, there may be little to save. The Chinese government is carrying out its genocide rapidly.

Lerner: Can you describe the personal transformation involved in going from writing a song like "Fight For Your Right to Party" [the first Beastie Boys hit] to fighting for freedom in Tibet, and how it relates to your personal quest for meaning?

LeVine: It seems so easy for people who go into the music business to lose their soul, not to find it. So how is it you became more spiritual?

Yauch: In some ways I was lucky enough to get to live out some of those fantasies that rest in our collective subconscious in the West—that is, that happiness flows from having a lot of money or attention or fame. I guess that I got to live that out for a minute and then realized how empty it ultimately was. I mean, of course it was fun. I had a blast, but there's no end. You don't ever arrive at that point that it feels like you're at peace or complete. If you pursue those things, you slowly become more and more unhappy. There's no actual time when you've gotten enough materially and you say, "Ah, all right. I'm satisfied."

Recently, I became Buddhist, but I studied Buddhism for a number of years before I chose to do that. During that time, I tried to live by Buddhist principles, and learned a lot from that experience. But I think what is most important is being kind to others. That is true spirituality; that is the core of all major religions.

LeVine: How do people in the music business react when you come to them with something that's spiritual? The last album that you did had something reminiscent of Carlos Santana, who radiates a kind of spirituality, or John McLaughlin way back when they first got into Eastern spirituality. Have you been able to detect that maybe at least a small part of your fans have followed you on your spiritual growth, that they've grown with you?

Yauch: Maybe some of them, but there's probably also a lot of younger people that are just getting into our music now for the first time. But a lot of people who were into the old stuff probably look at the newer stuff and think, "What are these guys giving me?" But let me ask you guys a question. How much do you know about Kabbalah [a Jewish mystical tradition]? Does Kabbalah go into subjects like reincarnation or karma?

LeVine: The funny thing is that in meetings between the Dalai Lama and Jewish leaders, one of the strongest points of conversation was around the idea of karma and reincarnation and how Judaism has very similar concepts. It's not called karma, but gilgul—the idea that a person or soul would be reborn more than once in order to complete its journey back into what the Kabbalah calls the Ein Sof, or the "limitless," that is, returning to God. You could be born many times in many different forms of existence, from being an angel to being an animal, until you reach the level where you don't have to be born again. It's very close to the Buddhist teachings on karma and reincarnation.

Lerner: *In the Torah, God warns the Jews that his love for them will last for generations, but if they turn against God's love, the repercussions will also be felt for generations. It is also possible to look at the Israelites' wanderings in the desert as a kind of karmic cycle, in which the Jews had to rid themselves of a certain entrenched slave mentality before being able to establish themselves in their land. But also central to Judaism is the notion that the cycle can be stopped or broken. Judaism has never accepted that pain and suffering are a necessary component to the universe, although our history seems to prove otherwise. Many of the stories in the Bible are about people who seem to be stuck in certain karmic cycles, but are able to break out of them. So there are similarities with karma; but like all things in Judaism, there are also tendencies toward opposite understandings of the interrelation between fate and agency.*

Yauch: I believe that spirituality does not necessarily have to be traditional or "religious"; that's a big part of the way I look at it. I look at spirituality as higher levels of consciousness. It's just continually raising your level of awareness to see how what you do affects other people, and how what they do affects you. It's about becoming more aware of why we perceive everything the way we do, and how our perceptions create our reality. It's better understanding what brings us happiness and what brings us suffering. Many people think of spirituality as being a far-off, intangible thing that you have to go to the mountains and meditate in order to find, and sometimes that can be a really limiting concept of what spirituality actually is.

LeVine: *Do you ever find when you're working in the hip-hop world that being Jewish is an issue?*

Yauch: Most of the time, not really. People who are around hip-hop don't really notice that. I think maybe they notice that we're white more than Jewish.

Lerner: *It's interesting to hear how the cultural perceptions differ from the reality, because I remember when you guys were first starting to hit it big, there were rumblings that the Beastie Boys represented yet another* *moment in a long history of Jews exploiting Blackness—in this case the deeply entrenched rhymes and rhythms of African-American culture—for your own personal aggrandizement.*

I remember in the mid-eighties when rap was first starting to hit, many whites were initially attracted and repelled by its erotic rhythms and overwhelming energy, but also felt frightened by its urban African-American expression. Some would argue that the Beastie Boys played an essential role in allowing whites to groove to rhythms that previously felt forbidden. But in playing this role there were accusations that a certain co-optation of an Afro-American discourse had taken place. I know that the Beastie Boys now are not only fully accepted in the hip-hop world but that you guys help set the standard and provide the cutting edge for the groove. But at the beginning, did any of these dynamics affect you or was it mostly media hype?

Yauch: When our first hip-hop records came out, there weren't really any other white kids out rhyming. This was before *Licensed to Ill*, when some twelve-inch singles came out. It's possible that there might have been other white kids who rhymed at block parties or whatever, but if so, it was a rare occurrence and they weren't making records. So, when we started making hip-hop records, it hit first in the Black community before it did at all with the white kids. Most white kids outside of New York had never heard of hip-hop. At the time, a lot of people, having just heard the music, thought we were Black. When people finally met us and saw that we were white, they were surprised, not that we sounded Black, but just because it was out of left field to have somebody rhyming who was white. It wasn't until later when *Licensed to Ill* came out and "Fight For Your Right to Party" that it started to flip to a white audience.

The first hip-hop twelve-inches were around '84 or '85. And then toward the end of 1986, the album came out. At the time, a lot of hip-hop lyrics spoke about unity between the races. There was little or no racial tension in hip-hop.

It wasn't until "Fight For Your Right to Party" came out that we started acting like drunken fools. At that point, our image shifted in a different direction, maybe turning off the kids that were strictly into hip-hop. It started off as a goof on that college mentality, but then we ended up personifying it.

Lerner: In many ways, your identity and your versatility with regard to first the hip-hop world and then later the struggle for a free Tibet seems to come out of being positioned within a Diaspora identity. I don't think it's purely an accident that three Jewish guys were able to succeed in grooving with a traditionally African-American discourse of celebration and resistance—rap—and at the same time have been able to become, within the counterculture, a spokesman for the Diaspora community of Tibetan exiles. Traditionally, Jews have been described as having a wandering, borderless, homeless quality which can never be fully inscribed within a particular national community except for perhaps modern Israel. This has been a cause for much anxiety for non-Jews and Jews alike, because it creates an identity that can't be readily located within standard notions of national or racial identities. This ambiguity has allowed Jews to produce a unique identity in the Diaspora. Because we partake in shaping the society in which we exist, but are also not locked in, we have had a certain versatility.

Perhaps this Diaspora aspect has allowed you to play a unique role in not only being accepted in both Diaspora communities, but also in setting the agenda and playing a leadership role. The same Diaspora positioning that allowed a bunch of white guys from New York to become cutting-edge in the world of hip-hop also created the sensitivity and ability to then connect with the deeper rhythms of the Tibetan freedom cause.

LeVine: *I know I've felt this way as a musician who happens to be Jewish but plays Black music—when I used to play with blues musicians or doing hip-hop—and then also meeting other people, like Palestinians, who are themselves diasporized. Is there something similar in your feeling, being in the world of hip-hop, some kind of similar energy and what music serves in terms of healing the wounds of being Black in America? And then just working with Tibet, is there something that goes between both situations whether it's doing music with one or working politically or spiritually with the other?*

Yauch: I never really noticed that. I don't know. It's interesting though. I know sometimes that Tibetans look to the Jews as a good example of how to preserve a diasporized culture. But personally, I don't really feel like an outsider in someone else's society. I feel more like a New Yorker than one who has been diasporized. I feel at home here. The great thing about New York City is that it is made up of all types of people—all cultures, races, and religions co-existing. Mike and Adam and I are of Jewish descent, but were not raised religiously. I didn't even notice that all three of us were Jewish until magazines started writing about it. Some were excited about us being Jewish, like the *Village Voice*, and others, especially the English press, were very anti-Semitic. I felt surprised by both. As far as I was concerned, we were just some friends making some music together. What does being Jewish have to do with that?

Well, since I've gotten older, I've come to feel that some of the Judaism came through to me by way of osmosis. Maybe things like my mother saying, "Do unto others as you would have them do unto you." And basic principles of respect. But going back to what you were saying about diasporism, I feel that much of that, for us as Jews, is just a frame of mind. Jews have been diasporized for so long that we should feel at home anywhere. The more we visualize ourselves as outsiders, as downtrodden, as oppressed, the more we will help to perpetuate that and create it for the future. If we think of ourselves as outsiders, we will project ourselves that way and people will see us that way. We are not any better than anyone else or any less than anyone else. To imagine either is to create our own suffering. We are just human beings trying to find happiness, as are all human beings.

Lerner: I'm sure your last comments will raise some eyebrows among those in the multiculturist camp who would claim that holding onto our identities as oppressed peoples is an essential element for genuine understanding and authentic co-existence. In fact, some would claim that their experience as a subjugated people is central to their self-understanding and identity. There are various reasons why people become invested in their people's subjugated histories, but the main one is because it gives some understanding of their current positioning in society. For example, I as a Jew, or as a woman, or as an African American continue to hold onto my history of oppression first, because second, because it helps to explain current situations of oppression that come out of historical memory but are experienced as reality. Seeing oneself as not fully accepted by society or as downtrodden usually is because there is a reality that creates these situations. So to the Jews who dwell on the Holocaust or construct an identity around their historical pariah status you would say, "Get off that trip." Or to the African Americans who still feel the scars of slavery you would say forget it and move on?

Yauch: I'm not saying forget about it. I'm saying remember it, forgive, and don't focus on it in a negative way. If it empowers you somehow in some positive way, if you can look at it and say "My people have been oppressed" or "are being oppressed" as Dr. Martin Luther King, Jr. did, and then do something positive with that, then that can be a great thing. But there are a huge number of us who make our lives a living hell by focusing on it in a negative way. If we see our people as downtrodden and alienated and combine that with negative emotions like hatred or depression, we will actually be reinforcing that situation. If we project ourselves that way in public it, in effect, makes others treat us that way. We need to remember histories of pain so that we can learn something from them and then get beyond them. The best way to do this is through forgiveness; forgiving ourselves for our own involvement, forgiving others for their involvement, and then in that way making sure that it doesn't happen again. Many people's fear is that if we forgive it will happen again, but in truth, through forgiveness we can do much more to make sure that it doesn't happen again. Forgiveness gives us a much more positive understanding of ourselves, which then allows us to see more clearly. That clarity will ensure that it doesn't happen again. If we stay angry or upset, we'll lose our clarity of mind and it is more likely to happen again.

Lerner: I agree with you that forgiveness is an important attribute for any healing process and eventual transcendence of the scars left historically or personally, but what about the claim that a reason for harping on historical experiences of degradation is because the pain and oppression still persists, maybe in a different form or to a different degree, but nonetheless it is still there? I refuse to believe that the oppression of African Americans is only because they project an attitude onto others, or that anti-Semitism continues because Jews talk too much about the Holocaust.

Yauch: I don't think it is solely because of the oppressed peoples' mentality. It is perpetuated through the momentum of collective consciousness. That is, thought processes that have been going on within the oppressors as well as the oppressed. But the way to change that begins within ourselves. Forgiveness and compassion will lead to that healing. Anger and fear will perpetuate it. The healing must begin within ourselves. If we change the way we perceive ourselves and the way we perceive our oppressors, then they too will begin to change.

Lerner: But there are people who are going to look down on you no matter how you behave. Again, oppression isn't simply a projection by the oppressed. Although we may all take part on different levels in our collective and personal subjugation, quiescence, and denigration, the oppres-

sion still rests in the hands of the perpetrators. The Tibetans may partici-pate on some levels in their persecution but still the Chinese are the main force behind oppression in Tibet.

Yauch: I guess that's one of the main reasons I'm so involved with the Tibetan struggle. Because the way they perceive themselves is their whole basis for trying to change their situation. They are just being open and honest about what is happening and hoping that the rest of the world will see that and help. It is like a test of whether non-violence and compassion can prevail over brutal oppression.

Lerner: Getting back to our earlier discussion about trying to get people involved in freeing Tibet, one issue that we who are involved in the poli-tics of meaning see as crucial for any liberatory movement is to address the issue of cynicism. The politics-of-meaning analysis of cynicism is that we are all caught in a tension between wanting to go with our highest ideals of what we think should happen in society and feeling that if we really try to go with those ideals we will be taken for a fool, a dreamer, a silly idealist who, according to other self- proclaimed pragmatists, isn't really dealing with reality and will hence become lost in the rat race of tak-ing care of personal selves regardless of the consequences. Being at the Tibetan Freedom Concert with more than 100,000 other people, mostly from my generation, was a very powerful experience. But what also struck me when I talked and listened to some of the other people in the audience was just how much the dynamic of cynicism had its grip on people's atti-tudes about what was possible in regard to Tibet. I would guess that the cynicism that some of those kids were expressing wasn't just about Tibet but was also tied into how much they thought changing the status quo was possible. I think the concert did a lot of good to turn kids onto social justice issues like freeing Tibet, but I think a lot of kids tuned out when the music wasn't playing. This was in part because their cynicism over being able to participate in real change was too deeply entrenched.

Yauch: In terms of going for one's highest ideals or holding back, I look at it like a chess game. We must just feel out when it is appropriate to make what move. Expressing an idea that makes sense one minute, may not the next. I think most cynicism is based on fear of how we will be per-ceived if we look into something like spirituality, or into any serious issue. People are afraid of being judged by their friends. But when we talk about cynicism we tend to look at it as an external factor, something outside of ourselves, someone else's cynicism, instead of seeing it as our own cynicism about cynicism.

The way to look at cynicism is how it exists in ourselves, because cynicism, in the context we are talking about, is really just our own insecurity. Sometimes you just have to be strong and stand up in the face of cynicism and speak out for what is right. And chances are if people stand up, eventually others will respect them for their integrity and join them.

Lerner: Some religious systems maintain that there are cycles of oppression or pain that are essential to the structure of how things are in the world. A secularized version of this form of ontologized cynicism is manifested in society through notions that either certain biological groups are destined to dominate, or that suffering is essential to progress.

Yauch: In Buddhist belief, which is also the way I perceive things, everything is constantly changing, nothing is fixed, every molecule is in the process of evolving, every bit of consciousness, everything physical, mental, emotional, is evolving. Who I am is constantly changing and evolving, because of our interactions. Just being here having this conversation has already changed who I am and who you are. This understanding helps break out of the cynical mind frame, because it reminds us not to accept the current conditions of things as eternally fixed.

Lerner: There seem to be a lot of similarities between what you are describing and the notion of God discussed in Michael Lerner's book, Jewish Renewal. *Similar to the concept of continual evolution we have in the Jewish tradition the story in which Moses asks God before going back to Egypt by what name he is being sent to demand freedom. To which God responds with "Tell them that 'I will be, whom I will be' sent you"— essentially, tell Pharaoh that the God of possibility has sent you. So maybe these two conceptions, one based in Buddhism, the other in Judaism, can provide the best theological approach for combating cynicism.*

One of the issues that you hope to raise in people's consciousness through the concert and through your work for a free Tibet is the need to protest China's human rights abuses by not consuming its products. Recently, we've witnessed China's Most Favored Nation trade status renewed, which attests to the strength of corporate America's demand that once again, human rights should be subordinated to economic prosperity and greed. This ethos of selfishness and greed on behalf of corporations isn't unique to their attitudes toward Tibet. If we look at the devastation of many communities in America due to either downsizing or jobs being shipped overseas, or to the huge impending ecological crises that are already starting to have a devastating effect on our planet, it becomes apparent that whether the issue is freeing Tibet or having clean air, greed is going to be one of the biggest obstacles to rectifying either of these tragedies. So if the struggle for Tibet is about confrontation through compassion, transformation through higher consciousness, why not tackle head-on the destructive behavior of corporations? Why not put on a concert to address the selfishness and greed that traps people in a cynical spiral, which then allows them to turn their backs on human-rights abuses and ecological devastation?

Yauch: Well, I feel we should be careful not to demonize all corporations. A corporation is a collection of human beings, which is really just a consolidation or reflection of the greed we all have. I believe that the main problem facing humanity is greed. It goes to every level, it's where our collective consciousness is at in the so-called modern world. We can point to the corporations and say they are acting from greed but they are just a manifestation of what's going on for almost all of us on different levels. Let's look at ourselves and see how we not only participate in that greed by buying from the corporations, but also look at how we perpetuate it. We've got to look at how we need to wear this week's Nike Jordans and not last week's. How many pairs of shoes and sneakers do we have in the closet? It's our selfish egos that fuel the greed of the corporations, which in turn support human-rights violations. Let's look within ourselves and see how we affect this on a daily basis.

Lerner: What you are saying is similar in many ways to one of the politics of meaning's tenets, which tries to focus on the ways in which greed and cynicism adversely affect everyone at all levels of society. This is not to be exculpatory. Some people, like some corporations, do play a disproportionally more destructive role than the rest of us, yet the ethos of greed and cynicism is something that we all live with and are all affected by. Therefore, it is important to try to change the bottom line in society rather than just focusing on villainizing a few. The truth is that nobody is safe when human rights are abused or the environment is polluted. It's important to educate people to acknowledge the ways we are all interconnected and therefore we all are in constant need of partnership with one another in order to survive.

LeVine: *Strategically, how does the Dalai Lama think he can actually get autonomy or earn some sort of freedom or end the oppression for Tibet? What is his thinking, from what you know, about how he can get the Chinese to stop oppressing and destroying his people?*

Yauch: I think right now a big part of what he is doing is raising people's awareness. Once someone starts learning about the situation, and that the Tibetans' approach is nonviolent and that there's genocide going on, this horrible destruction of Tibetan culture and Tibetan people and the depth of their culture, they see how terrifying what's going on there is. I think his idea is to appeal to people's hearts. When more people become aware of it, they can begin to help in different ways. Depending on what we do and who we know, there are different things that each of us can do to help. One thing that the Dalai Lama has said when people have asked him how can you not be angry at the Chinese, how can you not be enraged when you see your people being tortured by them, when you hear stories of nuns being raped with cattle prods and Tibetan women undergoing sterilizations and abortions against their will (there's a truck driving around doing forced abortions and sterilizations on women all over Tibet) . . . But his response was that he actually feels more compassion for the Chinese soldiers that are doing this than he does even for his own people who are getting tortured, because what he sees is his own people coming out of a cycle of karma, paying it off so to speak, and being done with it, whereas the soldiers are just entering into a very heavy cycle of karma.

Lerner: *When you bring up the issue of karma, it makes me think about how Tibet used to be a warrior culture. With this history in mind, wouldn't karma dictate that possibly the Tibetans are experiencing this current form of oppression because of their warrior past? If we keep to the traditional understanding of karma, isn't it necessary for the Tibetans to be going through this period of repression? And therefore, to play devil's advocate, if this is their karma that must be worked out through Chinese domination, why should we interfere? Couldn't our actions be perceived as Westerners once again claiming a higher ground and sticking their noses into issues they don't understand and shouldn't be involved with?*

Yauch: Maybe this is something the Tibetans have to go through. I don't know what the Dalai Lama's position is on this, but I would say that I believe that there is collective karma; just like there is collective consciousness, there is collective karma. So I believe there is some karma that the Tibetan people are working out. But that's not to say that just because someone is working out their karma that we should just leave them alone to their suffering. We are obligated as fellow human beings to help. And in fact, by not doing so when we are able to, we will just create bad karma for ourselves.

Lerner: Under karma logic, could it be conceivable that by stopping the karmic cycle that the Tibetans are now in, we could in fact bring onto ourselves bad karma through our interference?

Yauch: No, it's really all about our own intention (which, in Buddhism, is called *bodhicittd*). If your intention is to help somebody else out, it can only bring you positive karma. It's not the actions themselves that mean anything; the actions are symbolic, it's the intentions behind them. If you intend to be mean to someone, but to everyone else it appears that you are actually nice, because your motivation was not pure, you will still have that bad karma to deal with in yourself. Karma is not some outside force waiting to punish you, it's feelings within ourselves which we then generate into our reality. Imagine you and I are walking down the street. I see an open manhole cover in front of you, but you don't see it because you are talking to me. If I purposely don't tell you, and I let you fall and get hurt, then I'll feel guilty and responsible. On the other hand, if I stop you, and it turns out that it was karma you needed to work out, you will find some other way, on your own, perhaps slipping in the bathtub.

I believe we are here on this earth to learn that we are interdependent. To learn that what brings us lasting happiness is helping each other. The way I see it, we are all interconnected, and therefore by not helping the Tibetans it will ultimately reflect on us. Once we become incarnate in this world our actions, or lack thereof, affect it, and we are all thereby responsible.

Lerner: Let's go back for a minute to the discussion about recognition and respect and how someone in your position can help others to get away from a materialistic and manipulative ethos.

Yauch: Well, perhaps just by seeing other people that way, it begins to open them up to that level of interaction. That's what I was talking about when I spoke about being around the Dalai Lama. His perspective seems very clear to me. I believe his motivation is to help everything collectively.

Any time I've been with him discussing what can be done to help the Tibetan people, he immediately brings into it what can be done to help the Chinese people and even the people from the Chinese government—what can be done to help even them, his oppressors. He cited the leaders of China, the ones who are destroying his people, as being his teachers, because they have given him a chance to be compassionate even in the face of such extreme conditions. In meditation, he visualizes taking on their negativity, like hatred or anger, and sending them something positive he's acquired. Just being around someone like that makes you feel this overwhelming feeling of wanting to help, and to be positive.

LeVine: Can you explain for someone who doesn't know, what is meant by meditation or visualization?

Yauch: By visualization I mean taking a time where you're not focused on outside stimuli, where you unplug the phone and switch off the radio and don't answer the door and don't focus on any of your outside senses, and just visualize a situation in your head, for example, sending positivity to the Chinese authorities and taking away some of the negativity they're dealing with. It's like prayer, but rather than sending it to God, you're working it out within yourself.

LeVine: So, similar to a politics of meaning, the Dalai Lama feels that a necessary ingredient to the transformation in a society, be it Chinese, Tibetan, or American, is going to be a politics in which we realize that we're all in pain here, we are all crippled by a system that doesn't respect our spiritual and ethical needs. The Dalai Lama tries to embrace the energy of the Chinese people and also see them as hurt by the whole process. Instead of seeing the occupation of Tibet as just going one way, he sees it as a system that affects both peoples and is degrading to what's good in both peoples.

Yauch: Yeah; we have been trained to think of everything in terms of "us" and "them." We must remember that at the most basic level we're all human beings. To separate our "enemies" as those others whom we have to get rid of is a twisted idea. When I was on tour in Israel, I met young Jewish kids who were fifteen or sixteen years old, who were saying that they can't wait to get into the army and kill Palestinians. They were excited about going and murdering people, and to me that's just completely crazy. I mean, basically, it's easy to look at people and demonize them and see the Nazis, the Chinese, the Palestinians, whomever, as non-human, or to look at them as these distant, evil people who have nothing to do with us. But in many ways, they're just like we are.

In the case of the Nazis, the Germans were a poor, repressed people. They were fed a lot of misinformation and were dealing with a lot of anger, and the anger got expressed in a really crazy way toward whomever was the "other" of that society. It happened that that "other" was us. But I mean any people, even Jews, could take a wrong turn. Everyone is capable of insane acts. We must constantly keep close tabs on what we are doing and who we are becoming. And we must forgive those who have erred, just as we would hope they would forgive us. If we use violence to achieve our freedom, perhaps we will become the same as our enemies.

Lerner: We must always be careful not to use atrocities from the past to abuse the innocent of the present. Though justice must be served, it's important that the method is not one that approximates that of our oppressors and enemies. This is in part my fear of what is currently happening in Israel and in many of the Diaspora Jewish communities around the world. We've become so fatigued by the twentieth century, with its fires of exterminations, wars for survival, and terror on our streets that it's blinded us to seeing the ways in which we are participating in another people's persecution. Our pain, anger, and mistrust makes taking the more morally sensitive path all the scarier.

Right before Prime Minister Rabin was assassinated, Israeli society was beginning to open up, but now it's returned to its siege mentality. It's too bad that we didn't have a figure like the Dalai Lama when we were emerging from the ashes of Europe, who could have helped influence our process to re-establish ourselves in our ancient homeland with an ideology of compassion. While the enormity of the atrocities committed against us put compassion far from our consciousness, it could have helped our own healing and possibly helped us to deal with the Palestinian problem better than we did.

The challenge to the Tibetan people will be if they will be able to continue with an ideology of compassion once their homeland is returned. Like the Palestinians who represent the population that was established by the Islamic invasions, so too many ethnic Chinese have moved into Tibet and now see it as part of the national heritage. If power is ever returned to the Tibetan people, it remains to be seen whether they will be able to exercise the same restraint and compassion preached in Buddhism toward the ethnic Chinese.

It's great to see someone of your stature in the hip-hop world out there fighting for healing of the world. I hope that your example will inspire others in the music industry, and fans of your music, to focus more of their attention on the ills plaguing this planet. What's particularly exciting is that you take a politics of meaning perspective, insisting on the centrality of values and spiritual sensitivity, integrating this with your commitment to fight for human rights in Tibet, and challenging the greed and cynicism we find in so much of our society and our personal lives.

ANN POWERS

FREEING THE FESTIVAL

Village Voice, *June 17, 1997*

Tibetan Freedom Concert: Randall's Island, June 7 and 8

"So this whole thing is about joy," declared Radiohead singer Thom E. Yorke as he slouched, all in black, beneath the bright cumulus clouds of the banner adorning the Tibetan Freedom Concert's Blue Stage. Then he launched into "Paranoid Android." It was a weird move, Yorke's juxtaposition of bliss and anxiety, but it pinpointed the dilemma facing everyone this weekend. What was this whole thing about? Was it a political action? An information fair? An artistic experience? A party? Was this Woodstock? Live Aid? Lollapalooza? One by one, the shining lights of the alternative nation took the stage and entertained the options. The weekend rose and fell on the courage of their convictions.

Those convictions were not necessarily political. Six years after Perry Farrell recast the rock festival as a family reunion with a flea market attached, the nature of these big events remains contested. Bands that would never have occupied rooms bigger than Roseland now regularly play stadiums on modern-rock radio tours. Live Aid's notion of the charity gig as a superstar's night out has given way to the grassroots model of Rock for Choice. Older models pop up, too: the blues festival, the Reading-style European marathon. Free Tibet's lineup of rockers and rappers—Ben Harper, Jon Spencer Blues Explosion, Porno for Pyros, Radiohead, A Tribe Called Quest, U2, Noel Gallagher, Sonic Youth, Patti Smith, Foo Fighters, KRS-One, and Biz Markie on Saturday; The Mighty Mighty Bosstones, Pavement, Lee Perry, Taj Mahal, Blur, Michael Stipe & Mike Mills, Alanis Morissette, Björk, Rancid, and the Beastie Boys, with

Tibet Freedom Concert, '97.

Pearl Jam's Eddie Vedder and Mike McCready as unannounced guests on Sunday—included many veterans of these massive bills. They've come to understand the festival as a predetermined form, like a haiku or a blues. Each artist has to figure out how to fulfill it.

Everything about the weekend demanded that disparate elements be blended, as Beastie Boy Adam Yauch and his fellow organizers at the Milarepa Fund attempted to keep people thinking about China's oppression of Tibet while still enjoying themselves. Randall's Island was certainly a less bucolic setting than last year's Golden Gate Park, but artists were given 10 to 15 minutes more each for their sets, which allowed them to stretch out. On Saturday, the lineup was carefully arranged to create a warm, unhurried but always energetic vibe, with spacious rock flowing into tightly wound hip hop and big guitars into dance grooves. Sunday came off more haphazard due to two no-shows (De La Soul, the Wallflowers), longer breaks between sets, and nearly twice as many attendees, perhaps due to the day's flashier bill. The fair's marketplace, featuring Tibetan wares and other goods made by companies uninvolved in China, demonstrated Milarepa's plan for conscientious consumerism. And the monks' tent once again made for a mystical chill-out room.

As befits a Buddhist-oriented event, the best performances found a careful balance, matching humor with rage and achieving abandon through discipline. Farrell, that old master, took Porno for Pyros down the ancient festival road of the bacchanal, festooning the stage with flowers and a small troupe of scantily clad dancers (one horned god among them). Pyros poured out its world-punk groove like honey wine. Radiohead created a similar total environment with sound. Cranking the volume, these new kings of pop psycho-candy cast out their grand songs—most from their forthcoming album, *OK Computer*—like great invisible webs. At times, their three-guitar assault bespoke Pink Floyd, at other times the melodrama conjured Bowie. Without those artistes' theatrics, though, Radiohead demanded greater attention for the music itself, and their intricate compositions lived up to the scrutiny.

Sound-worlds veterans Sonic Youth spun their own sticky filament, with a set comprised entirely of instrumentals, save a last song, "Hits of Gay Sunshine," dedicated to Allen Ginsberg. The Youth numbered among the artists who approached the festival as a chance to relax, and in their case the mellow take worked—it was as if they'd never ended the set they'd begun at the cavernous Anchorage beneath the Brooklyn Bridge two nights earlier, simply stretched their drone to fill a new, huger space. U2, seeming very relieved to have an afternoon's escape from their burdensome PopMart tour, used songs from *Pop* and *Achtung Baby* to create a similar groundswell. Each tune became a lesson in controlled acceleration, with a smoky, drooly version of "Until the End of the World" packing the most sensual punch.

This was one way to smooth the savage festival beast: with sweet sounds. Tart ones work too. After a mud-wrestling match with the soundboard, the Foo Fighters came out loud and venomous, letting their pop melodies slide beneath an onslaught of tightly executed punk. Pavement, always inexplicably great at these big shows, clamored through a career-wide sampler with verve, even if Steven Malkmus was in one of his famous moods. (Fans got a chuckle when, at the end of the band's set, Malkmus poutily refused every suggestion for a last number until Spira Stairs took it on himself to launch into "Two States"—a song whose border-respecting message served as the band's only, if mostly conjectured, comment on Tibet.) Blur, who at first seemed as bored as Malkmus always is, must have gobbled some Vivarin a third of their way through. They hit a frantic high point, with the keyboard pumping hurdy-gurdy, their guitars tossed into the air, and lead Ritalin kid Damon Albarn babbling "Wee hoo!" Now that's a sound anybody can love.

Leave it to the weekend's most celebrated sound man, though, to best employ the festival conqueror's other main weapon: personality. Lee

"Scratch" Perry took the stage in a jumper made from an American flag, full face paint, Dennis Rodman hair, shoes spangled with compact discs, and a fanny pack. "I'm a punk and a monk, and I've got the funk," he bleated, covering all the bases. A thick dub carpet beneath his feet, Perry cooed and screeched and free associated, ranting, "Don't be a victim!" Ben Harper, the excellent vocalist and slide guitarist who served as the weekend's opener, had a clearer message but lacked Perry's charisma. He was best building a hypnotic psychedelic groove and most tedious raising his fist in the air. Harper's mentor Taj Mahal, who has experience to rival Perry's, erred in the opposite direction, declining the elder's wisdom he might have offered in favor if a good-time soul review.

Despite its overly relaxed tone, Mahal's performance would have been fine at any of the many of the blues festivals I'm sure he'll play this year. But by its very nature, the Tibet concert asked more from its artists. Yauch and Milarepa hoped to inundate festivalgoers with a sense of mission about Tibet, and the Randall's Island fairgrounds were crowded with information booths, the biggest of which was the monks' tent, which included an altar where monks and nuns prayed continuously and a few adepts drew a sand mandala. Palden Gyatso, a monk who was imprisoned and tortured by the Chinese for 30 years, appeared as he had last year, one of many speakers representing a panoply of nonviolent action groups. Public Enemy leader and longtime motivational speaker Chuck D offered a poem, "Male Ego/Overblown Testosterone." Tibetan performers brought home the message that a glorious culture is being annihilated. Singer Yungchen Lhamo, in white and gold with waist-long hair, seemed like a vestal goddess giving her blessing; in contrast the horn-and-drum duo Nawang Kechog were all earth and fire, this year's dynamic replacement for the Red Hot Chilli Peppers.

Finding a different way to keep Tibet in the faces of the crowd, Jon Spencer shouted, "All of you who want to get involved and free Tibet, I want you to HIT ME!!," working the blues tradition's time-honored connection between church and state, Jesse Jackson and James Brown. In monk's duds updated for the juke joint circuit—red dress shirt, orange hip-huggers—Spencer's Blues Explosion jumped the gap between entertainment and incitement to riot, using the day's message as a good reason to get people off their butts. In a seamless, bouncy set, A Tribe Called Quest employed similar integrative tactics, leading the crowd in a chant of "Oh my Gawd! Free Tibet!" and offering the declaration "Free Tibet! Free Kashmir! Free Africa! Free Japan!" (Don't ask about the last one.) KRS-One won the contest for most elaborate metaphor; after leading an old-school hip-hop revue that included some eye-boggling break dancing and muscular rhymes, he tossed a bagful of tennis balls, announcing, "I autographed these tennis balls 'cos they signify the whole world," which, he explained, we need to change. Oh yeah, and props to Gustavo Kuerten.

Patti Smith did the most to promote Tibet during her set, even singing a new song about the conflict. Nonetheless, she skewed the mood by letting her righteous attitude slip toward simple anger. She chose to target the photographers working the lip of the stage but her rants about media "parasites" felt inappropriate at a media event—the cameras seemed a small invasion compared to Chinese imperialism—and enveloped her set in a shroud of petty negativity. Alanis Morissette, who wouldn't know negativity if it slapped her, indulged herself in a different way, by laying back and delivering an unambitious acoustic set. At least her voice achieved some passion, which is more than you can say for Michael Stipe, who drifted through his superstar session with buddy Mills, Patti Smith bass player Tony Shanahan, Pearl Jam's McCready, and (on drums, briefly) Mike D. Singing in his weak midrange, Stipe seemed to be trying to create a whirlpool of placidity that would suck the crowd of all its negative energy. Mostly, though, it just sucked, rather like Noel Gallagher's perfunctory solo appearance on Saturday. Vedder, who stepped in for a ghostly cameo on one song, did nothing to remedy the situation, although he reportedly shared more wisdom and strength in the short set he and McCready performed on Sunday morning, before most people arrived.

These top seeds on the alternative circuit apparently all decided that "festival" means a chance to coast, to behave in ways they wouldn't dare if their own ticket sales were on the line. It's one thing to try something new, as Björk did, debuting several new songs with a string section; at first her dress, a cutaway coral-pink contraption, gained more attention than her soft-boiled set, but she and her ensemble eventually caught a groove through sheer determination. It's another thing to act like just showing up is enough. That's something Rancid would never do—music just means too much to them. Kicking through a set of greatest hits topped by a sing-along version of "The Harder They Come," joined onstage by a host of pals from the New York ska scene, they hit on an ideal blend of feistiness and showmanship. And they actually seemed to care about the situation that has brought them there.

It goes without saying that the Beastie Boys care, and Yauch and his homeys put out extra hard for the weekend's final set. The threesome burst forth in Day-Glo jumpsuits, like monks in a Japanimation movie, Mike D's hair in tiny braids and Ad-Rock's in a Young Einstein mop. From "Sure

Shot" all the way to the hardcore miniset that ended the show, the Beasties drove to the hoop over and over again. They were jesters, they were warriors, they were in it for the fun and the paradox of it all. They ended their set with a tune by the Ramones and one by Billy Joel. Balance had been achieved.

Sitting in the wings as the Beasties brought down the day, a ring of monks and nuns waited to give a final blessing. Bashful and coy, a little harried, they gave off the nervous aura of accidental celebrities. In their tent, they'd demonstrated that cultural expression can be introspective, intended not for consumption but to enrich the self. Now they watched their new friend and his buddies lead the crowd in a different kind of chant: "rock the house." Looking through my binoculars, I couldn't tell what they were thinking. Did they feel weird, like an endangered species on display? Did they feel superior? Most sat without moving. One monk bobbed his head in time with the beats. I wondered what he thought "festival" means. Maybe freedom.

ADAM HEIMLICH

SENSITIVE B-BOYS

The Stranger, *January 14, 1999*

The Beastie Boys' metamorphosis into sensitive boys began as early as 1992's *Check Your Head*, whereupon they expressed their "Gratitude" and a wish that the world might "Lighten Up." It was nearly complete by the release of 1994's *Ill Communication*, which featured a song about Tibetan Buddhism and, in the single "Sureshot," a heartfelt statement of "love and respect" for "mothers and sisters" delivered by the man who'd eight years earlier sang, in reference to a pair of "girlies," the line, "their father had AIDS so I shot him in the head."

By 1998 the Beastie Boys were omitting lines like that one (including but not limited to "I did it with the whiffle ball bat," "I grabbed the piano player and I punched him in the face," and "I got my barrel at your neck so what the fuck you gonna do?") from performances in support of their new, fifth album, *Hello Nasty*. The self-editing of old material to better suit a grown-up artist is not outside of rock tradition—Neil Young and Dylan have done it. But in August, the Beasties revealed the true extent of their discomfort with rude rap, and made clear exactly how sensitive they now are. At England's Reading Festival, the Boys asked co-headliners

Prodigy to excise the song "Smack My Bitch Up" from their set. Prodigy made a point of refusing the request—they introduced "Smack My Bitch Up" by telling the assembled crowd, "The Beastie Boys asked us not to play this song, but we do what the fuck we want."

The Beastie Boys' distaste for the song is shared by the National Organization for Women, who called for a boycott of Time-Warner (which owns Prodigy's label, Maverick) to protest "Smack My Bitch Up," and by Wal-Mart and Kmart, who refused to stock the album it's on. Prodigy's defense, as expressed in a press release, was, not unexpectedly, artistic license. It's undeniable that the song does not necessarily advocate violence against women—the title line isn't even sung by any member of Prodigy, but is sampled from a rhyme by Beastie *Licensed To Ill*-era contemporaries Ultramagnetic MCs. Prodigy may have used the line to comment on it. And nobody knows what Kool Keith was thinking when he wrote it— maybe the "bitch" is his dog. Arguing that something should be censored because its interpretation can prove hurtful is obviously problematic, as the Bible fits that bill. It's especially problematic for the Beastie Boys. Did Beastie Adam Horovitz inspire assaults when he bragged, "I smacked her in the puddy with a plank beam"? If so, the Boys perhaps ought to call for a boycott of their album *Paul's Boutique*, because those words are voiced on every single copy.

The Beastie Boys are probably far too dedicated to classic liberal tenets (and the proceeds from sales of their back catalog) to go out like that. But their conflict with Prodigy crystallizes a recurring dilemma for many rap fans. Obviously, a good deal of rap content is crude and offensive to adult sensibilities. It is also one of the primary modes of artistic expression for young, black, underclass males. It is to be expected that middle-class people aren't going to like everything they say. But at what point should reverence for free expression give way to abhorrence of the expressed? One obvious answer—the one the Beastie Boys hypocritically gave at Reading—is that artists who cross-culturally adopt poor black youths' words and style go too far.

It's crucial to note that the important boundary being crossed here is not the color line. In 1986 sensitive white critics collectively wrung their hands over the Beasties' supposed "minstrel show," but if the black hip hop world saw it that way, surely at least one rapper would have committed such feelings to wax. Instead, *Licensed To Ill* was widely sampled—by militantly pro-black artists like EPMD, N.W.A., Public Enemy and others—and the album is today an acknowledged hip hop classic. The criticism the album did receive (mostly in the rock press; the rap mags downplayed it) resonates more with rebukes later directed at gangsta rap by accomplished black professionals C. Delores Tucker, Wynton Marsalis, Chris Rock and Nelson George than the ones rappers aimed at Vanilla Ice and MC Hammer. Various shades of upright citizens proved hostile of middle-class artists in lower-class drag (see any rock magazine's review of *Licensed To Ill*, Kool Moe Dee's rap attacks on L.L. Cool J, or the Chris Rock/Nelson George-penned film *CB4*). Within the rap world, the big crime was watered-down attempts at "crossover." Uncensored street slang was understood to be inherently honest.

This duality was understood implicitly by sensitive b-boys in the late '80s and early '90s. Rap language was a way to let the world know who you are and where you come from. Expressions of violence—from Public Enemy and Boogie Down Productions' revolutionary rhetoric, to "De La Soul Is Dead"'s assertion that the group's members are not hippies and will in fact hit you for calling them such, to Ices Cube and T's poetic depictions of contemporary Western gunfights—were deemed authentic, and thus as culturally valuable as they were entertaining. Back then, to label Kool Keith "misogynist" for rhyming "change my pitch up" with "smack my bitch up" was to miss the forest through the trees. "All" hip hop culture was anathema to the mainstream because, offensive or not, it was exactly what it said it was.

Public Enemy's apparent anti-Semitism caused a momentary conundrum (that this was much more controversial than any anti-white or anti-woman rhymes perhaps reveals biases hidden within sensitive-boys' collective unconscious), but the sensitive-boy defense of every rappers' license to ill did not fall apart until the 1992 emergence of the Death Row label, and modern gangsta rap. Like many rappers before them, Snoop Dogg, Dr. Dre and Tupac, as well as East-Coast converts to the Death Row style like Biggie Smalls, rapped about being armed and ruthless. And there was plenty of evidence suggesting they really were just that (except in the case of Dr. Dre, who made a point of stating that he was just an entertainer and was subsequently branded a homosexual by Tupac). Their records sold in the millions, and the hardcore rap world abandoned its prohibition of crossover. By the time Tupac and Biggie were gunned down, many of the critics who'd praised hip hop in the '80s had given up on it. You didn't have to be all that sensitive to recognize that a moral element that had been present in hip hop even when N.W.A. and the Beasties were misbehaving had since disappeared.

This led quite naturally to the mature Beastie Boys' request for sensitivity at Reading. A new, left-activist hip hop underground, and an international revival of old-school party-rap styles are further evidence that at least some segments of hiphop culture want to disown rap stream-of-consciousness in favor of conscience. All of these scenes have, in effect, adopted the stance of the '80s-Beasties' and N.W.A.'s upper-class, middle-aged critics. This is hardly surprising considering that many erstwhile Beastie defenders have since grown old and rich. It's no doubt easier to divest yourself of the proposition that rap tells the truth, when it's not your truth it tells.

But the vast majority of rappers moved in a wholly different direction. Instead of conceding that rappers bore an ethical responsibility for what they said, the second great wave of sensitive b-boys only confessed that rap language could be misused—rappers could be liars. Hinging their argument on the hip hop verity that deigns all authentic, heartfelt, skillfully delivered rhymes inherently just, the third coming of hardcore (artists like Nas, Wu-Tang Clan, Outkast and Mobb Deep) pointed the finger at pretenders. In the third wave, the sort of middle-to-underclass dissemblers who'd inspired especial criticism in the '80s were the true enemies of hip hop—not because their tales of violence weren't immoral, but because they weren't "real." That most if not all of the great rappers of the previous period had been such sheep in wolves' clothing didn't matter, as this time rage at phonies was coming not down or across the class and generation totem-poles, but up from below.

If the Beastie Boys have trouble hearing "Smack My Bitch Up," one wonders how they'd feel about Wu-Tang Clan leader RZA's brutal, girl-friend-bashing "Domestic Violence," which appears on his new album *Bobby Digital In Stereo*. I imagine they'd find it as challenging as school-marms found *Licensed To Ill*. Neither, I'd point out, is as violent as *Saving Private Ryan*. When the context is young men at war, the content is never going to be pretty.

PRINCESS SUPERSTAR

YOU GOTTA FIGHT FOR YOUR RIGHT TO THE STAIRMASTER!

POPsmear, 14.0, March/April, 1998

I am staring at this really skinny guy in the X-large T-shirt. His eyes are closed and his legs are crossed. Funny, I think, people at the NY Health & Racquet Club don't usually wear X-large T-shirts. Usually it's old guys in "Advil 5K Run" T-shirts, or else old ladies wearing leotards and shiny tights and legwarmers, one of my favorite looks (and I am not being sarcastic). Hmmm, I think, that guy looks like Mike D. But that guy is doing yoga: NO WAY that's Mike D doing yoga!! Well, my friends, that's Mike D doing yoga. His legs are crossed and he's doing this funny breathing thing. "Rock the Bells" is going really loud in my walkman (I'm doing leglifts, really attractive) and I turn up the music even louder. STOP IT, MIKE D!! C'MON, SING ABOUT DOING DUST! PLEASE! I send a mental message, but I think he is too far gone. All I can think about is being 16 and seeing the Beastie Boys dumping champagne on sluts in cages. Maybe if I had a sack 'o White Castles and some Brass Monkey I could wave it all under his nose and he would become Mike D again. Oh god what is this world coming to?

I joined the NY Health & Racquet Club last year after scoring an $80 membership through my job. I was particularly excited about this club as opposed to say, Crunch, because while Crunch had all the good-looking actors/advertising execs/waitresses/ whatever with thongs up their asses, MY new club only had old boring people with money. This meant I could go to the gym reeking of cigarette smoke, half-asleep and wearing a ripped T-shirt (that also served as a nightgown the night before), and not have to worry about a thing. I'm sorry but when you're jumping around in aerobics class doing moves you wouldn't be caught dead doing even in the privacy of your own home (for those of you in the know, one word: grapevine!) the last thing you want is people you know watching you through that little glass window. And conversely, the last thing you want to see is people you know doing that shit. So imagine the absolute horror of seeing a respected idol, one who has enjoyed the fine reputation of being baaaaad, doing something as pussy as yoga?

You would think it couldn't get any worse, but then Mike D walked onto the treadmill next to mine. My ass was bouncing up and down from the impact of running on the treadmill—like bouncing in ten different directions. My hair was really dirty, and it doesn't get oily, you know? It gets dry and split and looks like a blonde Buckwheat. My eyes were puffy from lack of sleep. On top of that, and definitely the worst of all, I was doing that annoying thing of mouthing words to the song in my walkman and staring at every aspect of my person in the mirror while I was running. The song you may ask? FUCKING "Sure Shot." Yeah, I was wishing to die right there and then. Aha, gentle reader, but then Mike D started up the treadmill. And I haven't been able to listen to "Sure Shot" since. It wasn't like he was a bad runner or anything, but watching the great Mike D's spindly legs running really fast in oversized shorts like a 12 year old in PE class just kinda ruined the hallowed concept of the Beastie Boys.

THEN, Mike D ventured into the exercise room where I was stretching. Could I not get any peace? And, playing in my walkman was "Hold It Now, Hit It." I had a 90-minute hip hop mix tape with only two Beastie Boys songs and some marvelous god decided that they should play precisely when I am watching one of my favorite rock stars doing weird jerky arm stretches in the mirror. I suppose the overwhelmingness of it all compelled me to open my mouth. It came out almost in slow motion . . . "Hey, I'm listening to you right now!" As soon as it came out, I was transported to those good old days of high school—perennial dorkdom. GODDAMN it, what was wrong with me? "I suppose it's better than me listening to it," he smiled back. "Uh-huhh huuhh," my laugh was like Beavis', as I thought about how I listen to my band's music sometimes when I exercise—you know, to make sure the mixes are OK. (James, here is where you insert, "yeah, right.") "Oh," I said, "I suppose that could be embarrassing." Boy was I cool. So now I felt like the biggest asshole in front of a rock star that was doing weird jerky arm stretches in the mirror. MIKE D, GET THE HELL OUT OF MY GYM!!

Just a little end note: The next blow came when I was on the ass machine. The one where you have to lift your leg really far behind your butt—well let's just say it's not very pretty. And sure enough, in walks Russell Simins, the drummer from the Jon Spencer Blues Explosion, one of my most favorite drummers. He had on sweatpants, an oversize T-shirt and an oversize belly and was looking around at the equipment, obviously new to the gym. I must now silently pray that Russell Simins will not be in my step class. Who's next—Iggy, my punk rock idol? Oh wait, I think he belongs to Crunch.

EVERETT TRUE AND JON SLADE, WITH STEPHEN SWEET

BEASTIE BOYS

The following is drawn from e-mail correspondence between three friends living on both sides of the Atlantic. One is a critic, one is a musician, one is a photographer. One lives in Brighton, UK, another in Washington State, U.S. and the third in London, UK—although who lives where changes, depending on the date. The second correspondent has met Mike D on a number of occasions—most notably when the Beastie Boy grabbed him backstage at Lollapalooza '94 and solemnly informed him that, "Usually my main mission is to get on stage and rock the house. Today, it's to keep you and Billy Corgan apart." (A reference to a long-standing feud that began after the pop star wrote a song about our man on his dreadful Siamese Dream *album.) The first correspondent met Mike D and Ad-Rock in a club in New York in '97, but failed to recognize them. The third photographed Mike D for an article on Grand Royal in London. He found him to be an uncooperative, arrogant fuck who didn't take his headphones off once during the entire session.*

All correspondence is as it was originally written. Almost.

DATE: 21/3/99 0930.000
SUBJECT: VOLKSWAGEN WHEELS
FROM: JON SLADE

It's funny you should mention the Beastie Boys. . . .

They seem to've existed throughout my awareness of pop music, although they aren't much older than me—but that's a false memory because I was already stealing Volkswagen symbols in 1981. Not to wear them, to steal them. I wasn't aware of their music as such, just aware of their effect. I first learnt of the myth of the Beastie Boys when they were being obnoxious, sexist types—which was diagrammatically opposed to the way I was trying to live my life as a teenager—and I hated them for that reason. I might have been a thief, but I had my limits.

DATE: 25/3/99 17.45.000
SUBJECT: RE: VOLKSWAGEN WHEELS
FROM: EVERETT TRUE

Early on, I had any number of contradictory impulsive thoughts towards the Beasties. I appreciated their brattiness, the way they caused shock horror headlines in the tabloids—I even thought the idea of giant phallic symbols and naked dancing girls in cages on stage was pretty neat, cos it was all obviously so ironic. This, despite the fact I was even more sexless than you back then. It was only later I grew to despise the hypocrisy of those around the Beasties. It was only later I learnt that the vast populace has no sense of irony—especially those in America—and that the Beasties were simple bad frat boy humor (something I undoubtedly would've hated if I'd known what it was). But don't get me wrong: I fucking loved the first

With Weird Al, c. '85.

Beasties album—"Fight For Your Right To Party" had a great snotty feel to it, as did almost all of *Licensed To Ill*, and "No Sleep Till Brooklyn" was the greatest song Motorhead never wrote. Punk wasn't that far away that I hadn't forgotten the attraction of behaving badly for its own sake, and shocking people. Even then, I was aware that the Beasties' "violence against women" lyrics and bad-mouth boasting were only present because they were aping their black hip hop counterparts. They weren't serious, man. Yeah, I liked them (mainly because they were everything I wasn't: fun, frivolous and fanciable).

It was only later I realised I was a perfect target audience for the Beasties; a white middle class kid with aspirations to being an outsider, who'd never experienced black culture beyond the odd trendy late Seventies deep reggae outfit—and anything condoned by Abe Hoffman.

That was in retrospect, though. I was gutted when NME asked me to review the Beasties Brixton show in 1986 and I couldn't cos I was supporting the Shop Assistants in Switzerland at the time. I wanted to be BAD so badly. I thought it'd be a hoot, a slap across the face to those who thought of me in one way and one way alone. Even then, I knew I wanted to have fun. And the Beastie Boys—for better or for worse—seemed to be the living embodiment of fun.

DATE: 25/3/99 19.05.000
SUBJECT: LIVING EMBODIMENTS
FROM: JON SLADE

Was that '86?

It was around that time I made some new friends who were into Def Jam releases and could appreciate the Beastie Boys in an ironic way. Good for them. I never could. I bought the first Public Enemy LP and got off on its misogyny and obnoxiousness, but the Beasties were too Aerosmith for me. Buying the Public Enemy LP was a daring step, but the Beastie Boys were too traditional. I could've gone that route, but they were symbols of everything I despised. I was much too scared to go see Public Enemy play, though . . . .

DATE: 15/4/99 23.55.00
SUBJECT: BEASTIES AGAIN
FROM: EVERETT TRUE

I know what you mean by being scared . . . that's why the Beasties held so much appeal for us suburban kids. They gave their fans the veneer of street credibility, without any of the danger. Plus, you knew they were golden-hearted sorts underneath it all really—and incredibly smart.

I don't know when I first realised they were that smart—maybe it was in 1989, when *Paul's Boutique* flopped so massively—because I've always favoured bands who don't sell records. They seem so much more artistic, somehow. All of a sudden, I found myself loving the Beasties' arrogance even more—the way they thought that overnight they could change from being a loud-mouthed brat-rap act into something of worth! How excellent. (Even now I don't know anyone who's actually listened to "Paul's Boutique," although I know plenty of wannabe hipsters who claim to've done.) And it wasn't the Beasties' fault they almost ruined English culture by inspiring James Brown, first editor of proto-typical "new lad" magazine *Loaded*, to think he was clever. . . .

Whatever. There'll always be people around who'll always miss the point. And most of them will be journalists. . . .

I didn't realise how truly smart the Beasties were, though, until the early nineties, when they hooked up with all the credible alternative rock sorts— Sonic Youth and Nirvana and, er, all the other bands managed by their livewire manager John Silva—and started to really exploit their credibility. Well . . . how much credibility does it give you, from selling 10 million records to selling about 10 records in the space of three years? If the Beasties could come back from that, they could come back from anything, right?

(In fact, *Paul's Boutique* sold a cool million in the States alone—but because those sales came on the back of the seven million-selling *Licensed To Ill*, it was perceived as a flop. Some flop!)

John once flew me to San Francisco to witness their comeback gig, shortly before the release of their third album, 1992's *Check Your Head*, where they realigned their hip hop credentials and started to get a little too serious for my tastes. . . . I get to the venue, and there are kids outside on the street touting fucking sub-machine guns. I get told I'm not on the list. Fine, I think—and go back to the safety of my hotel porn-laden room. I don't need that fucking macho shit anyway.

DATE: 11/4/99 13.00.00
SUBJECT: ILL KNOWLEDGE
FROM: JON SLADE

My knowledge of the Beasties Boys in the early Nineties is almost non-existent—I don't know what I was doing at the time. Reading books, probably. I didn't know anyone who'd heard *Paul's Boutique* or *Check Your Head*. It's my favorite period of the Beastie Boys, though, because I was completely unaware of their existence. If I did hear about them at all, it seemed like they'd reformed their misogynist, boastful characters—and were now making friends with punks like the aforementioned Sonic Youth, and the Breeders. Again, another reason to dig the Beasties because . . . Punks Are Cool.

DATE: 11/4/99 13.05.00
SUBJECT: POINT OF ORDER
FROM: EVERETT TRUE

So you don't think they were punks already?

After all, the Beasties started off as a NYC thrash-core punk band, with a Luscious Jackson on drums, right?

Yes, but they were dreadful crap punks, like the Macc Lads [awful, early Eighties woman-hating, English joke-punk band]. The Beasties were hard-core when they started out—and hard-core is not punk.

Anyway, it was only when the next album *Ill Communication* came out in '95 that I finally started to get interested, because it contained a reference to a band I was in at the time [proto Riot Grrrls, Huggy Bear]. The line was "So I'll say it like the group Huggy Bear/There's a boy-grrl revolution of which you should be aware." It was in a song called "The Scoop." So I played the whole record, but it wasn't much cop—there were far too many horrible funky jams on it.

I saw them a couple of times round this record—once at Brixton Academy where they jammed with all their funk musicians for even longer than they did on the record. The other time was at an MTV Rough Trade Covent Garden show for all the skater kids. I hated the show, but I did get to stand next to Donovan's daughter Ione Skye (from *The Rachel Papers*)—which I liked very much.

That's about as far as my knowledge of the Beastie Boys goes—although obviously I've heard plenty of their pioneering whiny white boy rap in the last year or so, what with *Hello Nasty* being Number One in the UK and everything.

Plus, I like their magazine *Grand Royal* because it's dense, fannish, packed full of information about obscure subjects and has bad covers . . . and dislike it for exactly the same reasons. And that's about all I know on the Beasties. Sorry.

Fuck man. Let me clear my throat first. . . .

You can't skimp over *Ill Communication* like that—the Beasties' finest album, no shit. It was the perfect summer record, the kinda bomb you want blasting out of every tenement window, every car stereo as the long, hot, interminable months drag gloriously on. *Ill Communication* was the moment the Beasties finally gelled—before they started wearing their NYC street cynicism as a badge of cool, but long enough after their brash impetuous beginnings to realise that boasting about beating up women just isn't that funny. It was cool and aware, without being preachy or over-bearing. It casually threw the Beasties' rock influences into the fray while still remaining resolutely hip hop. It was funny, stylish and FUN! *Ill Communication* oozed cool from every pore—not put-on "hipster" fake sunglasses-after-dark cool, but the cool that only comes about when people are operating at the top of their form. And it's a record the Beasties are almost certainly doomed to copy forevermore . . . unless of course their projected *Full Country Album* ever comes out, and they "do a Beck" (another Silva signing, incidentally) and reinvent themselves as rootsy, 70-year-old, ornery Ol' Opry folks. But fuck, I hope they don't. Rather the jaded, business-like retreads of *Hello Nasty* than more indie cosmopolitan white-boys pretending to be Southern rednecks. Please!

DATE: 18/4/99 11.35.00
SUBJECT: THE ONE DEFINING MOMENT
FROM: STEPHEN SWEET

The Beasties did have one fantastic defining moment—the video to "Sabotage".

It was their one moment of class where they played to their strengths (confidence, humor, the funk) and knew when to quit. Its Seventies blaxploitation movie spoof was clever because it was restrained and spot-on. Their humor was implicit, it wasn't shoved in your face . . . which is where they let themselves down nowadays. The Beastie Boys seem to be growing ever more desperate, what with their recent Japanese boiler suits and protective eye-wear. Please! I'm not saying I like pure rap Beasties—I don't—the time I liked them was when they could collide different genres simultaneously, switch effortlessly between rock and rap, without it being contrived. *Hello Nasty* seems contrived; they don't hold much interest for anyone anymore. Just more corporate MTV stars, up there pretending to be young.

What's the point of the Beastie Boys in 1999? Why are they still around?

DATE: 18/4/99 23.56.00
SUBJECT: RE: THE ONE DEFINING MOMENT
FROM: EVERETT TRUE

I dunno.

Hello Nasty let the side down by using tired samples, by being in tune with a mentality which went out of fashion several years back . . . I'm not sure it was that contrived, more sadly out-of-touch. I guess one could've seen it coming during the long years of artistic wilderness after *Ill Communication*, where they reissued that compilation of early hard-core (punk) singles *Some Old Bullshit* best left festering in collector's vaults along the East Village, when they put out that unbelievably dull collection of instrumentals *The In Sound From Way Out* (which at least had the merit of proving that the funk only funks when it is kept under tight restraint . . . heresy for any funk musician).

Still, the Beasties managed to define the moment at least twice—with "No Sleep Till Brooklyn"/"Fight For Your Right," and "Sabotage"—which is twice more than almost anyone else. And I love 'em for that reason alone. Hey, who knows? *Hello Nasty* could well be a momentary aberration. Let's hope so . . .

DATE: 8/5/99 14.00.00
SUBJECT: SMARTNESS AND B-BOYS
FROM: EVERETT TRUE

I still contend the Beasties are smart. Why?

Because they once used a fish eye lens in a video.

Because they knew that if only they could get people to forget all their misogynist shit and reinvent themselves as caring, sharing men with an eye to the political action (Tibet) they could create a much longer-lasting audience.

Because they took full advantage of MTV's cluelessness in that channel's last dying days (1993, approx).

Because, with *Ill Communication*—the album no one expected—they effortlessly, cockily managed to capture the moment. That album defined that summer. That summer defined that album. Inventive, cheeky, riotous and—most importantly—not offensive. How could anyone resist it?

Because they mix art with commerce and manage to fool millions of people that the end result is worthwhile.

Because they know how to have fun!

NEIL STRAUSS

THE BEASTIE BOYS:
KEEN-EARED SURVIVORS

New York Times, *July 19, 1998*

There is a term in hip hop, flavor. It is a good thing. Rappers want to have flavor: panache, style, something extra that enables them to stand out from the pack. In their 17 years together, however, the Beastie Boys have developed something much better than flavor: taste. This is not a hip hop term. It is the key to survival in the mercurial world of pop. Musicians like David Bowie, Peter Gabriel and David Byrne have good taste; as most of their colleagues have fossilized, it has enabled them to remain relevant, even after their hit-making days ended.

The Beastie Boys are listeners as much as they are musicians, so any music they make is going to be interesting. This has enabled them to survive commercially while every rap act from their era has fallen by the wayside (with the exception of L.L. Cool J, whose grip on the mainstream has become tenuous as his taste has devolved into mimicry). That is, if one could still consider the Beastie Boys rap, because they've blown what little currency they did have in the hip-hop world by following their broader instincts instead of the orthodoxy of the rap mainstream.

The band's previous two albums were a collection of hardcore punk songs and an album of lighter instrumental music; its new record jams 22 tracks with 8 singers into 68 minutes. This is not the output of a group that sets out to make the perfect pop record like *Pet Sounds, Sgt. Pepper* or even *It Takes a Nation of Millions* (the rap classic by Public Enemy). This is the work of a band that aims to show how much it can do. *Hello Nasty* jumps from rap to easy listening to Latin to noise to soul to opera to rock without pausing for breath. As the band boasts on "Intergalactic," "I'm so versatile."

The Beastie Boys are emblematic of a new breed of artists who have emerged over the past decade, the collector-musicians. Where postmodern musicians slap different styles together noncommittally, as if they were all equivalent colors in the sonic palette, collector-musicians weld different sounds together with commitment and bias. Their songs are more tributes than statements. For example, the eccentric dub-reggae pioneer Lee (Scratch) Perry appears on *Hello Nasty*, not to make the album better, more commercial or more musical, but simply because the band likes him and wants to collect his voice like an audio autograph. It's not that collector-musicians (they also include Beck, the Dust Brothers, Stereolab and Cornelius) are fans more than artists. It's that being a fan is part of their art.

From their first full hip-hop album, *Licensed to Ill* in 1986, the Beastie Boys set themselves up as observers and emulators of rap culture, privileged white boys looking in from the outside, as they did as teen-agers in the years leading up to the record, running around Manhattan clubs where punk, new wave and rap were mingling. Since then, the Beastie Boys have transformed themselves from a band to an enterprise. Like Mr. Gabriel's Real World label or Mr. Byrne's Luaka Bop, the Beastie Boys developed Grand Royal, a record label and a magazine (plus a clothing company called X-Large) predicated on the notion that the Beastie Boys have good taste, that they know what is cool.

Another key to their survival is their ability to spot talented musicians and use them on their albums, whether it's the Dust Brothers' producing *Paul's Boutique* nine years ago or the contributions from the turntablist Mixmaster Mike and the keyboardist Money Mark on *Hello Nasty*. As music buffs, the Beastie Boys are also able to listen to current rap and rock and siphon off the elements that make them interesting, as evident in the snatches of violin and sped-up female voices on the new album, both tricks borrowed from the Wu-Tang producer known as RZA.

Hello Nasty sounds like a night with a disk jockey with a short attention span: samples of everything from Stravinsky to Tito Puente to earlier Beasties albums abound. Hip-hop beasts are mixed into Latin music. Songs skid to a halt as the sound of a needle scratching across the record interrupts. And all kind of turntable tricks—sirens, horns, electronic gurgles and sound effects—are mixed on top of the busy songs, as the band raps lines like, "Remote control, change the station." On the album, some of the stations are playing seething, energetic music, and some are playing directionless throwaways. It is the curse of the collector-musician: knowing too much and wanting to do it all.

The most often cited dilemma for the Beastie Boys is that their most popular music has been their goofiest—tongue-in-cheek frat anthems like "Fight for Your Right (to Party)" and "Girls." They may be too smart to fail these days, but they are also too smart to be a phenomenon again. Though some would place the Beastie Boys in the genre of alternative rock, they behave more like a classic-rock band, especially since the personalities of the three members have been diverging.

Though they tend to rap in unison, it's easy to pick out the three intertwined aesthetics at work. Lines like "Share your love with a friend" come from the member who has discovered spirituality, the aspiring Tibetan Buddhist Adam Yauch. Phrases like "money makin'" come from the member making the shift into the executive world, Mike Diamond. And the phrase "Dogs love me cause I'm crazy sniffable" probably came from the band's secret weapon, the clown and collector Adam Horovitz. Silly-smart lines like the Run-D.M.C. parody "I'm the king of Boggle, there is none higher/I get 11 points off the word quagmire," best fuse all their personalities.

On *Hello Nasty* there is probably something for everyone, but there is probably no one whom everything is for. Popular music is moving past the time when combining two genres is going to create something new. It is more the exposition of a distinct personal taste that is going to result in a new sound.

In other words, something unusual is less likely to arise from a combination of hip hop and Celtic music (that's flavor) than it is from someone mixing the sound of the Wu-Tang Clan and the Chieftains, along with a few favorites from a treasured record collection, like, say, Celia Cruz, Willie Nelson and a cocktail-music compilation on Rhino records (this is taste).

Flavor fades, but taste is a lifetime trait. And *Hello Nasty* is a testament to good taste, even if at times it does lack flavor.

GEORGE KAPLAN

KEEP WATCHING THE SKIES: AN ALIEN ABDUCTION INSPIRED REVIEW OF *HELLO NASTY*

What Ya Lookin' at, Mutherfucker, #17, 1999

NOTE: George Kaplan asked me to write a brief preface to his review of the Beastie Boys' Hello Nasty. *The reason for my intrusion here will become clearer as I relate the extraordinary circumstances surrounding the composition of the following. I commence with the events that occurred the dark night he wrote the review.*

I was dozing after having tea with Aunt Vera, a cigarette dangling from my fingertips as I reclined on the divan. It was a peaceful moment after a week of Kant and piles. The telephone rang.

L to r: Adam Horovitz, Michael Diamond, and Adam Yauch in '98: Mike D's basketball injury. © Glen E. Friedman.

"Hello," I said, hoping it wasn't George.

"Roger! Fuckin' Roger!" George screamed-choked on smoke.

"Yes."

"I need your help."

"Money again?"

"No . . . worse. I have to write a review of the new Beastie Boys new album."

"So?"

"I can't do it."

Interminable weeping. I opened a new bottle of scotch with my teeth, spat the cap across the carpet, and drank.

"Are you still there?"

"Yes," I said after about ten minutes.

"Well, I can't write it. I mean, I love the band and the album and I even asked for this assignment. But I just can't do it. I first thought it was because I hadn't smoked so I went over to Tom and Vin's. But then I still couldn't—"

"George, why the hell are you telling me all this? I didn't even know you had a job. I thought you just sucked money off of me and sniffed glue in the backyard."

"Listen you motherfuc—URUGHHGKKHHHH!!"

And the phone went dead. I drank half the bottle of scotch and put on a sweater. I packed my pipe and stuck it in my mouth as if I was about to tour my estate in Devonshire. I went out not for George who I distrusted, but for the image that had graced my heart and stirred my emotions. I had seen her the night before.

Kaplan lives down my block, and I had just helped carry him home from the bar again. *I quickly turned and was about to cross the street when I saw her. Her long blonde hair moved on the wind behind her as it does in commercials. She quickly glanced at me. She was carrying a half-finished Snapple iced tea. Dreamlike. I recalled* Citizen Kane *when the reporter interviews Mr. Bernstein and Bernstein—he's great when he falls asleep during the opera—tells him the story about the girl glanced at on a ferry whose image stayed with him for his entire life. Then I thought of a different woman who I saw in a movie theater with popcorn and soda in her hands. Her jeans were splattered with paint. She was a painter. She caught my look, and I looked away. I thought of the painting she was working on: a large rectangle filled with her nightmares and childhoods. Huggy Bear is on the soundtrack.*

But when I get there I don't see the women of my dreams. All I see is Kaplan's half-opened front door. I push the door open to call him an asshole, and I get the shock of my life. First thing I notice is the pulsating purple light, but I quickly forget about that when I see what's going on in Kaplan's empty-Forty-pizzabox-cig-arettebox littered hallway. Four mounds of green flesh with three arms and eyes all over the place were putting Kaplan back together. They were snapping his legs and arms back onto his torso. To get his head back on his neck, one of the mounds held the head while another screwed it back on. As soon as the head was on, Kaplan starts screaming—screaming not in pain, but in ecstasy. *All the mounds see me and drop Kaplan who is still screaming in* ecstasy. *An eye moves and the mounds are gone. Kaplan squirmed on the floor among the trash for forty-five minutes before I could get him up. I quickly poured a bottle of bad cognac down him. I asked him what happened.*

"What happened? What happened? didn't you see?"

"I don't know what I saw." We smoked a funny cigarette.

"They were aliens from another world who abducted me. They scooped me up right there when I was on the phone with you. They

took me up to their spaceship, and there were millions and millions of them in a small compartment—they have defeated the problem of space like Milton's fallen angels: "They but now who seemed/ In bigness to surpass Earth's giant sons,/ Now less than smallest dwarfs, in narrow room/ Throng numberless"— then they took me apart. They tore my arms and legs off, but they gave me something before and it felt great. Then they tore my head off and it was like having 10,000 orgasms at once through your head. They were kind and they told me what they were doing. They were just checking me out. They did all sorts of things with my body and brain and none of it hurt. It actually felt fantastic. What did the Knicks do tonight? To serve man."

Kaplan shot up and I thought he was going to have a fit. He demanded a pen and writing materials. He started writing furiously.

"They told me that I would forget the whole thing. It would become tangled up with my last moment of concentration. My memories of the aliens and the abduction will become a shadow under the other memory. But I can still remember. Must write down. Make money. Movie rights . . . "

He bent over the paper and wrote. But he stopped.

"Fuck. It's happening already. My memory of the aliens is getting mixed up with that review I was trying to write."

"Just write," I advised. "Get out as much as you can and we'll try to reconstruct the details."

Dear Reader, what you hold in your hand is the product of this writing. Yes, Kaplan reviews the album, but he also describes his abduction by beings from another planet. Remember, this is not an album review, it's a warning: KEEP WATCHING THE SKIES!!
—R. O. Thornhill

I was on the phone with Thornhill when a purple light grew above my head. Then I felt cold and then hot and then I was flying. And the voice spoke to me: EARHTLING! DO NOT FEAR US FOR WE COME IN PEACE JUST LIKE IN ALL THOSE MOVIES YOU WATCHED. NOW WE NEED TO TOUCH YOU TO SEE HOW YOU WORK TO HELP US HELP YOU, BUT WE HAVE CHANGED PAIN TO PLEASURE.

The appearance of a Beastie Boys album is anticipated much as the next Kubrick film. But Kubrick is gone and so is grunge and so is Starks and so is Oakley and here are the Beasties again with something astounding.

Just when you figure the Beasties have finally faded they come back with something like this. If we all were transported back to the old school days who would believe what the Beasties have transformed themselves into? Not me and I've been abducted by aliens from another universe! And I've also *really* tripped. And to beat all the tricks I saw the Mets win the series in '86! (Is there a coincidence that *Licensed to Ill* came out in the same year Mookie Wilson won it all for the Mets? I don't think so. Mookie's real first name is William, thus his name is William Wilson just like in that Poe story of doubles.) Not only were the Beasties not a one-shot-wonder, they transformed the culture. In doing so, they broke down genres and expectations. This latest installment in the Beasties discography is a major entry into pop culture: it's the Beasties peeling off their instruments and. . . .

I was in a huge tube with several other people—a woman, a little girl, a basketball player, a K-Mart manager—and we waited for the tests. Time is different up there in hyperfreakyspace: I was gone for 5 minutes here but it was weeks up there.

You just know the Beasties are big old-school *Star Trek* Fans. *Hello Nasty* is their SPACE album! The cover is them in a can heading straight for the "sun"! Just like that episode with the planet-eater-cone-monster and Kirk rammed an exploding starship down its throat! In another episode, the Enterprise runs into a floating Abe Lincoln.

The stars pass like posts on a frozen fence.

Lee Perry's appearance on the album is an astounding symbol: the Dub Master raps about the Boys on their fifth album, their fifth extension of their crashing together rock and rap, hardcore and hip hop, funk and samples. Spilled out over the Beastie-will-to-hardcore and in the tradition of *Paul's Boutique*, but with one important difference: in between came the Boys' mix of punk and hip hop. In between came the aliens to take me away.

Being torn apart was painful until the they started and they then I we it was great. Like a million Whipits at once. Gigantor!

OK. I'm happy. The Beastie Boys' album *Hello Nasty* is like a call from Eden: "Hello? This is Eve. I need three large pies. And a liter of diet Coke. Oh, and an apple from the Tree of Knowledge." The Beasties have proven my theory about sampling. It ain't stealing, it's Freudian. Or

Jungian. Or a part of the Force or something. When you listen to *Licensed to Ill* you get washed in the '70s and shot through with heavy metal. When you listen to *Paul's Boutique* you swim through an LA stuffed into a New York covered in flaking, smoky bombers. It's the greatest psychedelic album since Pink Floyd lost Roger Waters and the Dead's *Live/Dead*. The Beasties aren't the Beatles of their generation, they're our Grateful Dead—crazy trippy American noise in the hall. What *Hello Nasty* does is circle back to the old school daze and the Beasties come up sampling themselves, but with a soft-voiced MCA, Latin beats, Robot noises, writing rhymes *together, Krush Groove*, and all Five Boroughs in Stitches.

The music they have is made of colors. You pick a color and eat it and the music starts to play all over your body.

The Beastie Boys were the first to welcome Latrell Sprewell to the team. "Unite" is the greatest Knicks song in the history of songs.

Their notion of space travel comes from a different physics. They are connected to their ships through a narcotic they consume which powerfully alters their brain waves which are then harnessed and used in the ships' engines to spin the stars into one.

My theory of sampling: it's just a tool to connect into the unconscious mind of the listener. Thus, people who disrespect sampling ("anybody can do it," "it's just machines," "it's stealing other peoples' music") don't get plugged into the trip, and they should be pitied. When you hear the Beasties sample the Jazz Crusaders in 1999 it does something in the context of the album and your listening. You don't need mind-altering stuff (but it helps) to *feel* the sample, the reference, somewhere below your active, conscious mind. It gets you somewhere and you can't pinpoint it.

The aliens are interested in us for one thing: Art. They are fascinated by human art in all it's forms: music, painting, film, literature. They don't have art because they are not as fucked up as we are. Most of the famous paintings in the world's museums are fakes planted by the aliens who have stolen the originals. Their favorite artist of all time is Marcel Duchamp.

So fuck all those critics who don't give props to this new Beastie album. What are they thinking? Don't they see that the Beasties have refashioned music to suit their needs?

The aliens are also fascinated with the human fascination with sex. To them it's just like blowing your nose. They showed me three pictures during the interview part of the exam: the Eiffel Tower, Sylvia Saint, Alfred E. Newman. I told them: "The first is a radio station in Paris that only plays the Beastie Boys called 'Le Petit Mort.' The second is a European porn star who is also a big Beastie Boys fan. The Third is a character from a Beastie Boys album." Newman. Newman.

My theory is a theory of hip hop. It has a glistening surface and a depth unknown to other music. The best hip hop opens up and freaks the unconscious. But one has to be cerebral as well as an unconscious-driller to practice it well, hell, to sling the dope shit one must be righteous as well as touched with anger and magic (Amiri Baraka before the New York Art Quartet: "If Elvis is the King, then who is James Brown? God!" Amen!). These Beasties are righteous, and magical, and pissed off at the callousness of the American Night (Jim Morrison: "I pressed her thigh and death smiled.") Giuliani Sucks!

Space is NOT the final frontier. The aliens know this and they are happy about it. They tried to tell me about the REAL frontier, they tried to describe it to me, but I just couldn't understand it. They gave me a Heineken.

Beastie albums come in pairs: the opening/shattering *Licensed* JOINED to the hallucinogenic comeback *Paul's;* the funked mix of *Check* JOINED to the further funked punked *Ill Communication.* What will the Beasties' return to the future be paired with? "A shout that tore Hell's concave, and beyond/Frightened the reign of Chaos and old Night." KEEP WATCHING THE SKIES!! KEEP WATCHING THOSE GUYS!!

Selected Bibliography

Adler, Bill. *Rap: Portraits and Lyrics of a Generation of Black Rockers*. New York: St. Martin's Press, 1991.

———. *Tougher Than Leather: Run-D.M.C.* New York: Penguin, 1987.

Bangs, Lester. *Psychotic Reactions and Carburetor Dung*. Greil Marcus, ed. New York: Vintage, 1988.

Batey, Angus. *Rhyming & Stealing: A History of the Beastie Boys*. London: Independent Music Press, 1998.

Chuck D with Yusuf Jah. *Fight the Power: Rap, Race, and Reality*. New York: Delta, 1997.

Dick, Philip K. *The Shifting Realities of Philip K. Dick: Selected Literary and Philosophical Writings*. Lawrence Sutin, ed. New York: Vintage, 1995.

Foege, Alec. *Confusion Is Next: The Sonic Youth Story*. New York: St. Martin's Press, 1994.

Friedman, Glen E. *Fuck You Heroes: Photographs, 1976–1991*. New York: Burning Flags Press, 1991.

———. *Fuck You Too: The Extra & More Scrapbook*. New York: Burning Flags Press, 1997.

George, Nelson. *Hip Hop America*. New York: Viking, 1998.

Hagar, Steve. *Hip Hop: The Illustrated History of Breakdancing, Rap Music, and Graffiti*. New York: St. Martin's Press, 1984.

Heylin, Clinton. *From the Velvets to the Voidoids: A Pre-Punk History for a Post-Punk World*. New York: Penguin, 1993.

Jones, Leroi. *Blues People: The Negro Experience in White America and the Music That Developed from It*. New York: Morrow Quill, 1963.

Kerouac, Jack. *Good Blonde & Others*. Donald Allen, ed. San Francisco: Grey Fox Press, 1993.

———. *Mexico City Blues*. New York: Grove Press, 1959.

———. *On the Road*. New York: Signet, 1957.

———. *Visions of Cody*. New York: McGraw-Hill, 1972.

Kostelanetz, Richard. *John Cage (ex)plain(ed)*. New York: Schirmer Books, 1996.

Marcus, Greil. *Ranters and Crowd Pleasers: Punk in Pop Music, 1977–1992*. New York: Doubleday, 1993.

Oyewole, Abiodun and Umar Bin Hassan with Kim Green. *On a Mission: Selected Poems and a History of the Last Poets*. New York: Henry Holt, 1996.

Palmer, Robert. *Deep Blues*. New York: Penguin, 1991.

——. *Rock 'n' Roll: An Unruly History*. New York: Harmony Books, 1995.

Powell, Ricky. *Oh Snap!: The Rap Photography of Ricky Powell*. New York: St. Martin's Press, 1998.

Rocco, John, ed. *The Nirvana Companion*. New York: Schirmer Books, 1998.

Rose, Tricia. *Black Noise: Rap Music and Black Culture in Contemporary America*. Hanover and London: Wesleyan University Press, 1994.

Ross, Andrew and Tricia Rose, eds. *Microphone Fiends: Youth Music and Youth Culture*. New York and London: Routledge, 1994.

Savage, Jon. *England's Dreaming: Anarchy, Sex Pistols, Punk Rock, and Beyond*. New York: St. Martin's Press, 1992.

White, Armond. *Rebel for the Hell of It: The Life of Tupac Shakur*. New York: Thunder's Mouth Press, 1997.

A Beastie Boys Discography

Polly Wog Stew EP (Ratcage 1982)

Cookie Puss EP (Ratcage 1983)

Licensed to Ill (Def Jam 1986)

Love American Style EP (Capitol 1989)

Paul's Boutique (Capitol 1989)

An Exciting Evening At Home with Shadrach, Meshach and Abednego EP (Capitol 1990)

Check Your Head (Grand Royal/Capitol 1992)

Frozen Metal Music EP (Capitol 1992)

Gratitude EP (Capitol 1992)

Some Old Bullshit (Grand Royal 1994)

Ill Communication (Grand Royal/Capitol 1994)

Root Down EP (Grand Royal/Capitol 1995)

Agilo E Olio EP (Grand Royal/Capitol 1995)

The In Sound From Way Out! (Grand Royal/Capitol 1996)

Hello Nasty (Grand Royal/Capitol 1998)

VIDEOS

The Beastie Boys Video (CBS/Fox 1987)

The Skills to Pay the Bills (Capitol Video 1992)

Sabotage Video (Capitol Video 1994)

Beastie Web Sites

The Official Beastie Boys Web Site (http://www.beastieboys.com) is
stuffed with goodies (lyrics, news, photos) and it has links to
Grand Royal (http://www.grandroyal.com) and the Milarepa
Fund (http://www.milarepa.org).

For the complete *Grand Royal* magazine, issue #1 log onto
http://www.grandroyal.com/Magazine/Issue1

A good site for fan sites is Some Beastie Boys Links
(http://members.tripod.com/bin/roadmap?938110427570)

Check out Glen E. Friedman's photos and words at
http://www.southern.com/BURNINGFLAGS

About the Contributors

Sheena wrote for the late great Boston zine *Boston Rock.*

Joanne Carnegie wrote for *Creem.*

Tim Ross is a computer programmer and freelance music writer currently residing in the idyllic town of Carrboro, North Carolina. "Something Like a Phenomenon: The 99 Records Story" initially appeared in the fourth issue of *Tuba Frenzy*, a zine that Ross has sporadically published over the course of the last five years (see www.tubafrenzy.com for details). Ross's first rock band once did a cover of the Beastie Boys' "Gratitude."

Nelson George has written several books on African-American art and culture including *The Death of Rhythm & Blues, Elevating the Game: Black Men and Basketball, Buppies, B-Boys, Baps & Bohos: Notes on Post-Soul Black Culture*, and, most recently, *Hip Hop America.*

Dave DiMartino writes for *Billboard.*

Linda Moleski writes for *Billboard.*

Bill Holdship is the former executive editor of *BAM* magazine. He's also been an editor at *Radio & Records, Daily Variety*, and, of course, *Creem.* He currently freelances for numerous publications.

John Kordosh is currently a chemist and the technical director of an aerosol paint division for the Glidden Company (ICI Paints). He irregularly contributes to *Real Detroit*, and was an editor at *Creem.*

Chuck Eddy is a senior editor at the *Village Voice*, and the author of *The Accidental Evolution of Rock 'n' Roll: A Misguided Tour Through Popular Music.*

Adam Heimlich is a New York–based freelance writer who contributes to the *New York Press, The Stranger,* the *Newark Star-Ledger* and various magazines.

Chris Morris writes for *Billboard.*

Robert Christgau is one of the great heroes of rock writing. He is a senior editor at the *Village Voice.* His most recent book is *Grown Up All Wrong: 75 Great Rock & Pop Artists from Vaudeville to Techno.*

Havelock Nelson writes for *Billboard.*

Frank Owen met the Beastie Boys in 1992 and wrote about it for *Newsday.* He currently writes for the *Village Voice.*

Craig Rosen writes for *Billboard* and contributed to *The Nirvana Companion.*

Larry Kay writes for *Magnet.*

Adam Beyda writes about music production for *Mix.*

Kim France writes about pop culture and contributes to *New York Magazine* and the *New York Times.*

Matt Diehl writes about rock for various publications.

Jon Pareles is one of America's most respected music critics. He currently writes about pop music for the *New York Times.*

Akiba Lerner, a graduate of UC–Berkeley, has served in the Israeli paratroopers and is currently a writer living in the United States.

Mark LeVine is a professional guitarist who has worked with artists ranging from Mick Jagger and Dr. John to Israeli folk singer Sata Alexander. He teaches religion at Hunter College.

Ann Power's scintillating writing on pop music often appears in *The Village Voice* and the *New York Times.*

Princess Superstar (aka Concetta) writes for *POPsmear*.

Modfather Paul Weller once said of UK music critic **Everett True** that "if it was any other line of business, I'd punch the cunt out." Courtney Love once claimed that the freelance journalist, currently traveling around Australasia, "ran England."

Neil Strauss is the coauthor, with Marilyn Manson, of *The Long Hard Road Out of Hell*.

George Kaplan is a former member of the Blitzed Poets (New York chapter). After breaking with the BP after dreaming he should, Kaplan established the TERROARTISTS, a group who worship horror movies and get "inspired" by them. (Kaplan is currently viewing *Night of the Living Dead* nonstop for two weeks. At the end of this time period he plans on doing a painting or a novel or breaking something.) Kaplan's other interests include conspiracy theory, pornography, hallucinogenics, utopian fantasy, hip hop, Dada, drinking, and the Grateful Dead (he has the title of every GD song ever recorded tattooed on his body). He is the editor, writer, publisher, and distributor of *What You Lookin' At Mutherfucker?*, a literary periodical he puts out when he can.

Permissions

Grateful acknowledgment is made for permission to reprint the following:

"Beauty & the Beastie Boys" by Joanne Carnegie. Reprinted by permission.

"How Ya Like 'em Now?" by Robert Christgau. Copyright © 1989 by VV Publishing Corporation. Reprinted by permission of *the Village Voice*.

"When Will These Old Guys Shut Up?" by Matt Diehl. Copyright © 1994 by *New York* magazine. Reprinted by permission of the Los Angeles Times Syndicate.

"Beastie Boys Denied Right to Party in San Diego" by Dave DiMartino. Copyright © 1987 by BPI Communications, Inc. Reprinted by permission of BPI Communications, Inc.

"The Beastie Boys Take Over?" by Chuck Eddy. Copyright © 1987 by Chuck Eddy. Reprinted by permission of Chuck Eddy.

"Recording on the Fly" by Adam Beyda. © 1994 by Adam Beyda. Reprinted by permission of Adam Beyda.

"The Beauty of the Beasties" by Kim France. Copyright © 1994 by *New York Magazine*. Reprinted by permission of the Los Angeles Times Syndicate.

From "Rhythm & Blues" by Nelson George. Copyright © 1987 by BPI Communications, Inc. Reprinted by permission of BPI Communications, Inc.

"'Together Forever' Incites Good and Ill Will" by Nelson George. Copyright © 1987 by BPI Communications, Inc. Reprinted by permission of BPI Communications, Inc.

"Space Cake Cookie, I Discover Who I Am" by Adam Heimlich. Copyright © 1999 by Adam Heimlich. Reprinted by permission of Adam Heimlich.

"If I Played Guitar I'd Be Jimmy Page: On Being Young, White, and Beastial in Late-'80s Suburbia" by Adam Heimlich. Copyright © 1999. Reprinted by permission of Adam Heimlich.

"Senstive B-Boys" by Adam Heimlich. Copyright © 1999 by Adam Heimlich. Reprinted by permission of Adam Heimlich.

"High School Equivalency Test" by Bill Holdship and John Kordosh. Copyright © 1987 by Bill Holdship and John Kordosh. Reprinted by permission of Bill Holdship and John Kordosh.

About the Editors

John Rocco is the editor of *The Doors Companion*, *The Nirvana Companion*, and *Dead Reckonings: The Life and Times of the Grateful Dead*, all for Schirmer Books. He teaches English at SUNY Maritime.

Brian Rocco is the assistant editor of *The Nirvana Companion*. His mask is at the dry cleaners.

Index